The Religion of Life

Pitt Latin American Series

Catherine M. Conaghan, Editor

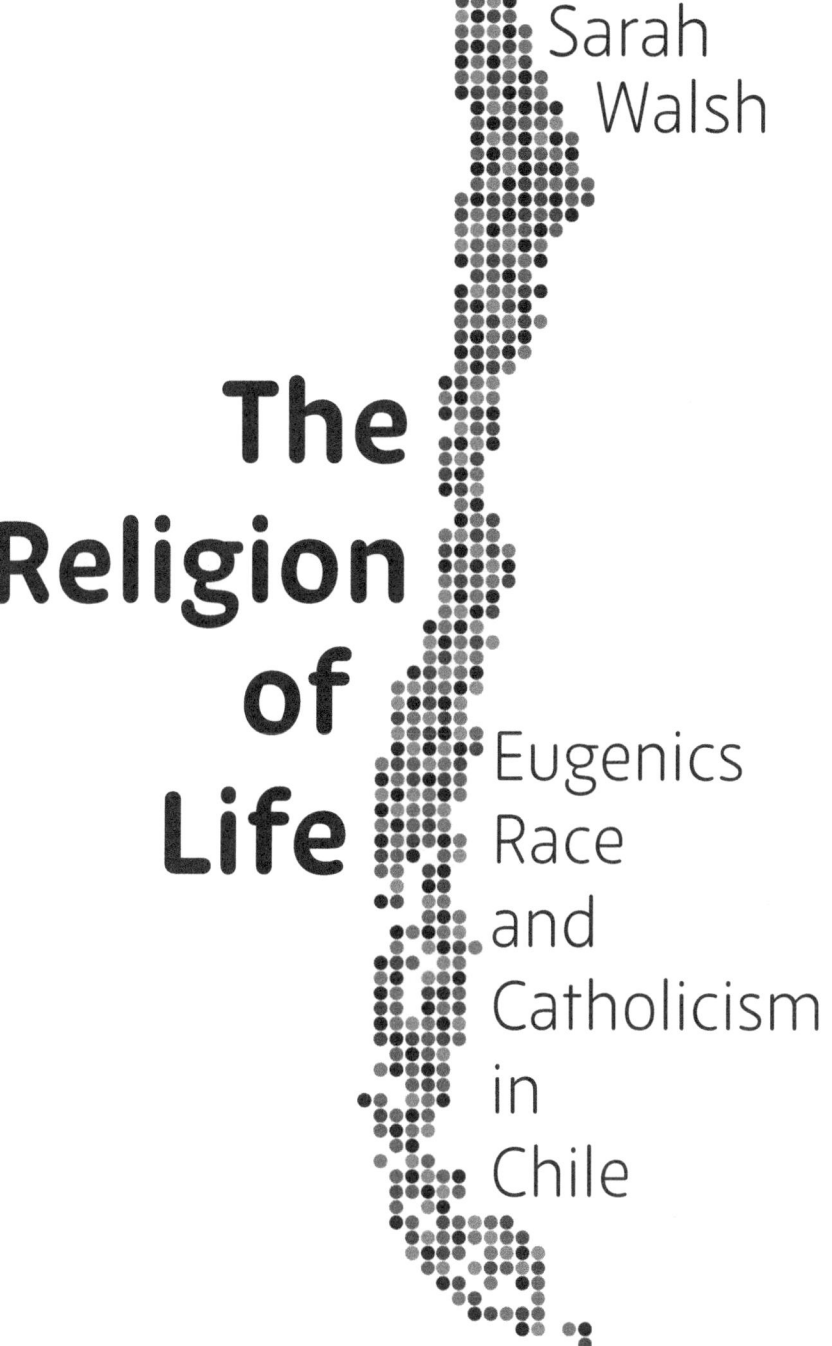

Sarah
Walsh

The
Religion
of
Life

Eugenics
Race
and
Catholicism
in
Chile

University of Pittsburgh Press

Published by the University of Pittsburgh Press, Pittsburgh, Pa., 15260
Copyright © 2021, University of Pittsburgh Press
All rights reserved
Manufactured in the United States of America
Printed on acid-free paper
10 9 8 7 6 5 4 3 2 1

Cataloging-in-Publication data is available from the Library of Congress

ISBN 13: 978-0-8229-4664-9
ISBN 10: 0-8229-4664-5

Cover design by Melissa Dias-Mandoly

For my family and for James

Contents

Acknowledgments

The road to this point has been a long one and this book has gone through many lives. Although my goal has always been to illuminate connections between Catholicism and eugenics in Latin America, it has taken a considerable amount of effort and time to do justice to the task. The support I received along the way, both material and emotional, has been essential.

The vast majority of research for this book occurred during my time as a graduate student at the University of Maryland, College Park, and the first funding I received for preliminary archival research was provided by the Department of History there. Longer-term research was supported by the National Science Foundation's Division of Social and Economic Sciences, Program in Science, Technology, and Society, Doctoral Dissertation Research Grant, Award Number 0959821. Additional research funding was provided by the Australian Research Council Laureate Project "Race and Ethnicity in the Global South" (PI: Warwick Anderson) and "The Colour of Labour: The Racialised Lives of Migrants" (ERC Advanced Grant no. 695573, PI: Cristiana Bastos). I am grateful to the Roots of Contemporary Issues Program at Washington State University, which gave me the push I needed to get the manuscript finished. My final months of revision were far better than I might have imagined, in the truly terrible year that was 2020, thanks to my new colleagues at the University of Melbourne.

Conceptually, a great many people influenced what this book has become. My graduate advisor, Karin Rosemblatt, was essential in seeing the value of this research and has remained a steadfast mentor and advocate in the years since. Barbara Weinstein played an important role in my earliest efforts to think these questions through. Erika Milam was a major early contributor regarding the history of biology. Mary Kay Vaughan was similarly important to early iterations of this project. Warwick Anderson's guidance was invaluable both on my moving to life as a professional historian and on how to transition this manuscript into a book. His impact is seen in my efforts to better understand Whiteness in Latin America. Miranda Johnson encouraged me to more fully consider the role of indigeneity in the story. Sebastián Gil-Riaño helped me to examine the bridge between Latin American history and the history of science.

Colleagues who volunteered their time to read and comment on different versions of these chapters are many and are much appreciated. Some of those include Warwick Anderson, Rebecca Ellis, Sebastián Gil-Riaño, Miranda Johnson, Benjamin Nobbs-Thiessen, Hans Pols, Karin Rosemblatt, Patience Schell (who also has given professional advice along the way), and Ben Silverstein. For those of you who do not appear on this list, this is the fault of my memory, and I remain grateful to you.

The list of colleagues and friends who played a role in maintaining my sanity during this process is extensive, but I will do my best at a representative list (of those not already mentioned): Ariana Azar-Farr, Julian Dodson, Marco Duranti, Jennifer Ferng, Lawrence Hatter, Philippa Hetherington, Stephanie Hinnershitz, Chin Jou, Sophie Loy-Wilson, Michelle Mann, Amanda Marzo, Nic Miller, Karen Milton, Katie Schultz, Alecia Simmonds, Eugene Smelyansky, Noah Tian, Brandi Townsend, Katy Whalen, and Jesse Zarley. The copious amounts of venting and wine were essential, and I was glad to share both with all of you.

None of any of this would have been possible without my family. My love of history and learning was first encouraged by my parents, Nancy Jenal and James Walsh. Thank you for never saying that I could find a more lucrative profession and for never asking why I kept leaving the United States. It is finally paying off. Amy Walsh, my sister and podcast cohost, is as near and dear to my heart as ever. To all my extended family, who are possibly still confused about what I do at work, you have been supportive all the same. The person who has been the biggest cheerleader and North Star during my entire career (and especially this past dreaded year) is my partner, James Herbert. Every time I thought of giving up, he helped me to keep going. I should probably be annoyed but am actually incredibly thankful.

The Religion of Life

Introduction

Our race was born as all those called historic races should be: from the combination of the vanquishing male element with the vanquished female, complying with the biblical sentence that woman will avenge her race, perpetuating the blood of the conquered lineage.

Palacios, *Raza chilena*

In his best-known work—the multivolume *Raza chilena: libro escrito por un chileno y para los chilenos*, first published anonymously in 1904—the Chilean physician Nicolás Palacios (1854–1911) wrote as a dedicated nationalist and sometime labor activist. His primary motivation was to question Chilean business leaders and politicians who were at that time creating a variety of schemes designed to welcome both foreign laborers and foreign capital into the national economy. Palacios agreed that the capital was welcome, but he was concerned that the immigration programs operated on the faulty assumption that foreigners were racially superior to domestic workers. To combat this belief, he argued in *Raza chilena* that Chileans had a unique biological profile that existed nowhere else on Earth, and therefore the country's leaders should protect the population from foreign racial incursion. Invoking a trope of colonial conquest and subsequent racial mixture that was familiar throughout Latin America, Palacios described the Chilean race as the biological result of the encounter between two distinct ethnic groups, one European and one indigenous.

Different versions of this type of racially mixed, or mestizo, origin story evolved and were celebrated throughout the nineteenth and twentieth centuries across Latin America as part of independence struggles and subsequent nationalism. Historians of racial thought in Latin America have studied these tropes and their specific national contexts extensively.[1] Less well studied has been what Palacios referred to as the "biblical" punishment of childbirth visited on Latin American women; specifically, that by the early twentieth century they were considered to be the primary conservators and reproducers of racial heritage. Although historians of race and gender have discussed the obvious disregard for the brutality suffered by indigenous women at the hands of European men in order to foster this mixture, the conceptual mixing of biblical imagery and biological claims in a work dedicated to eugenically inspired racial protectionism has often gone unremarked within the history of racial thought in Latin America.[2]

Yet Palacios was not the only Latin American writer to rely on these types of metaphors. They were commonplace, and their existence suggests a significant amount of discursive effort to make religious and scientific ideologies work together. In the case of Latin America, where the social, cultural, and political influence of Catholicism remains significant, it seems especially important that the impact of Catholicism on racial thought not be overlooked. By tracing connections and similarities across Catholic and secular eugenic writing in the early twentieth century in this book, I examine the interactions between Catholicism and eugenics as intellectual frameworks to highlight their symbiotic relationship in the construction of Latin American racial thought.

Doing so demonstrates that an essential component of this process, which Palacios captured in his prose, was the widespread belief among virtually all Chilean intellectuals, eugenicists, and public figures that women were the key to maintaining and improving the nation's supposedly exceptional racial heritage. Monitoring—and when necessary, modifying—women's behavior was therefore essential to the quality and longevity of what Palacios dubbed *la raza chilena*.[3] In other words, the modernization of patriarchy became a time-sensitive issue critical to the protection of the racial integrity of the Chilean populace in the first half of the twentieth century. Conceptual connections between eugenics and Catholicism were forged primarily through the shared belief that gender difference and patriarchal social structures were not merely biologically determined and therefore scientifically sound but also vital for the prevention of racial degeneration. Agreement regarding the importance of marriage, the appropriate roles of men and women in the home and outside it, and the need for sexual fidelity in women, all united Chilean eugenicists and their writing in ways they often failed to see themselves.

What Constitutes Eugenics in Latin America?

One of the main obstacles facing the historian of eugenics in Latin America is a generalized belief that the science never thrived there. Two ideas remain pervasive within the history of science that allow for this belief to persist. The first is that the term "eugenics" is best understood as the implementation of practices such as coerced sterilization, abortion, and euthanasia legislated and eventually mandated by the state.[4] Since the Catholic Church as a whole stood against these practices, no matter where they were proposed, and because Latin America compared to other regions is striking for its lack of eugenic legislation in the early-to-mid twentieth century, it is easy to assume that eugenics was not popular there. The second and more problematic assumption operating within the history of science is that eugenics was only of use or of interest to individuals identified as White and that Latin Americans of any persuasion cannot legitimately claim membership in that racial group.[5] Drawing together Chilean sources from the first decades of the twentieth century, in this book I show that the popularity of eugenics was in no way limited by the cultural influence of Catholicism nor by the presumed racial identity of its advocates. In fact, I seek to better illuminate the claims to White identity that writers of Chilean eugenic scholarship (both Catholic and secular) sought to strengthen and legitimize.

At first glance, treating Catholicism and eugenics as complementary intellectual frameworks makes for a surprising set of bedfellows. In the United States, in particular, the Catholic Church represented one of the few staunchly anti-eugenics public institutions operating in the early twentieth century.[6] In Latin America, however, historians of eugenics have been examining this interaction for quite some time; one of the first examples is Nancy Leys Stepan's *"The Hour of Eugenics": Race, Gender, and Nation in Latin America* (1991). Comparing eugenics in Argentina, Brazil, and Mexico, Stepan primarily illustrates the distinctive ideological differences between Latin American and North Atlantic eugenics. The two major differences were Latin Americans' overall skepticism regarding biological determinism, particularly when linked to race or ethnicity, and their enthusiasm for the future possibilities of race mixing.[7]

Stepan attributes these fundamental differences to the influence of Comtean positivism and neo-Lamarckian evolution among Latin American intellectuals and scientists intent on the orderly improvement of their respective nations in the nineteenth and twentieth centuries. Showing the intellectual connections across the Latin world, both strands of thought were developed by French scholars. Jean-Baptist Lamarck, a naturalist, rose to prominence at the turn of the nineteenth century as a result of a series of publications on zoology. In particular, Lamarck had an interest in taxonomy that would eventually cause him to consider the biological processes involved in speciation. In 1809 he published his treatise *Philosophie Zoologique* (*Zoological Philosophy*) where he proposed the idea of traits being acquired through use and disuse. Although he was not the first to suggest this type of change over time, his name became associated with one of the earliest modern theories of speciation and evolution known as Lamarckism.[8]

In French philosopher Auguste Comte's most famous published work, *The Course in Positive Philosophy* (published between 1830 and 1842), he sought to understand the universal concepts that formed the foundation of disciplines such as mathematics, physics, biology, and various social sciences. At its most basic, Comtean positivism broke human evolution into three progressive stages: theological, metaphysical, and positive. The positive stage, which he also referred to as "the scientific stage," was humanity's ultimate endpoint. In this cosmovision, human civilization was always progressing toward a positivist future, in which scientific exploration and experimentation would be used to determine human behavior. Needless to say, Comte did not believe that humanity had reached this stage during his lifetime.[9]

Yet Latin Americans familiar with his work were far more enthusiastic about its promise than Comte had been. The notion that progress could be achieved through careful study and human agency was especially inspiring in the young Latin American republics, in the midst of struggles with concerns about their potential turn toward barbarism in the wake of nineteenth-century independence.[10] Neo-Lamarckian environmentalism, and the eugenic theories it later influenced, fitted into the already popular positivist vision of the late-nineteenth-century because that theory implied that human beings had the ability to master their own destiny. The Darwinian version of evolution, despite its popularity among eugenicists in the North Atlantic, held little sway in Latin America because in it there seemed to be no place left for human agency.

According to Stepan, the preference for neo-Lamarckism in Latin America arose directly from a specifically Latin intellectual community whose members were influenced by French theories of human development, biology, and anthropology.[11] In her words: "This was less a matter of their being 'out' of the mainstream of genetics than of their being 'in' an alternative stream or tradition of Lamarckian hereditarian thought."[12] Characterizing the Latin American eugenicists as forming part of an alternative but equally valid scientific tradition meant recasting their scientific debates and contributions to the field as a whole. Rather than portraying their work as flawed or derivative, Stepan illuminates how eugenics could be widely appealing in a majority non-White, predominantly Catholic region. Ultimately, she argues, studying eugenics in Latin America disrupted the binary of positive and negative—hereditarian and environmental—divisions at work in the scholarship on eugenics in the late 1980s and early 1990s. Unfortunately, the canonical history of eugenics continues to be determined by this divide and still privileges the theories and work of North American and European eugenicists as representative of the discipline as a whole.

The case of Chile offers an opportunity to question the claim that North Atlantic eugenic theory and writing are representative of the entire field. For example, the continued salience of racial hierarchy in Chile and its links to biological determinism demonstrate that Darwinian ideas did impact Latin American eugenics, at least somewhat. In fact, I will show that it impacted some individual Chilean eugenicists quite a lot. It is more fitting to consider eugenics in the region as being founded upon a synthesis of neo-Lamarckism and Darwinism, which led to a widespread belief that individuals' environments as well as their biological ancestry were central to their overall eugenic fitness.[13] This mixture of evolutionary theories meant that notions of racial improvement and hierarchy coexisted with tolerance of racial mixture, which has so often been treated as proof of Latin America's disinterest in the field.

The Chilean, and Latin American, intellectual reckoning with eugenics highlights one of the more obvious aspects of eugenics as a whole—namely, that neo-Lamarckism was still a widely accepted scientific theory among eugenicists all over the world until well into the twentieth century.[14] French historian and philosopher of biology Jean Gayon argues this was because, prior to the 1930s, Darwinian evolutionary theory presented rather stubborn problems for its advocates. As he put it: "The long initial crisis of Darwinism was not only the result of external factors such as 'resistance' or the existence of rival evolutionary paradigms; it was also a consequence of a range of problems that were intrinsic to Darwin's central hypothesis. These difficulties, most of which were linked to the concept of heredity, could not be resolved by the biology of the time."[15]

Darwinists could provide little proof of how favorable traits were passed from parent to offspring, so neo-Lamarckian environmentalism or its variations remained appealing for many scientists, particularly for those interested in eugenics. Gayon argues that Darwin's own theory of evolution, until it was substantiated by the work of biologists and geneticists later in the twentieth century, was more accurately described as an extreme form of neo-Lamarckism.[16] Recognizing the international appeal of neo-Lamarckism—combined with the scientific obstacles to a functional evolutionary theory prior to the 1930s—helps to show that Latin American eugenicists were not isolated from larger transnational scientific trends, nor were they working with outdated concepts. The intellectual malleability of eugenic theory itself and the Latin American penchant for the reconstitution of scientific frameworks for local purposes both give context to Catholic involvement in the development of eugenics in Chile.

Stepan's work is also important because it inspired more scholars to research what aspects of Latin American eugenic theory and practice distinguished them from their North American counterparts. This research has led to better explanations of the reasons Latin American eugenicists consistently objected to methods usually considered quintessential to the field, such as coerced sterilization, euthanasia, and abortion. An example of this scholarship is Marius Turda and Aaron Gillette's *Latin Eugenics in Comparative Perspective* (2014). They demonstrate how eugenic science in what they identify as the Latin world was less affected by notions of biological determinism—and practice was therefore more interested in a wide variety of state-sponsored environmental interventions into individuals' lives such as maternal and infant health programs, preventive medicine instruction, and public health campaigns, in the name of racial improvement.[17] Their explanation for this difference is that Latin eugenics focused primarily on homogenizing national populations (understood to be racially similar) and concentrated less on purifying a specific racial group considered to be superior.[18] I argue that this concept of national homogenization held true for Chilean eugenicists as well, despite the significant racial and ethnic diversity of the national population. I also argue that the environmentally focused eugenic theory that was popular in Chile, Latin America, and the Latin world more broadly, despite its advocates' seeming altruism, was still driven by racist logics that considered European heritage superior.

This more complete picture of racism operating within Chilean racial thought allows the historian to grapple with the ideological fluidity related to concepts such as racial fitness, hierarchy, and mixture operating within eugenic theory itself. The overwhelming popularity of eugenics in the first half of the twentieth century (not only in Latin America) allowed for widely varied interpretations of the science's application and ultimate purpose. As Matthew Connelly states: "the idea of improving the genetic makeup of humankind counted adherents all over the world, including everyone from W. E. B. Du Bois to John Maynard Keynes. Eugenics was invoked to justify everything from free day care to forced sterilization."[19] The conceptual malleability of eugenics allowed historical actors from a wide swath of political, social, racial, and cultural subjectivities to use the discipline as a tool. Yet, there has been significantly less scholarship on how this ideological flexibility allowed non-White and mixed-race peoples to develop their own forms of racialization and discrimination.[20] My argument in this book is that a significant portion of Chilean eugenic writing was committed to creating a White identity for Chileans, which obscured the existence of racial and ethnic minorities while simultaneously discriminating against them.

The Complex Relationship between Catholicism and Eugenics

Stepan also argued that, "From the beginning, and alone of the major institutions of the West, the church opposed an extreme reproductive eugenics, for it took human reproduction as a sphere within its own rightful authority and did not cede that authority easily to secular science."[21] This power struggle has traditionally been portrayed as the reason Catholics objected to eugenic science whole cloth. However, state attempts to control human reproduction were only part of what constituted eugenic practice, which permitted more Catholic involvement in the science than has generally been recognized. The papal encyclical *Casti connubii: On Christian Marriage*, released December 31, 1930, speaks to this distinction. Written under the auspices of Pope Pius XI, the encyclical was mostly about protecting the sanctity of sacramental marriage in the face of growing efforts all over the world to popularize civil marriage and legislate divorce. Intriguingly, *Casti connubii* also included nine paragraphs about eugenics.[22] At first glance, those paragraphs seem to substantiate the claim that the main problem that eugenics posed for Catholics was when governments sought to prohibit specific individuals from marriage or childbearing: "there are some who[,] over solicitous for the cause of eugenics, not only give salutary counsel for more certainly procuring the strength and health of the future child—which, indeed, is not contrary to right reason—but put eugenics before aims of a higher order, and by public authority wish to prevent from marrying all those whom, even though naturally fit for marriage, they consider, according to the norms and conjectures of their investigations, would, through hereditary transmission, bring forth defective offspring."[23] Reading this passage more closely, however, reveals that Pius XI did not object to the central tenet of eugenic science—humanity can and should be improved. In fact, the endeavor to create stronger and healthier children was "not contrary to right reason." Rather, the encyclical states, the problem was with overzealous eugenicists or eugenic programs operating outside the purview of the Catholic Church. Distinguishing between eugenic practices that sought to control human reproduction through legislation or coercion and the larger goal of human perfection was not only an essential component of Catholic eugenic writing, it also explains how Catholics in Latin America (where negative eugenic legislation was never very popular even with secular eugenicists) were able to actively engage in framing the discipline's overall mission.[24]

This key distinction is the reason Turda and Gillette argue that "the relationship between eugenics and religion is of crucial importance when examining Latin eugenics."[25] For them, one of the defining features of Latin eugenic science is its ability to fit conceptually with the long-standing cultural and intellectual influence of Catholicism.[26] They contend that the development of a distinct network of eugenicists and eugenic literature in southern Europe and Latin America during the early twentieth century explicitly opposed the strict hereditarian eugenic theory associated with northern Europe and North America. In other words, understanding the interactions between Catholicism and eugenics, for Turda and Gillette, highlights the existence of a Latin scientific community. In this book I add to their work by demonstrating how Catholicism played a direct role in shaping racial thought in Latin America, not only as a cultural institution but as an intellectual framework.

This builds on the work of scholars such as Phillip M. Thompson who argues that the early twentieth century prompted a Catholic intellectual renaissance that "provided a coherent alternative to the culture of modernity."[27] For example, the papal encyclicals *Rerum novarum* (1891) and *Quadragesimo anno* (1931) alongside Pope Pius XI's establishment of the Pontifical Institute of Christian Archeology (1925) and the Pontifical Academy of Sciences (1936) attest to an obvious desire on the part of the Catholic Church to engage with science and society in new ways, even if the term "modernity" caused a certain panic among some Catholic writers.[28] Examining eugenics as a part of this intellectual renaissance, however, moves away from discussing both Latin American and Catholic knowledge production regarding race and ethnicity as alternative in the way that Thompson implies. Instead, it demonstrates that Catholic concepts about the body, the self, and the possibility of human improvement were central to the construction of racial thought in early twentieth-century Latin America.

Disrupting the idea that religious knowledge production is alternative is important because historians of science have a tradition of being particularly critical of the relationship between science and Catholicism.[29] This has been especially true in the context of nations perceived as non-White. Jorge Cañizares-Esguerra's *Nature, Empire, and Nation: Explorations of the History of Science in the Iberian World* (2006) illustrates how scientific achievements in botany conducted under the auspices of the Spanish and Portuguese empires were overlooked, and even attributed to other individuals, in the prevailing canonical historiographies. Those works, he notes, tend to emphasize the role of scientists from northern Europe and North America. Cañizares-Esguerra attributes this to "narratives of modernity inaugurated first by Protestantism and later by the Enlightenment, [which were] both profoundly hostile to Catholic Iberia."[30] Implicit in the critiques of Catholicism as an impediment to scientific discovery or innovation are also racialized and racist beliefs that portray northern European imperial expansion as neutral, or even benevolent, while the legacy of Iberian empires is characterized as perennial backwardness, scientific and otherwise.

Illuminating the scientific influence of the national church in the first half of the twentieth century is useful in the Chilean case because scholars often characterize this period as one of growing secularism and a corresponding decline of religious influence. Historian Hannah Stewart-Gambino has argued that "the post-1930s Chilean church did not wield the same degree of political power as did some other Latin American churches. The pattern of economic and political modernization in Chile resulted in a process of secularization and rationalization more common to Europe than to other Latin American countries."[31] While not untrue, these claims often point to the disestablishment of the Chilean Catholic Church in 1925 as the primary evidence of its waning political and cultural influence. As a result, the national church has been treated as an anachronistic institution with very little social relevance after that time. However, the founding of the Partido Demócrata Cristiano (Christian Democratic Party) in 1957 and the creation of the Vicaría de la Solidaridad (Vicariate of Solidarity) in response to the Pinochet regime belie the supposed irrelevance of the Chilean national church after 1925. Examining how Catholics engaged with eugenics is just one way to make visible their continued impact on, and engagement with, Chilean society throughout the twentieth century.

Sol Serrano's *Universidad y nación: Chile en el siglo XIX* (1993) describes this continued presence: "The Church was concerned with, as much in its discourse as in its educational practice, demonstrating that its opposition to secularization did not mean its opposition to scientific knowledge nor to technological advances."[32] Similarly, I will show that Catholic eugenic writers adopted and used the same scientific terminology and identified the same eugenic threats to *la raza chilena* as their secular counterparts. This illustrates how Catholic concepts and Catholic intellectuals remained active parts of Chilean public life and intellectual discourse by virtue of their contributions to the growing national interest in race as a biological category and in racial homogeneity as a pathway to progress.

Catholic eugenicists may have felt especially called upon because the most pressing threat affecting the Chilean race was increasingly considered to be blurred gender divisions—deviations that had typically been regulated within the confines of traditional family life. Catholic and secular eugenic texts both contended that modern life had drawn Chilean men and women away from their biologically determined—and therefore eugenically desirable—binary gender roles. As Thomas C. Holt writes: "Gender provided the most powerful language to describe national and racial relations. Whether invoked as metaphor, metonym, or allegory, the very idea of nation and national belonging is more often than not expressed in familial metaphors."[33] I will show that to be considered racially fit in early to mid-twentieth-century Chile, women and men had to conform to increasingly inflexible ideas about supposedly natural and healthy female and male behavior. That said, women were portrayed as the most important agents for maintaining racial health and therefore the subject of far more eugenic writing.

Catholics were not the only ones who used eugenic theories to legitimize a modernized form of patriarchy as the supposedly natural framework for organizing any society. In fact, the rise of eugenic science in Chile caused a wide variety of historical actors to insist that gender binaries were scientifically verifiable social realities. Building on the work of a number of scholars who have discussed the modernization of patriarchy in early twentieth century Latin America, I will demonstrate how emphasis on the maintenance of gender difference and the modernization of patriarchal social structures created a eugenic community of diverse historical actors who all agreed that a strict gender binary was essential to racial fitness.[34] The uniformity of agreement on this point among eugenicists cannot be overstated, as it emerged from my survey of hundreds of documents rather than from a predetermined interest in gender discourse.

In the scheme of women's centrality to the health of *la raza chilena*, it is particularly striking to note that coverage regarding indigenous women was relatively absent. After the recognition that their sexual exploitation in the colonial past was essential for the existence of a unique Chilean race in the present, most eugenic treatises were no longer interested in discussing indigenous women or their contributions to modern Chilean society. I will show that, time and again, discussions regarding Chilean racial identity were mostly about accessing Whiteness. The issue, for most of the texts and writers mentioned here, was always about how to prove that a history of mixed racial heritage need not preclude individuals (and the nation at large) from claiming a White identity in the present. This meant an overemphasis on *mestizaje* being the defining racial feature of the Chilean population, which effectively erased all but the "purest" indigenous Chileans from the eugenic landscape.

Racial Thought and Eugenics in Latin America

Indicative of the conceptual fluidity within Latin American racial thought, the same set of historical tropes were used to create supposedly singular national racial profiles rather than a regionalized ethnic identity. Throughout Latin America early twentieth-century race theorists such as Palacios looked to the colonial past as the origin point for a myriad of distinct racial types. This approach, however, was not new. Claims were widespread that the colonial encounter created new races.[35] Despite studying different geographic regions at different periods of time, scholars of early modern Latin

America all demonstrate how the imperial expansion of Spain and Portugal in the Americas created new types of colonial societies where racial and ethnic identity became increasingly important and formalized. Some historians argue that the very concept of race arose from the fact of the European colonial endeavor.[36]

By the first decades of the nineteenth century, this kind of thinking was updated. Founding fathers of Latin American nations often pointed to their racially mixed heritage or their ancestral connection to the land as central to the legitimacy of their claims for independence.[37] No matter where these concepts arose, a central component of them all was an understanding of the colonial past in which indigenous women became sexually involved with European men as the origin of national racial profiles.[38] Overlooking and obscuring the often coercive or abusive nature of these sexual relationships, national racial origin stories were celebrated and used as proof of Latin American pragmatism regarding race mixing. A number of early Latin American nationalists also claimed that the new republican nations would not permit the type of racial discrimination and prejudice that characterized the United States and previous imperial governments.[39] Although racial and ethnic difference in these societies remained a reality, Latin American nationalists contended that racial mixture was so deeply embedded in their respective cultures that, beyond its ability to legitimize political self-determination and independence from Europe, it remained irrelevant.

These stories continued to mature such that by the early twentieth century, many Latin American scholars had a strong conviction that their approach to race and ethnicity was unparalleled in a world increasingly divided by the color line.[40] Specifically, scholarship from Latin America in the first decades of the twentieth century began to reconsider racial mixture and suggest that it might not be degenerative.[41] Some scholars went so far as to contend that racial mixture actually improved the quality of human beings. Two figures most emblematic of this type of thinking were the Mexican philosopher and minister of education José Vasconcelos and the Brazilian anthropologist Gilberto Freyre.[42] In the Latin American context, they argued, skin color and racial heritage had no particular meaning for—or impact on—individuals. What was far more relevant was someone's cultural capital as evidenced by their education, income, or family history. This argument was so powerful and pervasive that the theme of cultural signifiers, particularly class, mattering more than physical traits has consistently played a central role in the study of Latin American racial thought since the mid-twentieth century.

Latin American area studies grew in prominence in the 1950s and 1960s among Anglo-American scholars precisely because of the widespread belief that biological race and racial purity held virtually no meaning there, in contrast to nations such as the United States.[43] The logic that these scholars relied on, as their Latin American counterparts had done before them, was that racism and prejudice manifested only in the context of White racial purity. If there was no one who could claim a "pure" White identity, which Latin Americans presumably could not, then racial hierarchy lost its meaning. However, beginning in the 1970s and maturing in the early 2000s, scholars of Latin America increasingly began to argue that, although Latin American racial ideology and practices did not seem to be based on physical traits alone, they still created conditions that were conducive to racial discrimination. This was especially noted by the writers of the literature about Brazil, who sought to document how prejudice and racialized identities persisted in the face of state-mandated antiracist programs that refused to recognize race at all.[44]

Histories of Latin America written in the early 2000s continued to build on the already considerable scholarship focused on how race was created primarily through socioeconomic conditions and cultural practices.[45] Despite the fact that this period saw the rise in immigration history and Whiteness studies in other fields, these questions were generally not incorporated into the larger remit of Latin American histories of race.[46] Similarly, histories of race science and eugenics proliferated but often remained focused on intellectual communities and practices in North America and northern Europe.[47] As a result, in various ways the notion persists that Latin American tolerance of racial mixture serves to undermine racial hierarchy. Histories of race science in Latin America that emphasize the influence of neo-Lamarckism unintentionally contribute to this situation as they seem to explain why Latin Americans might be more likely to focus on social standing rather than on phenotypical "realities" of race, despite the knowledge that this preference did not protect citizens from state-sponsored eugenic interventions into their lives.[48]

In the past decade, there has been a renaissance in the study of biological race in the region. For example, there is a good deal of writing about the development of genomics in contemporary Latin America and about the impact of long-standing racialized concepts in those studies.[49] Similarly, there is a growing awareness that ascriptions of racial identity are at least somewhat determined by physical traits such as one's hair, eye, and skin color.[50] Most relevant to my argument, there have been increasing efforts to incorporate questions from US Whiteness and immigration studies into considerations of race in Latin American contexts.[51] This is more than timely, as Latin American nations share similar histories regarding selective immigration schemes, the dispossession and annihilation of indigenous groups, and reliance on the labor of enslaved African-descended peoples.

Despite the similarities, there is considerably less scholarship on racial thought in Chile specifically. This is mostly because of a long-held belief, among many scholars and average Chileans alike, that the Chilean population has been racially homogeneous until relatively recently.[52] In terms of biological components, *la raza chilena* is considered to be exclusively and predominantly mestizo.[53] Widespread acceptance of racial mixture as a foundational myth was not without its problems, however. The Chilean case is especially valuable as it demonstrates how ideas of race mixing existed alongside more pernicious forms of racism and racial hierarchy. Chilean eugenic writers, both Catholic and secular, often implied that the Chilean mixture of European and indigenous ancestry was superior to that of other Latin American nations. This presumed superiority was based primarily on two claims: that the national population was racially homogeneous and that the period of active racial mixture was over. Chilean eugenic scientists combined elements from European, North American, and Latin American racial theory and refashioned them to create a particular blend of tolerance for racial mixture in the abstract and a preference for European heritage in reality. Thus my purpose here is not to write a history of the Chilean reception of European or North American eugenic principles or ideas but, rather, to analyze important nuances in the national eugenic discourse regarding Chilean racial thought.[54]

A Snapshot of Chile between 1891 and 1952

Rather than being organized chronologically, these chapters concern a number of themes at work in Catholicism, eugenics, and racial thought in early twentieth-century Chile. The earliest document discussed in the text, the papal encyclical *Rerum novarum: On Capital and Labor* was published in 1891, and this document impacted Catholic social activism and science all over the world (see chapter 2). The year 1891 was also an important year in the national context of Chilean history. It was almost entirely consumed by civil war, which began in January when then President José Manuel Balmaceda tried to wrest political control from congress with the support of the Chilean army. The war was quick and bloody and concluded in August with Balmaceda's surrender and suicide. These events led to the birth to the so-called Parliamentary Era in which the country was effectively ruled by congressional oligarchy.[55]

Growing political dissatisfaction with the parliamentary system ushered in a new era in 1924 when a group of military officials, including General Carlos Ibáñez del Campo, seized government control in protest over the treatment of the Chilean armed forces. Initially, the military leaders objected only to certain key congressional and cabinet figures and kept Arturo Alessandri Palma in the presidency. However, by September, Alessandri resigned as he felt increasingly like a puppet for the powerful military junta. He returned to the presidency in March 1925 but was not to last in the office much beyond the creation of a new constitution that same year. The political situation between 1925 and 1932 was especially precarious, as Ibáñez operated as a shadow dictator throughout those years. This period left its mark on the Chilean political landscape, as the strengthened executive style of government created during these seven years remained in place until the September 11, 1973, coup against President Salvador Allende.[56] The emphasis on presidential power encouraged the rise of coalitions between political parties in the 1930s and 1940s, such as the left-leaning Frente Popular (Popular Front) and the conservative Falange Nacional (National Phalanx).[57]

Another defining feature of the period between 1891 and 1952 was an explosion in the size of the country's urban population. Men and women from throughout the country came to cities such as Santiago, Valparaíso, and Concepción, to find work. In 1895, the number of Chileans living in cities with populations of more than twenty thousand was 34 percent. By 1930, that number was closer to half.[58] This new urban working class demanded new government services and protections.[59] Their numbers also made social issues such as poverty, disease, and infant mortality much harder to ignore. In 1920, the average Chilean had a life expectancy of only thirty years, which demonstrates just how unhealthy the population actually was.[60] These very real health threats caused a variety of politicians, priests, medical doctors, and average citizens to fear for the future of the Chilean race and its viability in the modern world.

This period was also characterized by internal struggles among the historical actors identified here as Catholic. A significant amount of the conflict had to do with the role of the Partido Conservador (Conservative Party), the traditional political home of most Catholics since the mid-nineteenth century. Catholic writers who came of age before the First World War were typically more closely aligned with the Partido Conservador than their younger counterparts. An individual who will appear a number of times in this book, Gilberto Fuenzalida Guzmán strongly believed that working with the Partido Conservador was the only proper means by which to realize Catholic social reform.[61] Younger Catholics, however, questioned this close relationship and indeed some of the organizing principles of the party itself, and they created the Falange Nacional in 1935, which they felt more accurately represented their supposedly enlightened views about the relationship between church and state.[62]

This generational difference was exacerbated when the Chilean Catholic Church was disestablished in 1925, which seemed to confirm the younger Catholics' fears about relying too heavily on state indulgence and protection.[63] The separation of church and state in Chile came as the result of the new constitution Ibañez demanded.[64] Prior to the coup, Catholicism had been the official state religion. This meant that religious practice and belief of any sort other than Catholic could only be observed privately. It also meant that the national church received state funding to support its various properties and endeavors while simultaneously avoiding taxes.[65] The combination of these material benefits, the close relationship with the state more generally, and the oligarchic nature of the Chilean state at the time served as driving forces of Ibáñez's coup.[66] Older Catholics saw the separation of church and state as a concerning development not only for the loss of prestige but also for the growing need to reckon with secularization as a social and political reality.[67]

Just as the Catholic individuals discussed here should not be treated as uniform in their perspectives and experiences, so too the overall category of "eugenicist" is not monolithic. Texts from popular periodicals, medical journals, monographs, and visual images produced by Catholic and secular writers and publishers show that eugenicists hailed from many walks of life. The eugenicists discussed here were selected by virtue of their ability to publish in one of these mediums, not because of their politics, prestige, or privilege, though many Chilean eugenicists came from privileged positions. What united eugenicists in Chile, and indeed all over the world, was their belief that the human race could be improved through human intervention and that intervention was necessary. Both of these elements are basic requirements to believing in eugenic science, but despite this foundational agreement among Chilean eugenicists, eugenic theory and practice were the subject of considerable debate.

It should be noted that medical training generally facilitated an interest in eugenics, and many of the eugenic texts discussed here were written by physicians from a variety of different specialties. This fits with trends for the region as a whole, as most Latin American eugenicists found their way to the discipline through the study and practice of medicine.[68] Medical schools were often incubators for various scientific disciplines in Latin America at the turn of the twentieth century, because of the relatively small set of scientific institutions there, which created an intimately connected local scientific community. However, this should not indicate a lack of scientific sophistication or interest. Indeed, Thomas Glick has argued for Spain that a small scientific community served to facilitate the "conductivity of scientific ideas" there.[69] In Chile, the relatively small size of the scientific community also created a certain porousness, allowing for self-taught experts, religious figures, and social reformers to make up a significant portion of the national eugenic movement alongside those with medical degrees. Eugenicists committed enough to put pen to paper and publish (those who are examined here) considered themselves experts, though their expertise might have been achieved in a variety of ways. In this book I illuminate just how fluid this expert category was—expanding even beyond the scope some of them believed it should to include Catholics.

By the early 1950s, political coalitions such as the Frente Popular and the Falange Nacional no longer commanded the same control as they had in the 1930s and 1940s.[70] The shifts in political priorities were probably best represented by the fact that Ibáñez, representing the center-right Partido Agrario Laborista (Agrarian Labor Party), was legitimately elected president in 1952 concluding a period of generally left-leaning political control.[71] It was also in the early 1950s that the papal encyclical *Humani generis* was published. Released on August 12, 1950, by Pope Pius XII, this encyclical recognized evolutionary theory as true, officially concluding any remaining internal conflict in the Catholic intellectual community on this issue. This only furthered the possibility of Catholic involvement in eugenic science, which continued to thrive in the region (and elsewhere) far beyond the end of the Second World War as is traditionally argued.

Chapter Summaries

The book is divided into two parts. The first is focused on illuminating how Catholicism and eugenic science reckoned with each other. To be clear, while belief and faith are essential to Catholicism as religious practice, the concern here is with how Catholicism as an intellectual framework was able to engage with eugenic concepts and theories. In this sense, both Catholicism and eugenics are treated as ideologies, which gained adherents by offering similar ideas regarding gender difference, family formation, and racial health in early twentieth-century Chile. In the first three chapters I address how these conceptual similarities fostered an unexpected link between ideologies that are often treated as oppositional. In chapter 1, I compare the writings of Catholic and secular eugenicists regarding the supposed marriage crisis of the interwar years so as to demonstrate that both groups identified similar issues as threats to the health and future of *la raza chilena*. In chapter 2 the focus is on exploring how Chilean intellectuals discussed the relationship between Catholicism and science generally. Although most secular eugenicists argued that Catholics had no place in Chile's racial renewal, most Catholic eugenic writers questioned this exclusion. They generally argued that Catholicism and science were mutually beneficial and that both worked to reveal the same laws prescribing human life and experience. In chapter 3, I demonstrate how Catholic eugenic writers contributed to the development of eugenic science in Chile by modifying the concepts and practices that were considered the most ethically dubious from a Catholic perspective.

The second half of the book is dedicated to a discussion of how Chilean racial theorists, both Catholic and secular, supported the contention that there was such a thing as a singular and homogeneous Chilean race. Shared ideas regarding the racial exceptionalism of the Chilean biotype not only further illustrate connections between Catholic and secular intellectual circles, they also give insight into a specific type of racial thought in Latin America that was quite different from other nations. The claim in Chilean eugenic literature was that the national racial character was the product of *mestizaje*, much like counterparts in Brazil or Mexico, but the contention was also that the Chilean mixture was Whiter and more complete than others elsewhere in the region. My primary purpose here is to better understand the formation of a distinctive "Chileanness" and how that racial identity functioned much like Whiteness in other contexts. To do this, my analysis begins with the work of Palacios. Although his book *Raza chilena* has mostly been forgotten, I show how it had a profound impact on Chilean racial thought throughout the twentieth century. In chapter 5 the discussion centers on how controlling female sexuality was treated as essential to both the continuation and the protection of the Chilean race. In chapter 6, I examine Chilean visual culture in order to illuminate how Whiteness could exist in conjunction with mestizo heritage, a contention that set Chilean racial theorists apart from their Latin American counterparts.

Despite scholarly and popular claims to the contrary, eugenics as a discipline had not yet fallen out of favor by the early 1950s, at the end of the period examined here. In 1953, Reverend Father Yves M. J. Congar wrote a short booklet entitled *The Catholic Church and the Race Question*, which was published by the UN Educational, Scientific, and Cultural Organization as part of a series on race and racism in various religious traditions and scientific disciplines. In it, Congar argued: "True eugenics is a matter involving the solution of the social problem (slums, drunkenness, prostitution, pauperism), the general respect of ethics . . . [and] constructive health legislation."[72] He also decried racism and wrote at length about how Catholicism stood in direct opposition to racist conceits. Echoing claims made decades later by historians of eugenics and Catholicism, he argued that the Catholic Church had been one of the few institutions to oppose coerced sterilization.[73] Yet, he still maintained that eugenics was a legitimate science with noble goals. "The Church has no idea of prohibiting eugenic practices or research," he wrote. A few sentences later, he stated: "It holds that, even on the animal side of his nature, man is not an animal. . . . This is overlooked not only by racist doctrine but also by that unconsciously materialistic attitude towards eugenics that racial feeling inspires."[74] His ability to disconnect eugenic science from racism and discrimination speaks to the conceptual malleability of the discipline. It also demonstrates how concepts often associated with Latin American racial flexibility not only were the result of cultural predispositions or pragmatism but were actively fostered by Catholic intellectual traditions. If anything, in this monograph I hope to illuminate how elements of eugenic science and racial thought became palatable through their active disconnection from obviously racist sentiments. The Chilean case, in particular, offers an important opportunity to consider how racialized concepts and tropes can be made invisible.

Chapter 1

"The Girl Is Not Pursued"

Shared Perspectives and Threats to the Chilean Race

On December 15, 1901, *La Revista Católica* (*LRC*; The Catholic review) published an article entitled "Guerra al Alcoholismo" (War on alcoholism). The article was part of the magazine's "Variedades" (Variety) section, which featured brief articles on issues of special interest to the periodical's primarily Catholic readership both lay and clerical. The article began: "Alcoholism is a social plague: it destroys health, relaxes morality; [it] peoples hospitals, asylums and jails, and it wounds and punishes its victims up to and including their offspring. It is not strange, then, that moralists have united with physicians and economists to wage all-out war against [it]."[1] Going on to discuss how this war would be won primarily through moral uplift programs and temperance, the anonymous author expressed sentiments that matched those of temperance advocates all over the world at the turn of the twentieth century.[2] Despite the relatively unremarkable laments over alcoholism, however, this article highlights one of the more notable aspects of the eugenic movement in Latin America. Depicting moralists, physicians, and economists as equally vital in the fight for Chilean public health, the author illustrates a phenomenon that permeated debates in Latin American eugenics and racial thought for at least the next four decades. Specifically, the author's language demonstrated just how pervasive eugenic concepts had become in Catholic periodicals at the turn of the twentieth century and also the relatively small size and dynamism of the Chilean scientific community.

Reflecting upon the extent of this interaction between Catholicism and eugenics, some of the most important concerns discussed in Chilean eugenic literature, Catholic and secular, were regarding the future of the national racial body. In particular, the Chilean family was often characterized as the first line of defense against racial degeneration. Placing such an onus on the family not only reinforced the importance of traditional gender roles for both men and women but also forged intellectual bridges between secular and Catholic perspectives on eugenics as conceptualized and practiced in Chile and Latin America more generally. In other words, regardless of religious persuasion, belief in eugenic policies and theories tended to demand a belief in patriarchal family structures and traditional gender roles that Catholic institutions and representatives had been advocating for centuries. Eugenic writing that appeared in Catholic periodicals eagerly pointed out this similarity and sought to capitalize upon it, while secular articles often portrayed religious belief as antiquated, at best, and at worst, dangerous to the future of the Chilean race.

Gender as a Shared Site of Concern

A primary conceptual space in which Catholic and eugenic interests merged was in the reification of the patriarchal family structure and the roles women and men played within it. Eugenic writers regularly covered a variety of gender-based issues that threatened the racial health of Chileans. One of the more troubling concerns they raised was the supposed infertility of the most eugenically fit members of the race.[3] The physician Christian Van Lennep, a member of the Sociedad Médica de Valparaíso (Valparaíso Medical Society), discussed this in his September 1917 article entitled "Esterilidad del Matrimonio" (Matrimonial infertility). Appearing in the *Revista Médica de Chile* (*RMC*; The Chilean medical review), this article was written for physicians who in their practice might encounter couples with fertility problems. In continuous print since 1872, the *RMC* served as one of the primary journals for Chilean physicians and medical professionals. Like a significant number of the prominent physicians working in the country in the early twentieth century, Van Lennep was not Chilean by birth. In fact, he was born in the Netherlands in 1886. He studied medicine and upon his graduation from medical school in 1907 was given a place in the prestigious Boherhaave Clinic in Amsterdam. However, he was obliged to emigrate when it came to light that he was having an affair with his supervisor's wife. He chose Chile in 1911 after seeing an advertisement in *The Lancet* calling for specialists to move to the country. Once in Valparaíso, Van Lennep worked as an obstetrician, and it was in this capacity that he wrote his article for the *RMC*.[4]

In "Esterilidad del matrimonio," Van Lennep argued that most physicians typically blamed women for fertility problems although, medically speaking, men were just as likely to be the cause.[5] He also implied that this was not necessarily the result of natural conditions. Rather, he contended that a common cause of female infertility, problems affecting the fallopian tubes, were "generally acquired by infections caused by the husband."[6] More often than not, Van Lennep believed, husbands carried sexually transmitted infections that affected their wives' reproductive systems without suffering any physical consequences themselves. This was doubly repugnant, in his opinion, because men often contracted these infections by engaging in sexual relationships with women other than their wives. The implication was that most men regularly engaged the services of prostitutes, who at the time were understood as known vectors of venereal disease.[7] In this context of presumed marital infidelity, Van Lennep thought that physicians should not permit men to blame their wives if they were having difficulty conceiving.

Nor should doctors be inclined to see the problem as primarily one of female physical dysfunction. As physicians, he wrote, "it is important to communicate to [the husband], the wife being many times treated poorly [and] being accused of being useless, that the first cause [of infertility] is in him, even though his sperm may appear normal."[8] He implied that it was a poorly trained physician who looked only at female patients as the cause of matrimonial infertility. This approach certainly shows that Van Lennep had empathy for his female patients, but it should also be understood as reaffirming the eugenic notion that maintaining a strict gender binary was essential to racial health. While holding men accountable for their sexual indiscretions, he still placed a premium on supposedly normal female sexuality as being almost exclusively reproductive. Female prostitutes were inherently sexually aberrant, so they did not figure into this argument. This would prove to be the overwhelming consensus in Chilean eugenic texts of the period regarding infertility.

Federico Ankelen Haussen, an obstetrician, also wrote about Chilean physicians' apparent enthusiasm for holding women solely responsible for fertility problems within married couples. His article on the subject, "Esterilidad femenina" (Female infertility), appeared in the January 1934 issue of *Medicina Moderna* (Modern medicine), another periodical aimed at physicians, which was published between 1927 and 1943. Then working at the Hospital San Agustín in Valparaíso, Ankelen would go on to head the Escuela Universitaria de Obstetricia y Puericultura (University School of Obstetrics and Puericulture) of the Universidad de Valparaíso in 1961.[9] Suggesting that the supposed crisis of fertility in Chile was, at least partially, perpetuated by sexism, he wrote: "The sexual pride characteristic of the man means that the woman is almost always blamed for infertility. In reality it is demonstrated that in half of these cases the man is responsible." Ankelen's statement demonstrates that male sexuality was associated more with sexual bravado and less with an actual desire to have children, unlike that of women. He insisted that this pride in male sexuality was not restricted to male patients alone. It also affected Chilean physicians (by and large a majority male population) in their ability to do their jobs effectively. The notion that women were mostly responsible for infertility problems was so deeply entrenched among Chilean physicians that Ankelen felt compelled to write, in bold text: "No woman should be considered infertile while a microscopic examination of the husband's semen [for defects] goes undone and live sperm have been found."[10]

Infertility among those perceived to be Chile's most racially fit was also linked to another concern raised in eugenic texts—about the use and availability of birth control. One of the earliest mentions of birth control and the supposed threat it posed to the Chilean race was in Pierre Barbet's 1924 monograph, *Preparación del joven al matrimonio* (Preparation of the young man for marriage). Barbet was a French physician and the chief surgeon at Saint Joseph Hospital in Paris.[11] Even further illustrating the already strong linkage between eugenics and Catholicism within the Latin scientific community, he became best known for his book *La passion de N.-S. Jésus-Christ selon le chirurgien* (*Doctor at Calvary: The Passion of Our Lord Jesus Christ as Described by a Surgeon*), published in 1950, which contended that the Shroud of Turin was authentic.[12] Still many years away from this success though, it is unclear why the Liga Chilena de Higiene Social (Chilean Social Hygiene League) decided to translate and publish *Preparación*.

Barbet argued that birth control for married couples allowed them to enjoy the physical pleasures of sex without the responsibility of bearing children, which presented a significant threat to the Chilean race by encouraging an indulgent and immoral attitude. "If the [betrothed] only look to marriage for the satisfaction of their sensual appetites, they will fall into the very sad practice of neo-Malthusianism and anti-conceptive precautions."[13] He also contended that this casual attitude toward sex would result in the increased use of prostitutes among men.[14] This behavior would further threaten the integrity of the Chilean race, as writers such as Van Lennep seemed to substantiate when discussing sexually transmitted diseases affecting women's reproductive systems. Barbet's Catholic background, medical training, and experience led him to advocate for sexual continence for all people. Yet his book was directed at men only, intimating that he believed they had more difficulty with this than women.

Marital infertility was also perceived to be the result of the increasing availability of birth control and Chilean eugenic texts made a variety of arguments against its use. One of the more intriguing approaches focused on the fact that birth control was the result of a misunderstanding and a misreading of contemporary societal problems. Alejandro Huneeus Cox wrote an entire article dedicated to his belief that social scientists had misinterpreted English cleric and economist Thomas Malthus's work related to population and food production. This article is significant not only because of its content but also because of its inclusion in the August 1933 issue of *Estudios* (Studies). The magazine was published by the Centro de Estudios Religiosos de Santiago (Center of Religious Studies of Santiago)—founded in 1928 by Partido Conservador (Conservative Party) member Ricardo Cox Méndez—and was designed to publicize the work of those affiliated with the center.[15] Aiming at a fairly academic readership, *Estudios* went through a run of 255 issues spanning twenty-five years from 1932 to 1957. Jaime Eyzaguirre, conservative lawyer and historian, was cofounder and served as editor of the periodical for its lifetime.[16] Due to the power and influence of both Cox and Eyzaguirre, *Estudios* represented an important site of Catholic intellectual development and knowledge production in mid-twentieth-century Chile. Notably, articles about eugenics, health, and science made regular appearances throughout the magazine's run.

On the very first page of the August 1933 article, Huneeus argued: "Modern ideas about the maximum density of the population absolutely differ from the Malthusian theory. For Malthus the problem only consisted of the relationship between the increase in population and that of subsistence; today it is a matter of population density and the productivity of human industry."[17] In other words, Huneeus insisted that modern scholars had applied Malthus's original theory incorrectly by glossing over the difference between population growth and density as well as availability of food and industrial productivity. These latter concepts were not what Malthus had discussed, so his ideas regarding scarcity or population management were not relevant to more modern-day discussions that went beyond his original intent and scope.

Huneeus ultimately argued that advocates for birth control were mistaken. Rather than attempting to limit the population, which he insisted nature could regulate on its own, experts should be working to develop new types of technologies to facilitate the growth and distribution of food for the world's population. He blamed irresponsible capitalist economic expansion for the supposed need for birth control. The difficulties in which many working people found themselves were not, according to Huneeus, because they had too many children but, rather, because capitalist economic logics punished the lower classes.[18] In fact, those logics were pushed to their extreme limit in the debates regarding birth control. He wrote: "Now then, the advocates of Birth-Control, far from ensuring the worker the benefits of a just salary to which he has the rights, they want to deprive him of that other unalienable right of all human beings, which is to start a family."[19] Arguments like these should be read not only in terms of the explicit critique of class differences operating in early-twentieth-century Chile but also as a more subtle racial and ethnic critique as well. The working and lower classes were often implicitly understood to be racially less fit because of their environmental circumstances as well as their supposedly undesirable physical characteristics such as dark hair and skin.

One of the more intriguing discussions of birth control methods as self-imposed infertility appeared in the January 1934 issue of *Medicina Moderna*. In an article entitled "Esterilidad fisiológica" (Physiological infertility), the Argentine physician and psychiatrist Arturo Guitarte adamantly opposed the use of the rhythm method, arguing that it had no basis in medical fact and that doctors should not recommend it to their patients. He seemed especially committed to the idea that female patients not be counseled to avoid pregnancy in this way, even when becoming pregnant presented significant health risks. For Guitarte, encouraging women to avoid pregnancy was akin to recommending a therapeutic abortion, which, he hastened to say, the Catholic Church frowned upon.[20] Of the rhythm method, or other practices involving periods of avoiding sexual contact, he wrote: "The Church sees the justification of marriage and its subsequent cohabitation in procreation; such that it prohibits all artificial methods that might diminish it. Starting from this strictly religious point of view, temporary chastity would not have the value of true chastity, but rather would be considered a subterfuge to avoid conception, and, even though some confessors have advised this with negative results, this method would not differentiate itself from other forms of birth control."[21] It seems that Guitarte was led to this rather extreme position because he believed, based on his research, that only 10–15 percent of sexual encounters resulted in pregnancy.[22] Since the numbers were so low to begin with, from his perspective the idea that fit individuals might attempt to limit their fertility even further was unconscionable.

The rhythm method was a particular focus in the debates surrounding birth control in Chile during this period. In a 1936 issue of the *Boletín Médico Social* (*BMS*; Social medicine bulletin), an author identified only as "E. M. S." wrote a review of the book *Grave problema conyugal: El número de los hijos* (The serious conjugal problem: The number of children) by Armand Dorsaz, André Rendu, and Raoul de Guchteneere. The *BMS* was published by the Caja de Seguro Obligatorio (Social Security Fund) for two decades, from 1936 to 1956, and its overall mission was dedicated to improving the general welfare of the Chilean populace through public health education. Originally published the year before in France under the title *Le contrôle rationnel des naissances*, the book championed the use of the rhythm method as the best way to avoid pregnancy.[23] Despite stipulating that married couples were not obligated to have children, E. M. S. did not share the same enthusiasm for the project as its authors, indicating that Latin eugenics was not a uniform intellectual landscape.[24] E. M. S. wrote: "given the conditions of contemporary social organization and the existing sexual freedom, under the false protection that DORSAZ's book gives, would give rise to a resurgence in free sexual unions, legal and extralegal, and with that, a good number of those condemned and abominable abortions that would be directly attributed to the inopportune initiative of the Catholic Church."[25] Like Huneeus before him, E. M. S. said that birth control overlooked serious aspects of modern society that needed to be addressed instead. Using neo-Malthusian logic to support birth control efforts while simultaneously obscuring the real causes of poverty and human suffering was a popular claim in Chilean eugenic writing.

Eduardo Keymer F. made similar claims. His chapter "Uso de anti-concepcionales—Problema económico-social" (Contraceptive use—a socioeconomic problem) in the 1938 edited volume *Estudios médicos* (Medical studies) argued that birth control arose from the "Anglo-Saxon mentality," which treated children as responsibilities to be endured. He wrote: "Children, far from being the glorious coronation of maternity, are a heavy burden that has to be overcome."[26] Keymer attributed concern over the amount of pregnancies a woman could, or should, responsibly have during her lifetime to an Anglo-Saxon perspective—because Malthus, an Englishman, was the first to consider the relationship between birth rate and the availability of resources.[27] This, in itself, is suggestive of the growing consciousness among Latin American scientists of the supposed intellectual differences between "Latin" and "Anglo-Saxon" eugenics and racial thought.

Keymer went on to wax eloquent about the ability of the female body to produce multiple children without negative consequences. He insisted that there was significant evidence that having multiple pregnancies actually led to women having longer lives.[28] He went on to argue that women were psychologically damaged by birth control because they had a "subconscious desire to be mothers despite having expressed the will to avoid conception."[29] Claiming that women subconsciously desired to become and stay pregnant, even if they said they did not, Keymer not only effectively applied the "no means yes" argument to birth control but, like Van Lennep and Ankelen before him, also diminished the status of women to little more than walking wombs. So sure was he that a woman's primary purpose in life was to have children, he also asserted that all sexual encounters must result in male ejaculation. Surprisingly, this was not to ensure the health of men but, rather, that of women. He wrote: "Semen, as well as masculine gametes, contains other complementary substances that when absorbed by the vaginal epithelium and especially the uterine mucosa will pass to the circulatory system where they interact with the metabolism. . . . It is this true masculine therapy that is responsible for the somatic and psychic changes in the female newlywed. On the other hand, many conditions of the skin, psyche, nervous and gynecological systems have been cured by injections of sperm extract."[30]

The claim that intercourse including male ejaculation into the vagina was essential for both male and female health seemed to be widespread in texts by Chilean eugenic authors skeptical of birth control. Although it is worth reflecting on the claims that birth control was a distraction from the true inequalities caused by capitalist economic structures (and perhaps inherently racialized logics, as Keymer's Anglo-Saxon comment suggests), the deep commitment to pronatalism (to the point of fanaticism) in these documents should not be downplayed. In an article entitled "Sobre patología del fraude sexual" (On the pathology of sexual fraud), appearing in the *Revista de Medicina* (previously *Medicina Moderna*) in November 1943, Carlos Thonet Ingles argued the same points as both E. M. S. and Keymer. As he put it: "Maternity, the fundamental biological tendency of the woman, forms an integral part of the feminine sexual instinct."[31] Here, Thonet elided the differences between biology, gender, and sexuality, again with the result that women were diminished exclusively to their reproductive abilities. The fact that this article appeared in the *Revista de Medicina* shows that these opinions were not exclusive to the Catholic medical community alone. Thonet then discussed the supposed physical results of "sexual fraud" for female patients. "Tricking" the female body to avoid pregnancy had dire consequences, and thus, he asserted, the rhythm method should only be recommended in the most serious of cases.[32] Though not entirely clear what these were, this presumably meant only when pregnancy would threaten the woman's life.

Concerns regarding the use of various birth control methods also held within them a deeper fear about Chilean race suicide in comparison to the world at large. In a brief review of the article "Current Comment—Ineffectiveness of Contraceptive Methods," which originally appeared in the *Journal of the American Medical Association* in November 1936, René Miranda Tirado related the findings of his American peers in the January 1937 issue of the *RMC*.[33] According to the Chilean version of the article, most women did not correctly apply the principles of birth control, so the effect on birth rates was almost negligible. This was especially true among African American women. As Miranda put it: "This last fact demonstrates the extremely inexact nature of the ordinary methods of birth control when employed by negro women."[34] This finding was important in the grand scheme of the birth control debate not only internationally, where many European-descended eugenicists insisted that White people would be outpaced by the fertility of supposedly lesser races, but also in Chile where these types of concerns could be applied to poor women who were typically thought to have more ties to indigenous heritage.

Infertility and birth control were linked by the overall concern regarding infant mortality and population size, but there was another issue discussed at length in eugenic literature. Alcoholism was thought to have perhaps an equally damaging effect on Chilean racial integrity as infertility and birth control. Carlos Alberto Castaño's May 1935 article in *Estudios*, for example, was titled "El alcoholismo aristocrático y la cura de hambre para adelgazar" (Aristocratic alcoholism and the hunger cure to slim down). Based originally on a lecture given as part of the Cursos de Cultura Católica de Buenos Aires (Catholic culture courses of Buenos Aires), the article that appeared in *Estudios* soon after featured selections from that talk.[35] Castaño focused on "aristocratic" alcoholism and dieting, which he characterized as exclusively female problems, to show how these two behaviors had catastrophic results for the birth rate. From this perspective, women seemingly held complete responsibility for population growth or depletion. Issues affecting male potency were not discussed at all.

The Catholic influence in this talk becomes apparent when Castaño argues that to overindulge in alcohol or in excessive dieting was not only unhealthy for women but actually sinful. He pointed out that these behaviors indicated a knowing abuse of one's own body and, as such, were in direct contravention of the Fifth Commandment: thou shalt not kill.[36] To have too many drinks or too little food effectively amounted to killing oneself one day at a time. Dieting in particular, he felt, was problematic: "There exists a great percentage of infertile women today for this reason: you do not see those large families of five children or more, there is a true decrease in birth rate, equally because of contraception practices that we have discussed as well as the poor state of the female organism due to the frequency of dieting."[37] Castaño insisted throughout the talk in the Catholic lecture series that shaming women for their problematic behavior was not enough. Doctors must take these issues seriously, he insisted, and priests also had to be informed of the dangers that drink and dieting posed specifically to women and, by extension, national populations.[38]

A significantly different approach to alcoholism appeared in Antonio Cifuentes Grez's article "El Proyecto de Represión del Alcoholismo" (The Project to Repress Alcoholism). Published in *Estudios* in July 1937, the article was written in response to a newly proposed government effort to curb the public's enthusiasm for drinking. While his colleagues bemoaned the fact that birth control was mere theater to distract from capitalist greed, Cifuentes instead argued that the reason alcoholism had become such a problem in Chile was because workers were so able to find well-paid jobs that they had too much available cash with which to buy alcohol.[39] Unlike government officials, who were working to reduce the amount of alcohol produced in the country so that less would be consumed, Cifuentes felt the real problem was the low breeding of the Chilean working classes.[40] He argued that Chilean workers drank less than their equivalents in France, Spain, and Italy but somehow managed to become more inebriated.[41] The best response to this state of affairs was not to reduce the amount of alcohol produced in the country but, rather, to educate the working classes so they would no longer find drunkenness appealing. "This in itself reflects the low cultural and moral level of our worker and the existing necessity of paying attention to his education if we want to see him free from alcoholism."[42]

Cifuentes's writing implied that the existence of alcoholism in Chile was evidence of an inherent racial failing. In this, he was not alone among experts who sought to rid the Chilean race of this specific problem. In his thesis to become a surgeon, Hernan Bennett Leay argued a similar position. With this text, evaluated and published in 1940 by the Universidad de Chile's Facultad de Biología y Ciencias Médicas (Faculty of Biology and Medical Sciences), Bennett fulfilled the requirements necessary for him to become a practicing surgeon. For his subject matter he decided to study the relationship between alcoholism and mental illness. When discussing how environment shaped and affected alcoholism, he wrote: "The lack of culture and discipline has meant that for a very long time we have not learned to see alcohol as anything more than a vice. Generation after generation of our race has suffered the onslaught of this veritable degenerative wave."[43] The Chilean affinity for alcohol—or, perhaps better said, the lack of appreciation for its potential dangers—would ultimately doom the race. This was even more likely, it seemed, because Bennett portrayed the negative effects of alcoholism as cumulative not only over an individual's lifetime but over the lifetimes of his or her children: "These fathers will fall further and further . . . in large part due to alcohol . . . [and] they will leave their children to follow in their footsteps."[44] Although these discussions of infertility, birth control, and alcoholism all evoked different perspectives and made different recommendations, what they all had in common was a foundational belief in the vulnerability of the Chilean family structure, which allowed for increasingly inappropriate behavior in both women and men. In this light, it makes sense that quite a lot eugenic writing started to focus on marriage as a central means of addressing all of these problems.

The Chilean Marriage Crisis as a Threat to Gender Norms

In addition to the generalized concerns regarding infertility, birth control, and alcoholism, there was also a more focused concern on the institution of marriage in the 1910s through the 1930s. Much like the more general issues, press coverage related to the so-called marriage crisis of the interwar years highlights the overlap in secular and Catholic eugenic perspectives. Intriguingly, this crisis moment represented a recapitulation of an earlier panic. Though the texts discussed in this section were written between 1918 and 1933, the first wave of widespread concern about the state of Chilean marriage began in the 1880s. At that time, then president and Partido Liberal de Chile (Liberal Party) member Domingo Santa María instituted a group of "leyes laícas" (secular laws) designed to curb the national church's influence. These laws secularized public cemeteries (1883), formed the Civil Registry, which recorded births, deaths, and marriages (1884), and established civil marriage (1884), provoking a vociferous Catholic debate about the nature of marriage in a secularizing state.[45]

The civil marriage law neither prohibited religious ceremonies nor mandated civil ones to formalize partnerships, and Catholic social commentators of the late nineteenth century contended that it effectively allowed individuals to practice a legal form of bigamy. An individual could marry one person in a religious ceremony and another in a civil ceremony with seemingly no repercussions. Furthermore, Catholic detractors pointed out that civil marriage was not commensurate with sacramental marriage in the eyes of the Catholic Church. However, the new law suggested they were interchangeable, which spiritually threatened the institution of marriage itself in addition to the legal ambiguities the new laws raised. The problem was exacerbated when, in protest, Bishop Joaquín Larraín Gandarillas encouraged Catholics to avoid having a civil ceremony entirely. The wrangling between church and state over who had true authority resulted in increasingly confusing legal situations, which became so involved as to require papal intervention. In 1897, the Vatican warned Chilean clergy members that they must encourage their parishioners to obtain a civil marriage immediately after the religious ceremony.[46]

The marriage crisis of the 1880s divided the upper echelons of the Chilean intelligentsia regarding the relationship between church and state, but that of the interwar years seemed to unify them, because the interwar crisis built upon widespread fears regarding the degeneration of the Chilean race.

Yet, the marriage crisis was not simply attributed to racial degeneration. Rather, by focusing on supposedly inappropriate gender behavior among young people, discourse surrounding the crisis reinforced the idea that traditional gender roles were essential to racial health. The pervasive belief that maintenance of patriarchal social structures and gender difference protected the racial health of the nation united socially conservative eugenicists, regardless of their religious beliefs. Both secular and Catholic periodicals published articles about this issue and its impact on the racial fate of the nation and demonstrated a striking uniformity of opinion when it came to the presumed relationship between racial health and gender difference.

"Un problema social" (A social problem), an article appearing in a 1918 edition of the national daily newspaper of record, El Mercurio (The Mercury), is a good example of how secular eugenic texts described concerns regarding supposedly decreasing marriage rates. Identified as "Merlin," the author placed the blame on male reticence. He claimed that Chilean men no longer seemed capable of establishing marital relationships with women; the prerequisite for creating a eugenic family that would contribute to the nation's racial health. "The man cowers; the girl calls and is not pursued."[47] "Un problema social" is a rare example of men being held accountable for the destabilization of family and society due to their collective inaction and implied effeminacy rather than alcoholism or overt sexuality.[48] In this case, men were the ones who had moved away from their biologically determined gender roles since every aspect of eugenic theory and practice relied upon the idea that male sexual desire and female submissiveness was nature's way of ensuring offspring.[49] However, according to Merlin, Chilean men had become detached from their natural urges.

To prove his point, Merlin discussed a thirty-year-old single man as a harbinger of Chilean racial degeneracy. He described the man as bald and weak from both hereditary causes and poor environmental conditions. This rather unflattering physical description was meant to illustrate that the young man was already losing his virility at the very age that most Chilean physicians contended that men were at their biological prime for having children.[50] "Un problema social" went on to quote the man as saying that he was not interested in getting married because "the girls are pretty and mature; but very badly raised, they spend a lot on clothes, they want cars, they are all the same, and they do not know one useful thing."[51] Merlin did not disagree with the unlucky young man in his assessment of modern women as frivolous, but he did blame him for fulfilling neither his biological duty to procreate nor his societal obligation to marry.

Merlin's article, a fairly light treatment of a serious problem, provoked a number of letters to El Mercurio's editor. As the editor wrote in the next day's issue, "the sincerity of [the letters] reveals that we have really touched upon a sensitive point, even though our language has not been as delicate as it should be in these matters."[52] The editor then went on to quote one letter in its entirety. Much like Merlin's article before it, the letter was submitted under a pen name, "Eugenia Grandet," alluding to the heroine in Honoré Balzac's *Eugénie Grandet* (1833). This author agreed that there was a marriage crisis of vast proportions affecting not only Chile but the entire world. In her words: "Is this phenomenon limited only to Santiago? Or has the marriage crisis that was noted across the globe before the war finally arrived at its apogee in this remote country, which receives ideas, fashions, and even post [parcels] with considerable delay?"[53] Aside from this rather bleak estimation of Chile's connection to the wider world, Grandet's claim demonstrates that the marriage crisis was perceived to be a significant problem at both international and local levels.

Unlike Merlin, however, Grandet placed the blame more equally on both genders. Perhaps explaining her choice of pen name, the author argued that mothers no longer properly educated their daughters in the choice of marriage partner and that the rise in the number of families with "new" money only worsened this problem.[54] According to Grandet, Chilean families were now much more willing to accept moral or eugenic failings in potential marriage partners if they could offer significant financial advantages. She went on to write that this fostered the notion of a marriage market where the richest partner was the most attractive, which was only further convoluted by a Darwinian understanding of sexual attraction. To prove her point, Grandet mentioned that a recently published article in *El Mercurio* stated: "Darwin had observed that the female in nature was that which adorned herself to attract a mate." While this made women's interest in fashion seem less capricious, it also had the unfortunate effect of making all young women seem interchangeable. And this, Grandet claimed, was the fundamental point of Merlin's article with which she agreed. In the face of dozens of women with similar tastes, ideas, and manners, men found themselves paralyzed and decided that it was better not to marry at all. Ultimately, Grandet seemed to agree with Merlin that male disinterest in marriage stood in the way of the development and improvement of the Chilean race.[55]

Fifteen years after the previous exchange, *El Mercurio* published another article about the marriage crisis, but the issue had changed somewhat. In this article the author argued that divorce legislation then under consideration in the Chilean Senate was an example of the current crisis facing marriage and represented a step backward in terms of national progress.[56] The author, feminist activist María Besa de Díaz Garcés, attributed this development to a larger trend in Chilean society in which "anti-family ideas float in the air like miasmas over swamps." Though her involvement in the founding of the Partido Feminino de Chile (Chilean Women's Party) showed her commitment to secularism, feminism, and progressivism more generally, Besa de Díaz contended that political radicals were trying to make Chileans reject family obligation for a life of individualism and indulgence, a position regularly taken in Catholic writing of the period as well. Although she did not blame Chilean women for this state of affairs, she did hold them solely accountable for solving the problem: "Finally, the woman who knows society's conscience, feels upon her the weight of that high calling of saving it, lending it her quiet experience of centuries, her honor and sincerity to help man untangle the complicated skein of life."[57] Here, she characterized the natural relationship between men and women as a timeless interaction between masters and helpmates that was best realized through marriage.

The marriage crisis of the interwar period had the unintended result of further opening the door to Catholic assessments of what should be done to protect Chilean racial integrity because, throughout Latin America, both clergy and the Catholic Church as an institution had advocated for the formalization of sexual relationships that produced offspring since the colonial period.[58] In this context, it is not surprising that the interwar years saw a significant debate within Catholic publications about the marriage crisis. In January 1920, *LRC* published a circular letter from the Chilean Diocese.[59] In it, Crescente Errázuriz Valdivieso Archbishop of Santiago, along with Luis Antonio Castro Alvarez Bishop of San Carlos de Ancud, Gilberto Fuenzalida Guzmán Bishop of Concepción, Carlos Silva Cotapos Bishop of La Serena, and Rafael Edwards Salas Bishop of the Vicaría General de la República Chilena (General Vicariate of the Chilean Republic), all stated that Catholics were required to register their marriages with civil authorities, which suggests that the papal intervention twenty-three years before had not had much effect. In the circular the authors argued that registering religious unions with the state would support the moral health of parishioners as well as the physical health of the entire nation.[60] Registering would also avoid the possible issue of being married to two individuals simultaneously: "We especially remind [priests and parishioners] of the prohibition of marriage for those who are inscribed in the Civil Registry as married to a different person than they intend to marry [in a religious service]."[61] Showing the seriousness of this effort, the circular ordered priests to read it to their congregations four Sundays in a row.[62]

Despite official calls for registering their marriages with state authorities and for ensuring that those seeking sacramental marriage were not already civilly married to someone else, the issue remained unresolved among clergy members. For example, in his November 1920 *LRC* article entitled "Deberes de los católicos en los momentos actuales" (The duties of Catholics in contemporary times), Gilberto Fuenzalida Guzmán Bishop of Concepción argued that Chileans had moved away from Catholic teachings and that this was especially evident in their cavalier attitudes toward sacramental marriage. Fuenzalida was one of the more prolific writers of the Chilean clergy during the interwar period.[63] In this article, which was mostly about the threats of secularism and socialism to modern Catholicism, Fuenzalida claimed that the availability of civil marriage had caused "the relaxation of familial ties, the corruption of the home, the illegitimacy of children, the abandonment of wives, the moral and physical ruin of the family."[64] He argued that the only way to stamp out the improprieties encouraged by civil marriage was to insist on making marriage a strictly religious matter, in contrast to the current situation in which both the state and the Catholic Church offered avenues to formalized unions.

His position was striking because, only eleven months earlier, Fuenzalida had signed the circular requiring Catholics to register their marriages with civil authorities. His change of heart is surprising.[65] Yet it seems that what he really wanted was to adjust the procedures by which civil and sacramental marriages were contracted. Fuenzalida claimed that those who sought out sacramental marriage before registering with the state were being persecuted by secular government officials, who "wanted to punish those faithful who appeared before God in a temple to implore benedictions prior to appearing before a civil functionary to register the marriage."[66] The solution to this problem, in his view, was to allow sacramental marriage to occur before registering with government officials. He felt that the current situation was untenable because it created obstacles for couples who wanted to marry but who might be intimidated by bureaucratic procedures, resulting in not formalizing their unions at all.

While secular publications generally argued that gender confusion was the cause of the marriage crisis, Catholic publications generally argued that it was a lack of religious conviction. A 1930 *LRC* article managed to combine these concerns. In "El problema social del matrimonio" (The social problem of marriage), Mario Gorostarzu argued that the cause of the current marriage crisis had to do with crumbling patriarchal traditions: "The modesty of the patriarchal habits stamped out vanity with the seal of austerity in the domestic economy."[67] According to Gorostarzu, the loss of patriarchal social structures and values caused both men and women to treat marriage as little more than a game of chance. Echoing concerns raised by both Merlin and Grandet, he wrote, "because in the end she believes that all of them are the same, and because he, with good reason, believes that any of them will be better than the ones he had in [his] libertinage."[68] Marriage partnerships started under these conditions could hardly be expected to thrive or contribute to the overall health of the Chilean race.

Yet Gorostarzu did not believe that the decline of the patriarchal social order was the result of racial degeneration, as secular texts often suggested. Rather, the decline in patriarchal social values was indicative of a
much larger social problem. The real issue, in his view, was a general move
away from faithful religious practice: "The abuse of men in the exertion of
marital authority, much like the feminine error in the misplaced [effort] at
achieving independence, are nothing more than two consequences of the
profound imbalance produced by the juridical looting of marriage's religious nature. . . . Reduced to the category of a simple civil contract, marriage lacks the unique force that makes a perfect union between the bride
and groom."[69] Gorostarzu's characterization of the cause of the marriage
crisis was quite different from that of his secular counterparts, but it is
clear that a significant number of eugenic authors at the time attributed
Chilean racial degeneration to changing gender roles and behaviors. In this
sense, Gorostarzu's emphasis on the return to religious practice was part
of a much wider spectrum of social conservatism captured in the pages
of publications speaking to a diverse audience of Chileans—Catholic and
otherwise—who took as its first priority the protection of *la raza chilena*.

Secular Critiques of Catholic Eugenics

The zeal of writers in the Catholic publications for addressing the marriage
crisis and racial degeneration was not met with enthusiasm by secular proponents of eugenics, who consistently argued that Catholic opinions were
irrelevant to scientific debates regarding racial health. An example of this
perspective appeared in the socialist feminist writer Clara de la Luz's speech
*La mujer y la especie (trabajo leido en el Centro Demócrata de Santiago el
3 de Mayo de 1913)* (Woman and the species, an essay read in Santiago's
Democratic Center on May 3, 1913). De la Luz argued that, "with a woman
who only knows *La historia sagrada* [The sacred history, a selection of Bible
stories], *Las vidas de los santos* [The lives of the saints] and who only goes
to mass, leaving abandoned her duties as housewife, one cannot make a
nation, nor form a family."[70] Her opinion demonstrated that even a secular
eugenicist like herself saw women as contributors to the racial health of the
nation only through their gendered roles as wives and mothers. However,
unlike Catholic eugenic writers, de la Luz contended that these duties were
hindered by religious belief and practice.

The physician Cora Mayers Gley expressed a similar view in her September 1924 article for the *Revista de Beneficencia Pública* (*RBP*; Public
welfare review). Renamed the *Revista de Asistencia Social* in 1932, the magazine lasted from 1917 to 1944, growing alongside the increasingly pro-
fessionalized social welfare and public health community in Chile. In "La

educacion higiénica de la nacion" (The hygienic education of the nation), Mayers mostly discussed her recent trip to the United States. In particular, she focused on how schools there were able to successfully indoctrinate tenets of hygienic practice into the lives of their students. This model was vital to solving many eugenic problems in Chile, she wrote, because "the value of [public health] means absolutely nothing while the collective spirit does not perfectly fathom that these measures . . . are indispensable to social welfare." Mayers then outlined the spaces in which Chileans might best learn hygienic practices such as "sanitary services, schools, hospitals, sanatoriums, dispensaries, the armed services, large factories and warehouses, life and health insurance companies, mutual benefit societies, cooperatives, civic centers, etc., etc."[71] In her lengthy list of public institutions that might contribute to the eugenic improvement of the population, churches were conspicuously absent—perhaps especially so in a country where Catholicism was the predominant religion and means by which quite a lot of social services were provided. Mayers's focus on the school as the best space for hygienic instruction was not casual. It fit with a larger effort among other segments of the secular social reform movement to create a mandatory public elementary school system in Chile in order to challenge a perceived Catholic monopoly on education.[72]

Identifying the school as the primary site for public health instruction served another purpose as well. It allowed Mayers the opportunity to obliquely critique Catholic charitable organizations that had previously offered the care she felt secular, state-run social welfare programs should now provide: "We have demonstrated then that the primary source from which hygiene should emanate is *the school*, and that only when this has been able to foment the civic spirit of future citizens will we be sure that the measures taken by Public Powers will yield the expected [results] and that the monies spent on public health will not be thrown away in the street."[73] In this image alluding to beggars and vagabonds who depended upon charity to survive, she conveyed one of the more powerful anti-Catholic arguments secular eugenicists made—that Catholic charitable organizations lacked the necessary scientific methodologies to adequately address modern social problems such as racial degeneration.

Discussing Catholic charity as lacking any reliable scientific foundation was a common trope in secular eugenic periodicals. In the 1927 inaugural issue of the professional journal *Servicio Social* (Social work), produced by the Junta de Beneficencia de Santiago's Escuela de Servicio Social (Santiago Welfare Committee's School of Social Work), for example, Belgian social worker Leo Cordemans published an article entitled "De la caridad al servicio social" (From charity to social work). Cordemans contended that "Assistance has evolved from Charity, which is an immediate donation, without worrying about tomorrow, calming the call of hunger, cold, pain, Philanthropy which has an organization and a defined purpose . . . and, finally, Social Assistance whose purpose is the most perfect adaptation possible of the individual to his environment."[74] Cordemans wrote this article while working as director of the Escuela de Servicio Social. Founded by Belgian social worker Jenny Bernier in 1925, this was the first school of its kind in Latin America.[75]

According to Cordemans, social work was far better than charity for the nation's racial health because it taught individuals to fend for themselves, which would render future welfare efforts unnecessary. Social work was superior to charity not only because of its planned obsolescence but also because of its reliance on scientific methodology.[76] "The system that demands this assistance is *Social Work*, a true science that encapsulates the rubrics of social diagnosis, those of treatment based on preventative and curative measures, with the exception of the procedures mentioned above that are simply palliative."[77] As Cordemans saw it, social work did not simply ameliorate existing social problems; it used the tools of the social sciences to anticipate and solve them. She believed that social work, when properly applied, would eradicate social problems and fundamentally improve the country's racial profile in perpetuity, something charity never attempted to do. This argument implied not only that the national church fostered an exploitative relationship with the marginalized communities it supposedly served but also that Catholic belief was not compatible with scientific problem solving or science more generally. Catholic publications vehemently disagreed with all of these claims.

Catholic Responses to Secular Skepticism

Although Catholic eugenic supporters did not see religion as antiscientific, the repetitiveness of their writing on the subject suggests that this was a pervasive assumption they combatted in their work. One of the most voluble proponents of the idea that Catholicism was not antiscientific was the Partido Conservador member Ricardo Cox Méndez. Cox originally studied medicine and was awarded his degree in 1895 from the Universidad de Chile. However, because his family needed to maintain their agricultural holdings, he was unable to practice as a physician. Instead, he pursued his various interests in science, medicine, and religion on his own time, becoming a member of the Sociedad Científica de Chile (Chilean Scientific Society), creating the magazine *Estudios*, and writing for a number of other Catholic periodicals as well at the turn of the twentieth century.[78]

In his September 1909 *El Mercurio* article "Orientaciones contemporáneas del catolicismo" (Contemporary aspects of Catholicism), Cox argued that Catholic interest in the eugenic movement grew out of the fact that the Catholic Church was a dynamic and vibrant social institution that always played a role in contemporary society. "But the Church lives in the world and lives in history, that is, lives between the waves of human generation and the vicissitudes of events: and in the midst of this perpetually agitated sea, as all boats on the move, it inclines to one side, and then the other; more, with the prow always pointed to the far horizon, where the sun of eternal justice shines."[79] Cox felt that Catholic involvement in eugenics was evidence of popular demand for that involvement. Therefore, he argued, Catholic efforts to engage in debates regarding racial health were not the result of self-interest or staunch traditionalism but, rather, grew from an authentic desire to serve.

This sentiment was echoed in a similar article that appeared in *LRC* in 1910. Father Samuel de Santa Teresa considered this issue in his article "El católico de hoy" (Today's Catholic). A friar of the Discalced Carmelite Order in the beachside city of Viña del Mar, de Santa Teresa was a regular contributor to the magazine between 1905 and 1910. In this article he argued, "today's Catholic has to develop his behavior today, in the day in which he lives, in the century in which he lives and in the country in which he lives, exactly the same as those Catholics of all days, centuries and countries."[80] De Santa Teresa believed that it was Catholics' duty to actively participate in the national and historical context in which they lived. In fact, the consistent emphasis on the national church's pastoral role helped socially conscious Catholics in Chile to extend that mission into more strictly scientific debates related to eugenics and racial health.

One of the most typical ways of insisting on the right of Catholics to engage in scientific debates related to social issues was to invoke the papal encyclical *Rerum novarum*, published in 1891. Historians such as María Luisa Aspe Armella, Patience A. Schell, and Ericka Verba all argue that throughout Latin America the *Rerum novarum* set the stage for Catholic intervention into social reform over the next fifty years.[81] In a January 1917 article appearing in *LRC* entitled "Orientaciones de acción social Con motivo del XXV aniversario de la Encíclica *RERUM NOVARUM*" (Aspects of social action in light of the twenty-fifth anniversary of the encyclical *Rerum novarum*), for example, Martin Rucker Sotomayor (then rector of the Pontificia Universidad Católica de Chile), argued that "the Encyclical '*Rerum Novarum*' provoked an enormous scientific movement [among Catholics]. The largest social issues were studied with determination; the principles were set in a precise way and the notable document commentators immediately enlightened the mind in order to penetrate the teachings emanating from the Papal See."[82] He contended that the encyclical paved the way for Catholic scientific inquiry in the modern age and that Catholic contributions to the human and social sciences would restore the church's reputation as a scientific institution. In other words, religious men—and, to some extent, women—might once again be seen as contributing to the development of scientific disciplines as they had done for fields such as astronomy, botany, and mathematics in the early modern era.[83]

Secular detractors focused so much on charitable institutions' supposed lack of scientific qualifications that Catholic eugenic authors considered this issue at length, typically, discussing the relationship between social work and charity in genealogical terms. In the 1931 *LRC* article "El concepto de caridad en la asistencia social" (The concept of charity in social work), Luisa Jörinssen argued that, "before all, that which we have to make clear is that there is *no charity that exists that does not have a religious background.*"[84] Like Cordemans, Jörinssen (a German) was writing as the European director of a Chilean school of social work. She headed the Escuela de Servicio Social "Elvira Matta de Cruchaga" at the Pontificia Universidad Católica de Chile from 1929 to 1933.[85] It was not surprising, then, that Jörinssen conflated religious charity with the science of social work. Positing that there was no distinction between the two, and that both originated from the same sort of altruism, was a strike at naysayers such as de la Luz, Mayers, and Cordemans, who argued that Catholics had no business in the interpretation and application of eugenic principles. However, despite these efforts in Catholic periodicals, the contentious relationship between secular and Catholic eugenicists did not dissipate with time. Rather, Catholic concepts that did not disrupt secular eugenic ones became imbricated so deeply into these larger narratives as to be rendered virtually invisible.

Clearly, problems associated with racial health and degeneration—such as the so-called marriage crisis of the 1910s through the 1930s—inspired a variety of historical actors to engage with eugenic theory in the early twentieth century. Eugenics as a discipline carried within it socially conservative ideas regarding the importance of gender difference to racial health, which facilitated agreement in secular and Catholic eugenic texts. This idea goes very much against what secular eugenic writers claimed to be true, as well as what modern scholars often expect regarding the relationship between Catholicism and eugenics. Examining specific eugenic concerns such as infertility, marriage rates, and alcoholism shows how socially conservative ideas regarding racial health and gender difference helped to sustain each other. Illuminating the connections between Catholicism and eugenics in Chile helps to unpack the development of a distinctive type of racial thought in Latin America, contextualizing the Latin American emphasis on women's gender roles and behavior in discussion of racial types and traits.

Yet focusing on the relationship between gender and racial degeneration is only part of the work Catholic writing about eugenics had to do.

More often than not, secular eugenicists felt that Catholics grossly misunderstood the pressures of modern living and the corresponding eugenic demands placed on individuals and families. In fact, doubt regarding Catholicism's ability to function in the modern world went beyond the field of eugenics and became part of an open debate in a number of different disciplines throughout the first half of the twentieth century all over the world.[86] The Catholic response to these critiques was immediate, vociferous, and extensive. In the Chilean case, Catholic eugenic supporters first approached this issue by insisting on the mutually beneficial relationship between science and religion.

Chapter 2

The Two Truths

"Harmonizing" Catholicism and Science

Pope Leo XIII's 1891 encyclical *Rerum novarum* had an impact on both the sciences and social activism for Catholics in Latin America.[1] The primary focus of the text was on how the expansion and maturation of industrial capitalism had encouraged income inequality and class conflict. Thus it inspired Catholic social activism aimed at improving the living conditions of lower-class Catholics all over the world, including those in Latin America. However, this encyclical was also read as a document encouraging Catholics to expand their reach into a variety of fields in the human and social sciences. Taking cues from the encyclical, many Catholic authors contended that science and religion, despite what might be generally believed, were mutually supportive.

The conflation of scientific logics with social activism was possible because of the encyclical itself. When affirming that private property would not be threatened by the construction of socially conscious welfare programs, Leo XIII did not only rely on the precedents provided in scripture. In fact, before even mentioning biblical passages related to the issue of charity or altruism, he turned to natural law or, more accurately, his understanding of Darwinian evolutionary principles. He wrote: "every man has by nature the right to possess property as his own. This is one of the chief points of distinction between man and the animal creation, for the brute has no power of self-direction, but is governed by two main instincts. . . . One of these instincts is self-preservation, the other the propagation of the species."[2] He went on to state that human beings had evolved beyond the needs merely to exist and procreate. Private property and ownership were distinctly human features that set Homo sapiens above other life on Earth, and Leo XIII made clear that no institution or individual should seek to remove these concepts from human society. Although his understanding of speciation, natural selection, and evolutionary biology were certainly limited, Leo XIII relied on the metaphor of survival of the fittest to support his claim that altruism and private property could coexist. This shows just how pervasive the use of scientific language to explain human behavior and society had become by the end of the nineteenth century. Indeed, his use of Darwinian concepts demonstrates a common approach in Chilean Catholic writing that portrayed science and religion as mutually constitutive.

Catholic and secular eugenic texts identified and discussed similar perceived threats to the health of the Chilean race because Catholic involvement in eugenic debates was predicated on a larger body of writing that conceptualized the relationship between science and religion as symbiotic. On the one hand, the texts examined here represent a local variation of a larger international movement in the Catholic press in response to the increasing political power of secular social reform everywhere. On the other hand, these texts were also central to understanding how Chilean Catholics explained their right to participate in national debates regarding racial health. As such, Chilean texts of the early twentieth century demonstrate how much variation there was in Catholic writing regarding the interaction between religion and science and how that variation fostered an intellectual environment that was especially open to eugenic concepts and theories.

Showing the open engagement of Catholics with eugenic ideas in Chile contributes to a more nuanced treatment of the "conflict thesis" in the history of science and religion.[3] Catholic writers there were unified only in their overwhelming rejection of the notion that science and religion operated in opposition to each other, which has come to be known as the conflict thesis. Some Chilean Catholic writers argued that science and religion rarely interacted, so there was no need to discuss conflict at all. Others contended that science and religion worked together to allow human beings to make the best practical use of the natural world and its resources. Others insisted that religion dealt with matters of the supernatural and therefore was superior to science (though science did seem to have its more mundane uses). Regardless of approach, Chilean Catholic authors did not accept the contention that religious commitment rendered one incapable of scientific thinking or unsuited to the task of weighing in on scientific matters. Instead, these authors posited a symbiotic—or to use their word, "harmonious"—relationship between religion and science, which created a space where Catholic eugenic supporters were welcome to participate. If a generalized belief in the gendered basis for threats to national racial health opened the door to eugenics for Catholics, a desire to remain relevant in an increasingly secular society that privileged science demanded that they walk through.

Transnational Secularism and Local Iterations of the Conflict Thesis

Chilean Catholic eugenic supporters confronted a vast amount of internationally and locally produced literature that was simultaneously critical and suspicious of their involvement in scientific debates of any sort. Participating in the regional shift toward democratic liberalism and corresponding anticlericalism across Latin America, some nineteenth- and early twentieth-century Chilean writers insisted that secularism was essential to modern society in general and to scientific inquiry in particular.[4] The conceptual clash between Catholic and secular eugenic writers highlights the transnational and local currents at work in the formulation of a specifically Chilean discourse regarding racial hygiene and eugenic theory. Almost immediately after independence from Spain, a number of Latin American leaders and politicians advocated for anticlerical measures in order to make a break from the colonial past. Some of the more notable individuals associated with this turn are Antonio Guzmán Blanco, the president of Venezuela for a total of three, nonconsecutive years; Benito Juárez, the president of Mexico from 1858 to 1871; and Plutarco Elías Calles, the president of Mexico from 1924 to 1928.[5] Calles was so vehement in his efforts to oust the Mexican Catholic Church from its privileged position that he enacted what came to be known as the Ley Calles (the Calles Law), a penal reform statute that fined priests for wearing clerical garb in public and threatened a five-year prison sentence if any priest criticized the government. In Mexico, Calles's anticlericalism sparked the bloody Cristero War, which pitted Catholic peasants against government forces.[6] In Chile, anticlerical viewpoints were primarily associated with the Partido Radical (Radical Party), though the Partido Liberal also advocated for various efforts at tamping down the power and influence of the national church. As Cristián Gazmuri argues, the main thrust of these efforts was to increase lay education and to end Catholicism as the state religion in order to secularize Chilean society.[7]

In addition to regional suspicion regarding the relationship between Catholicism and science, Chilean secular texts were also influenced by anticlericalist writers from the North Atlantic, who were often even more suspicious of Catholic claims to power and authority than their Latin American counterparts. John William Draper's *History of the Conflict between Religion and Science* (1874) and Andrew Dickson White's *A History of the Warfare of Science with Theology in Christendom* (1896) were particularly important foundational texts for the modern understanding of the relationship between science and religion in the English-speaking world. Both writers characterized the relationship as oppositional and held a skeptical view of the ability of religious institutions to contribute to the advancement of scientific pursuits. Leaving very little to the imagination, Draper wrote: "The history of Science is not a mere record of isolated discoveries; it is a narrative of the conflict of two contending powers, the expansive force of the human intellect on one side, and the compression arising from traditionary faith and human interest on the other."[8] Claims such as this were common throughout the latter half of the nineteenth century, so much so that by the early twentieth century many secular writers, scientists, and public intellectuals considered religious practice as indicative of an active rejection of modernity in all of its valences, including science.[9] Draper's and White's works were first published in the United States (and in English), seemingly quite far from the Chilean context of this study, but their opinions formed part of a transnational anticlerical community of scholars who were predisposed to skepticism that elicited Catholic responses in many nations.[10]

Chileans who preferred secular scientific practices were less polemic than White or Draper but no less certain of the fact that science and Catholicism did not mix, as is shown, for example, in the minutes from the first Latin American Scientific Congress held in Buenos Aires in 1898. The Chilean delegate and president of the proceedings, Paulino Alfonso del Barrio, noted that "science is the necessary condition for the complete emancipation of the body and spirit which promote the progress and abundance of the faculties."[11] Alfonso was no stranger to large international conferences. As a young man he accompanied his father, the former Minister of Foreign Affairs José Alfonso Cavada, to the first International Pan-American Conference, which was held in Washington, DC, between October 1889 and April 1890. He had also served as a member of the Chilean congress.[12] Although his comments about the relationship between science and religion were milder in tone than those of Draper or White, he still made clear in this statement that, in his opinion, science had no room for religious notions. The combination of international and local discourse insisting that religion was unable to positively engage with scientific endeavors created a situation in which Chilean Catholic scientific writers considered themselves to be almost constantly under attack. The situation was exacerbated by the very real loss of power and prestige suffered by the national church as a result of its disestablishment in 1925. As such, Catholic scientific writers developed a number of ways to combat these critiques.

Materialism as Religion and the Primary Cause of Conflict

One of the most popular ways in which Catholic writers argued for their place in the sciences was to insist that the strict materialist readings of the natural world that had been gaining popularity within the secular scientific community were fundamentally flawed. Materialist philosophy had increasingly informed scientific disciplines since the eighteenth century and, at its most basic, posited that the metaphysical did not exist, that the physical world was the only world, and that its laws were concrete, knowable, and immutable.[13] In the materialist origin story, life resulted quite by accident from a series of random interactions of matter. The divine played no role in creation, evolution, or natural laws regarding life on Earth. Thus, there was no place for religion in scientific debate or practice.

In contrast, Catholic texts tended to argue that the creation of life was part of a divine plan and that human beings represented the realization of that plan. An early form of this antimaterialist approach appeared in a 1910 article in the *LRC*, "El materialismo y la origen de las cosas" (Materialism and the origin of things), by Rodolfo Vergara Antúnez. At the time of the article's publication, Vergara was presiding bishop's officer and rector of the Pontificia Universidad Católica de Chile.[14] In both capacities, he played a critical role in shaping educational programs and policies that had national impact as "la Católica" was one of the two major national universities.[15] In his article, Vergara contended that racial degeneration in Chile was the result of materialist attempts to separate Catholicism from lived experience. Specifically, he claimed that materialism created a false perception of reality: "Materialism has accorded to matter divine attributes, and has made matter divine. But nature, indignantly refusing the undeserved honor that [the materialists] try to bestow upon her, proclaims the name and grandeur of her Author."[16] He argued that the scientific study of the physical world revealed its divine origins by illuminating the existence of its natural laws and the perfection of its balance. Who better to interpret the divine laws of nature than those who had already dedicated themselves to religious study?

Vergara also argued that it was materialists, not Catholics, who fought against the realities of modernity so obviously in front of them. It was materialists who were actually the intransigent dogmatists they accused Catholics of being. To prove this, Vergara contrasted his own willingness to engage in scientific debates with the supposed ideological rigidity of materialists: "Materialism, arrogant and boastful, claims to represent the sciences, and presumes to dazzle the unlearned multitudes with the vain apparatus of scientific formulas." Materialism promised easy, predictable results through the application of scientific principles. This was precisely how eugenic practice could go badly wrong, according to Vergara. Scientific findings were indeed valuable, but relying on science alone was not enough because it seemed to suggest that morality was unnecessary. Science was also potentially dangerous because materialists were not to be trusted. If left to their own devices, "they would say only they possess science's secrets, or that it is a patrimony that is exclusively their own."[17] Of course, this is exactly what most secular eugenic supporters did claim, so Vergara's concerns seem quite prescient.

"El materialismo" is also a good example of another common tactic deployed by many Catholic intellectuals to claim space in scientific debates. Vergara contended that materialism was actually a different type of faith and not the purely rational philosophy its supporters claimed it was. Catholicism as a religious faith and practice had coped for centuries with the existence of other religions, so portraying materialism as an alternative (and incorrect) system of belief allowed Catholic writers to address the problems it engendered in familiar ways. In his article, Vergara set out to prove that materialism was simply a new form of belief by contending that materialists *believed* that random interactions of matter had led to the creation of the universe, but had no physical proof of this claim—something strict materialism would supposedly demand.[18] Just as Catholics could not irrefutably prove their belief that a divine being was the creator, materialists were unable to substantiate their counter position.[19] For Vergara, this demonstrated that materialists differed from Catholics in content but not in form. Neither group had physical proof of their beliefs. Materialists ought to recognize the fact that they were equally motivated by their faith in science, he argued, rather than being the arbiters of impartiality they claimed to be.

A central element of the antimaterialist tool kit, as "El materialismo" demonstrates, revolved around the origin of life. Specifically, Vergara argued, materialists' insistence that organic life arose from bits of matter smashing into each other at random was actually based on an outdated and disproved scientific theory, spontaneous generation: "But, if everything begins with the atom, that was supposedly the beginning; and, if it had a beginning, it is not eternal; and, if it is not eternal, someone had to create it."[20] He contended that human reason did not support the belief that the matter necessary to create life could arise from nothing. Indeed, the theory of spontaneous generation in which matter might develop in a sterile environment (such as a test tube) had been disproved decades before by the French scientist and devout Catholic Louis Pasteur.[21] Something had to create the physical matter to which materialists were so devoted. For Vergara, then, the existence of a creator was implicit and a far more rational belief than that of materialists. To him, the existence of the natural world itself was proof of a divine plan. Natural laws, the existence of human life, and the seeming order of nature spoke to this reality. In this light, insisting on the random origin of life on Earth seemed almost purposeful obtuseness on the part of materialists.

A brief article that appeared in the *LRC* four years later, in 1914, similarly discussed spontaneous generation in order to discredit materialist belief. In the section dedicated to foreign events, the anonymous author discussed recent attempts by the English physician and neurologist Henry Charlton Bastian to prove that spontaneous generation could happen.[22] By this time, Bastian's experiments seem surprisingly out of step, as spontaneous generation had been a pet project of scientists of both materialist and religious persuasions in the first half of the nineteenth century.[23] Typically, these experiments were designed to see if life arose from nonliving matter such as purified air or water. If some kind of bacteria or simple organism appeared, then that supposedly proved the materialist contention that physical matter can arise from nothing. If nothing appeared, it purportedly indicated that divine intervention was the necessary spark to create life. Although both conclusions were dubious at best, partially because obtaining truly pure air or water samples in this period presented real challenges, spontaneous generation captured the minds of a generation of scientists.[24] Ultimately, Pasteur's 1859 experiments with water and broth and the Irish physicist John Tyndall's subsequent investigations in the following years proved that only living matter could produce organic life.[25] These experiments effectively proved that spontaneous generation did not occur in nature, closing the book on this particular path of scientific inquiry. In that light, it is strange that Bastian would attempt these types of experiments again over forty years later.

Bastian's experiments, because of their dated subject matter, received more coverage in the Chilean press than might be expected, speaking to their importance to the Catholic scientific community there. The *LRC* in particular followed this story rather closely in order to use spontaneous generation as a specific site to debunk materialism. According to an article titled "De nuevo la generación espontánea" (Spontaneous generation again), published in the same year as Vergara's article, Bastian submitted a paper to the French *Revue Scientifique* supposedly proving spontaneous generation.[26] That paper "had been accepted, without the benefit of consideration, by our colleague 'El Mercurio,' which has made its own the frightful news so as to impress this upon its readership as the last word in science." The implication was clear. Bastian labored to prove a point that had been well settled within the scientific community since at least the 1860s in order to bolster his own materialist beliefs in the 1910s. The article's author also stated that the

Royal Society, the United Kingdom's premier scientific professional organization, had rejected Bastian's article. In fact, he or she claimed, the Royal Society had stated it "did not consider [the article] worthy of acceptance."[27] That *El Mercurio*, the national daily newspaper of record, touted Bastian's results, even when his own scientific colleagues would not, seemed to prove that materialists were motivated by blind faith and political ambition, not rationality.

Those who argued against materialism not only became increasingly skeptical of the supposed objectivity of secular texts and writers, they also became distinctly anticapitalist as socialist movements garnered more political power in Chile. In *La muerte del materialismo: conferencia dedicada a las clases dirigentes y a los estudiantes de ambas universidades* (The death of materialism: A conference dedicated to the upper classes and the students of both universities), published in 1919, Victor Depassier actively linked the popularity of materialism to social movements such as socialism that were dedicated to addressing the harsh economic realities of capitalist industrialization. "Thus, it is explained why our workers and day laborers believe that religion symbolizes ignorance, deceit, misery, and how science implies the progressive concept of impiety, meaning the right to all sorts of grievances."[28] Depassier believed that materialists were telling the working classes that religious leaders and the national church supported the status quo that facilitated their exploitation. According to him, working-class Chileans had become increasingly intransigent and disinterested in Catholic efforts to address modern social problems.[29] Depassier was concerned that the working classes were looking for new, politically progressive guardians and that those guardians painted religion as the cause of increasing social decay and discontent rather than the cure.

He argued that materialists misrepresented the Catholic Church's calls for a return to social order as regressive and exploitative, when in fact they called for a social order based on the very scientific principles that materialists claimed to support. Echoing the themes used in the *Rerum novarum* twenty-eight years earlier, Depassier posited that social difference was a biological fact, as evidenced in the works of Darwin and other scientists. "When teaching the Darwinist doctrine, professors are obligated to implicitly recognize that the differences of all types that they observe in both organic and inorganic materials, are things that are necessary and natural to the social organism, just as bread and water are to the individual organism."[30] In other words, materialists who proposed that social difference was the result of capitalist industrialization alone were manipulating the facts in order to get more workers to follow them. The allusion to Darwin in the above passage is striking. Depassier used one of the scientists most responsible for, and identified with, materialist scientific interpretations of the natural world to question the motivations of materialism's proponents in Chile. Biologically speaking, according to Depassier's understanding of Darwin, social difference was natural. Indeed, it was critical to the evolution of all species. Thus, materialists who incited class tension did so for their own political gain, not because they were more modern or scientific.

The "Harmonious" Scientific-Religious Symbiosis

The thesis that materialism was its own new form of religious belief was typical, but it was rarely the only assertion made in Catholic eugenic texts. Antimaterialist arguments often appeared in conjunction with more expansive discussions about the symbiotic relationship between religion and science. Antimaterialist treatises posited that the connection between Catholicism and science was historically based, and that it was vital in the responsible management of newly developing social welfare and racial improvement programs. By characterizing religion and science as complementary Catholic writers posited that Catholicism was critical to the appropriate application of the human sciences, especially eugenics.

Catholic publications about the symbiotic or "harmonious" relationship between religion and science proliferated in the early twentieth century. In 1915, for example, Alejandro Vicuña published a monograph entitled *Armonía de la ciencia y la fe: conferencias científico-religiosas* (The harmony of science and religion: Scientific-religious conferences). Vicuña was a priest and the presiding bishop's officer in the Santiago archdiocese, and his pedigree within the Catholic intellectual community in Chile was similar to that of Vergara. Unlike Vergara, however, his influence also reached well beyond the local Catholic eugenic community. He served as director of the Dirección de Bibliotecas, Archivos y Museos (Directorate of Libraries, Archives, and Museums) between 1932 and 1935, a period in which the global economic crisis significantly limited his ability to support the types of programming he wanted to pursue. Nonetheless, a variety of improvements and public education initiatives were realized under his aegis as director. Vicuña was an important member of the Chilean intelligentsia, both Catholic and secular and his oversight of the reopening of the Museo Nacional de Historia Natural (National Museum of Natural History) in 1934 after a six-year closure denotes the close relationship between Catholicism and the sciences in Chile at this time.[31]

Originally delivered as a lecture and then published as a monograph, *Armonía de la ciencia y la fe* was aimed at the upper echelons of the Chilean intellectual community. It seemed particularly dedicated to convincing secular members of the community that Catholic involvement was essential to reliable scientific knowledge production. Vicuña contended that religion and science had to work together and could not be separated without serious consequences: "It is clear, then, that religious truth has the same characteristics as scientific truth; it is universal, immutable, firm, impersonal. . . . The cult of truth, in a word, is served by two worshippers: Religion and Science."[32] To truly understand human experience and the natural world, Vicuña believed, individuals needed both scientific and religious knowledge. Failing that, one's perception of reality would be skewed.

He bolstered this claim by adding that both religious and scientific findings were the result of meticulous vetting, noting that religious and scientific "truths" were only settled upon after thorough examination and consensus on the part of a community of experts. "The conduct of science and religion appear identical to me. Before admitting any truth, both are subject to rigorous examination which, when passed, begins to shape the patrimony of philosophical or religious reason."[33] He portrayed both religion and science as the result of rigorous examination and then communal acceptance of its findings. Catholic doctrine and scientific theory were both the result of knowledge production that privileged testing, reflection, and consensus among experts. Many Chilean intellectuals considered this to be true for scientific inquiries, but Vicuña extended this to apply to religious concepts as well in order to show that Catholics were not dogmatists who blindly followed clerical authority. Rather, what became Catholic ideology grew out of a series of increasingly specific hypotheses just as, he argued, scientific theories did.

Vicuña's efforts to draw parallels between scientific and Catholic knowledge production represented one of the most common and diplomatic approaches used by Catholic eugenic supporters when describing the relationship between science and religion. But there were Catholics who did not believe in the existence of this harmonious relationship. One such individual was the physician and ophthalmologist Carlos Charlín Correa. He studied medicine at the Universidad de Chile and went on to teach there in the late 1920s. Over the course of the 1930s, he helped to found the Sociedad Oftalmológica de Chile (Chilean Ophthalmological Society) and contributed to a number of Chilean periodicals.[34] In his 1934 essay in *Estudios* titled "Las dos verdades" (The two truths), Charlín outlined his relatively unusual opinion that science and religion had no shared common features. "The scientific man looks at the world with open eyes, with eyes that are amplified and multiplied through the use of the microscope; he is an observer. The philosopher looks at the world with spirit, he sees the Earth through closed eyes; he does not study it, he considers it; he does not observe, he meditates; his mind does not take note or speculate. The one is a realist, only the fact and its immediate cause and its relationship to other facts interest him; the other is contemplative and lives in abstraction."[35]

Although he was not describing the relationship as one of conflict (in keeping with the overall trends of Chilean Catholic writing on this subject), Charlín claimed that philosophers and scientists were not meant to share similar interests because their social functions were fundamentally different. Philosophers pondered life without being able to provide definitive answers. Scientists could provide definitive answers about *how* natural laws worked, but they could not explain *why* those laws existed. Recognizing and respecting these separate spheres of influence and their limitations was of paramount importance to the proper functioning of both. But, unlike the symbiotic model advocated by Vicuña, Charlín's argument created a situation in which Catholic involvement in eugenics specifically and in the sciences in general became problematic. By arguing for separate spheres of influence for religion and science, he potentially threatened the sociopolitical influence of the very group he sought to support. This was surprising considering his own background both as a devout Catholic and as a medical practitioner.

To mitigate against this possible interpretation, he explained how he felt Catholics could appropriately engage in scientific debates and developments using the French entomologist Jean-Henri Fabré as an example. Mostly active between 1862 and 1913, Fabré was a contemporary of Darwin who was known for the ethological study of insects. Charlín claimed that Fabré collected large amounts of detailed information regarding how insects behaved, but he never tried to answer why insects behaved as they did. "He scrupulously noted what he saw but he never pretended to understand the why, the causal factor of the very curious facts he had discovered. And he contented himself by attributing all of that to the 'vital phenomenon,' that is, he accepted the mystery." To explain the mystery would make Fabré a philosopher and, for Charlín, philosophers were not equipped to practice science, because "science and philosophy . . . have different, antagonistic, disciplines that annul each other."[36] Describing neither a conflict nor a symbiosis, Charlín leads the reader to believe Fabré recognized the limitations of his scientific discipline because he was Catholic.

Charlín championed Fabré as a model of scientific practice. His experiments and findings were beyond reproach in their methodology and exactitude, standing up to the scrutiny of the scientific community, but they did not veer into metaphysical territory. Thus, despite the supposed lack of connection between religion and science, Charlín was able to protect Catholic involvement in the sciences by arguing that Fabré's Catholic belief informed his scientific practice to ensure that it was done properly—essentially, that Fabré's Catholicism stopped him from pursuing metaphysical inquiries best left to clerics. So, although not advocating for the harmony between science and religion in the same way as Vicuña, Charlín still contended that Catholic scientists had just as much to contribute to their disciplines as any secular scientist did (and perhaps more).

Despite this rather unusual claim, scientific-religious symbiosis discourse was so pervasive in Catholic writing in the early twentieth century that it managed to creep into "Las dos verdades" all the same. In an exceptional passage, Charlín used his understanding of evolutionary adaptation to support his claim that science and religion shared no common features. When discussing the continued survival of a type of fern in southern Chile despite multiple efforts to exterminate it, he argued that the fern thrived there because it had adapted so successfully to that environment. Charlín attributed this ability to adapt rather than be annihilated to intelligent design. "These small facts are the manifestation of a fundamental truth, of a first principle, of the great truth, of the divine phenomenon, just as the small truths of the biological sciences are the manifestation of a first principle, the vital phenomenon." Using facts tied to Darwinian evolutionary principles to support the existence of religious truth was an approach employed by other Catholic writers to support the symbiosis model. Charlín even went on to say that being Catholic allowed one to see the relationship between scientific findings and religious beliefs more easily.[37] In "Las dos verdades," he began by arguing that religion and science had no relationship with each other and then concluded on a more ambiguous note demonstrating the discursive power of religious and scientific symbiosis in Chilean Catholic writing of the early twentieth century.

It was not only Catholic texts that recognized the seeming complementarity between religion and science. Descriptions of the origin of life and evolution in ostensibly secular texts also often highlighted the discursive similarities between secular and Catholic eugenic writing in Chile. This was, in part, the result of the ideological clash and subsequent reconciliation of Darwinism and positivism as philosophies of human development among Latin American intellectuals. Most Latin Americans, regardless of religious inclination, had trouble accepting the harsh individualism and fatalism suggested in a strict Darwinian approach to evolution.[38] Older traditions of positivist philosophy insisted on the potential of the human race to control its fate and the power of human reason in that effort.[39] Secular or not, many Latin American scientists and eugenicists could not fully embrace Darwinism because of its seemingly complete disregard for human agency and the contention that humans were not unique among other forms of organic life on Earth. Bernardino Quijada Burr's two major works—*Curso de zoolojía* (Course of zoology) and *La teoría de la evolución* (The theory of evolution)—exemplify this predicament for Chilean secular scientists.[40] Quijada was a professor of the natural sciences who served as director of the zoology and botany division of the Museo Nacional de Chile

(Chilean National Museum). His family hailed from the small island of Chiloé, one of the southernmost parts of Chilean territory.[41]

Quijada's enthusiasm for both the study and teaching of biology is evident throughout the pages of both works, which were produced as standard university texts for decades.[42] But it was in his discussion of Darwinism that he indicated the points of connection between secular and Catholic biological understandings in this period. In *La teoría de la evolución* (the first edition published in 1902, with eleven subsequent editions published through 1934), he argued that there was no conflict between evolutionary theory and religious belief. "This idea that an *evolution* or gradual progressive development of the species in the diverse paleontological ages is a very ancient philosophical concept and it has never invaded religious terrain nor has it ever attempted to alter the essence of the sacred books, as is generally believed."[43] To prove his claim, Quijada specifically noted that Saint Augustine of Hippo (354–430) had developed a theory of evolution long before Darwin did. Saint Augustine posited that the word "day" in Genesis was meant to imply an incalculable amount of geological time, which facilitated reconciliation between the Catholic origin story and evolutionary theory.[44] Quijada also argued that Saint Augustine believed life on Earth evolved from "original germs," which were created by God.[45] Thus, Quijada argued, Catholic scientists already accepted that evolution occurred from simple to complex life forms and objections to Darwinian evolutionary theory premised on religious orthodoxy were misplaced. Instead, he stated, Catholic scholars had actually been arguing for centuries that something like evolution existed.

Although Quijada's argument presupposed that most Catholics reading his book rejected evolution, a standard motif in scientific writing of the era, his argument actually mirrored those made by his Catholic contemporaries.[46] In 1917, the same year the fourth edition of Quijada's *La teoría de la evolución* was published, the *LRC* published an article entitled "Conferencia sobre el origen del hombre dada por el Sr. Obispo D. José María Caro R." (Lecture on the origin of man given by Bishop D. José María Caro R.), in which Caro wrote: "we do not reject an evolutionary movement that has God at its origin, Supreme Being, independently intelligent, *we do not reject that living organisms have been born from inorganic material, but [rather] obeying the creative will of God*."[47] His argument was strikingly similar to Quijada's interpretation of Saint Augustine's original germ theory.

That Caro professed this opinion was important, as he represented the highest levels of the Chilean Catholic clergy. Ordained in 1890, he was the first Chilean to be made cardinal after serving as Bishop of La Serena (1925–1939) and as Archbishop of Santiago (1939–1945).[48] Although he advocated for a modified version of evolution, this clearly did not preclude his rising within the ranks of the Chilean clergy over the course of his exceptionally long career. Caro's acceptance of life arising from inert material also suggests that at least some Chilean Catholics saw the origin of life on Earth in much the same way as scientists who identified as secular. The difference lay in the fact that most Catholic discourse attributed evolution to the power of God, whereas secular and materialist writing contended that evolution was the result of a random series of events.

Caro argued that believing in evolution actually proved God's existence, thus further supporting the widespread insistence on scientific-religious symbiosis that was popular among Catholic writers.[49] After all, if one accepted that humans were the ultimate expression of evolutionary development, as Quijada seemed to, then there had to be some sort of ordering force or principle organizing the evolutionary process. Because humans were so clearly the pinnacle of evolution, this result could not have happened at random. Human reason affirmed humanity's special place among the various forms of life on Earth, and this implied the existence of a divine plan and possibly a creator. Human exceptionalism created common ground because very few Chilean scientists, secular or religious, could accept the idea that humans were not the preeminent result of evolution.

Although virtually all Chilean scientists agreed that humans were the most superior species on Earth, there was still disagreement about the mechanisms of evolution. Materialism was simply not something Catholic scientific writers could accept. In the "Conferencia," Caro used the term "materialist" to discuss those individuals who believed evolution was the result of random chance. This terminology was widely used by early twentieth-century Catholic scientific writers when seeking to denounce strict Darwinian evolution and the more biologically determined eugenic theory and practice growing from it. Materialists, Caro argued, often favored the most uncompromising negative eugenic measures to preserve racial health and integrity. Needless to say, this is where he most strongly disagreed with materialist philosophy. Negative eugenic practices, such as coerced sterilization, went against the Catholic ideal that all humans have free will and must be afforded the ability to exercise it.[50] Catholics believed in a divine plan as represented through an orderly society, but they also stressed that individual free will and the dignity of the human person were central to this larger plan. This explains the potential for confrontation between negative eugenic thought and Catholic eugenic approaches. According to Caro, eugenics based primarily on hereditarianism operated on the assumption that no one was free from their biological ancestry, and as a result, people should be monitored and controlled by outside parties in order to ensure that the eugenically fit would reproduce effectively. This was in conflict with virtually all established Catholic teachings regarding free will, family, and choice of marriage partner.[51]

The Catholic Scientist as a Symbol of Symbiosis

Another common way in which Catholic scientific writers demonstrated the harmonious relationship between religion and science was by discussing famous Catholic scientists. In "El materialismo," for example, Vergara argued that religion played a fundamental role in the lives of important scientists throughout history. Referring to the likes of Nicolaus Copernicus, Isaac Newton, and Carl Linnaeus, he wrote: "And yet I see that the most incredible geniuses of science, those who have enriched it with positive advances and without pretension have made pronouncements that have yet to be challenged, they did not stop being wise because they believed in God." Choosing historical examples of notable scientists who were also devout Catholics (or Christians) was a strategy used by various Catholic writers to highlight the mutually supportive relationship between science and religion. But Vergara's choice of historical figures was not casual, as each individual had undeniably shaped a variety of scientific disciplines. Copernicus was responsible for shifting the entirety of astronomy to its modern iteration. Newton was the father of the earliest form of physics. Linnaeus was credited with the invention of taxonomy. In this way, Vergara was convincingly able to argue: "They were wise men and Christians; and being wise was not an obstacle to being Christian, and being Christian did not extinguish from their brows the halo of science."[52]

Charlín's discussion of Fabré, Quijada's invocation of Saint Augustine, and Vergara's reference to multiple Christian scientists show just how pervasive this approach was within the Chilean discourse regarding scientific-religious symbiosis. Profiles of Catholic scientists were written to counter secular rhetoric that denied Catholic contributions to scientific development in both the past and the present. Although many scientists were discussed in this way, the French chemist and microbiologist Louis Pasteur was the most widely used in Chilean Catholic texts, because his work in epidemiology and vaccination in the latter half of the nineteenth century was groundbreaking on an international scale, making him unequivocally one of the most important scientists of the nineteenth century.[53] Additionally, Pasteur's involvement in disproving the theory of spontaneous generation strengthened his appeal for Catholic scientific writers. Pasteur was also a devout Catholic, whose work in disease prevention was directly influenced by his religious belief and was repeatedly used as the best example of the harmonious relationship between Catholicism and science.

His popularity as an exemplary Catholic scientist was linked to his work with vaccines, characterized specifically as motivated by his Catholic altruism and desire to do good works. Appearing in *El Diario Popular* (The popular daily), a Santiago newspaper directed at working-class Catholics, a brief 1902 article stated that Pasteur "was stimulated by the thought of diminishing, through his works, the miseries and the pains of humanity." According to the anonymous author, Pasteur's Catholic obligation to do good works motivated him to study disease in order to ease human suffering. For those writing in favor of Catholic involvement in eugenics, this was the best example of how the relationship between science and Catholicism could benefit humanity. Pasteur was quoted as saying: "It will be truly beautiful and useful to use this part of my heart in the progress of science."[54] This suggests that Catholic scientific writing celebrated scientific experimentation simply for the sake of discovery, but science designed to help the Catholic mission to address perceived social problems and public health issues was all the more warmly received.

In addition to Pasteur's altruism in scientific exploration, this author emphasized his reliance on common sense in his experiments, and this theme would have increasing importance as the debate regarding evolution continued to rage. "All his work is nothing more than the application of a method that is within everyone's reach, that does not boast of being [newly] invented, and which honors the great experimenters of centuries past."[55] Pasteur's appeal lay not only in his religious belief but also in the seeming simplicity of his scientific methodology.[56] His work and findings were tied to a long tradition of Catholic scientific scholarship that preceded him. More important, much like Fabré, Pasteur recognized his limitations. He knew that he could not elucidate the origins of life or of humanity through scientific experimentation, and he did not try, though his efforts to disprove spontaneous generation suggest a bit more religious motivation than the author of this article chose to discuss.[57]

The trend of discussing Catholic scientists in Catholic periodicals continued in much the same way throughout the first half of the twentieth century, with a notable emphasis on scholars working in the life sciences. Appearing in a September 1926 issue of the *LRC*, an article entitled "Crónica científica–Los trabajos de P. Wasmann SJ" (Scientific chronicle— The works of Fr. Wasmann, SJ) highlighted the work of an Austrian Jesuit entomologist, Erich Wasmann. The author, identified as "A.F.L.," seems to have been the Chilean science journalist Arturo Fontecilla Larraín. In the article, Fontecilla credited Wasmann with providing convincing proof against materialist monogenism, the premise that all life on Earth arose from one original single-celled organism. "Thus refuted absolute evolution, that from a single cell all forms of life arose, as says Haeckelian monism,

Father [Wasmann] constructed his system, that is also evolutionist to a point, in that it admits the possibility of transformism that is not in conflict with sane philosophy."[58] According to Fontecilla, Wasmann was able to discredit materialist evolutionary theory while still providing Catholic biologists with an acceptable form of species transformation over time. This illuminates how Catholics might enter into the field of biology, related disciplines, and debates regarding evolution with relative ease. The fact that Wasmann turned out to be wrong is not terribly important, as many other secular scientists across the globe in this period also objected to the idea of monogenism, especially when applied to human beings.[59] Fontecilla's celebration of Wasmann's commitment to polygenism is also important in the context of the overtly White supremacist logic of that theory of human origins—demonstrating the racist elements operating in Chilean eugenic thought generally.

A final example of using the heroic Catholic scientist as discursive trope to illustrate the harmonious relationship between religion and science appeared in a 1936 article in *Estudios* entitled "Los católicos ante el problema científico de la eugenesia" (Catholics before the scientific problem of eugenics). Similar to previous authors, Roberto Barahona Silva rejected the idea that the Catholic Church was antiscience. The difference in this case was that he was discussing the field of genetics. While more general comments about the mutually beneficial relationship between science and religion certainly helped to create an intellectual environment open to Catholic involvement, Barahona's discussion of the origins of genetics was especially important to Catholic involvement in eugenics in Chile. He wrote: "Those hordes do not have, then, scientific or moral authority to say that the Church opposes scientific advancement, much less when they owe to [Gregor] Mendel, Augustinian friar from Moravia, the discovery of the laws of genetics."[60] Born in 1822, Mendel undertook experimentation with pea plants between 1856 and 1863 that would eventually become the foundation of modern genetics.[61] Barahona felt it was entirely unfair that secular writers touted Mendel as an impeccable scientist while simultaneously ignoring the fact that he was a religious man and a member of the Order of Saint Augustine. According to Barahona, these writers were lying to themselves and being disingenuous to their intellectual acolytes. Catholicism, and Christianity more generally, had been essential to numerous scientific developments. This was perhaps especially true in the human sciences such as eugenics, which was founded on the work of religious men like Mendel.

The Chilean Catholic writers examined here were deeply interested in discussing at length the relationship between science and religion. Although some insisted on separate spheres, many more contended that science and Catholicism were fundamentally intertwined and mutually reinforcing.

Therefore Catholic eugenicists could not sit by and let scientific debates regarding the fate of the Chilean race occur without them. In fact, in these articles they insisted that their presence was central to the proper functioning and application of scientific principles. The opinions articulated by men such as Charlín, Depassier, Vergara, and others provide new ways of looking at the relationship between Catholicism and science not only in Chile but throughout Latin America. Their work created new opportunities for the construction and elaboration of Catholic charitable organizations, social activism, and racial thought with a specifically scientific character. This foundational literature was critical for Chilean Catholics who wanted to use science to address the issue of racial health. By characterizing the relationship between Catholicism and science as symbiotic or harmonious, Catholic discourse portrayed Catholics as being central to larger national and international debates about eugenic science and its application to human beings. This manifested in a eugenic science that incorporated both secular and Catholic ideas, and those ideas contributed to the creation of *la raza chilena*.

Chapter 3

What Is Eugenics in Chile?

Formulating a National Discipline
from a Transnational Movement

In the April 1938 edition of *Medicina Moderna*, the physician Juan Astorquizo Sazzo contributed an article titled "Eugenesia" (Eugenics). Spanning twenty pages, the article, written for other medical practitioners, was a detailed overview of the state of the field at the time. In it, Astorquizo examined some of the more pernicious threats to the Chilean race (alcoholism, infant mortality, and birth control) and added some additional health conditions of concern, such as syphilis and tuberculosis. Astorquizo's writing was exemplary of the Chilean approach to eugenics in the twentieth century in his ability to blur the distinctions between biological determinism and environmentalism operating in eugenic theory and practice. For example, he described eugenics as "the effort to improve the biological characteristics of the race, using methods adapted deliberately for this end. It is the ideal type and practice of human selection." Emphasizing the desire to create and encourage the proliferation of specific biological traits shows that many Chilean eugenic writers did indeed argue that fitness was linked to heredity. But Astorquizo opened by stating that the primary reason undesirable traits had expanded across the human family was because of environmental factors, not biological failings. Specifically, and like many Catholic commentators, he blamed capitalism for the increasing racial degeneration apparent in the Chilean population. "The net and tragic reality is that the lack of space and the lack of food is because too many people have survived in the face of the mechanization that capitalism has driven."[1]

The fear that modern living somehow caused racial degeneration and could be combated with modern scientific techniques was not unique to Chilean eugenic writing and served as the bedrock of eugenic theory and practice all over the world. However, scientific writers in Chile highlight the fact that eugenics was equally founded upon environmentalist concepts. Belief in (or preference for) eugenics based on biological determinism did not preclude the possibility that the environment had the power to influence human beings for better or worse. Eugenic discourse in Chile blurred the boundaries between Darwinian biological determinism and neo-Lamarckian environmentalism, and this blurring allowed Catholics to play an active role in the construction of racial thought.

Catholic supporters could engage with eugenic debates, in Chile and elsewhere, because of the conceptual imprecision within the discipline itself concerning the relationship between heredity, environment, and eugenic fitness. The impact of education, upbringing, and access to resources could never be fully discounted, even among eugenicists who were more committed to biological inheritance as the critical component to determining fitness. Certain eugenic texts written by foreign eugenicists were available in Chile and demonstrate how this internal conflict was managed in the eugenic literature produced in North America and northern Europe, regions most closely associated with a preference for biological determinism. The work of these foreign eugenicists not only highlights ambiguities within the discipline itself but also illustrates that Chilean eugenic knowledge production was not the result of simple intellectual diffusion. While the pervasiveness of concepts related to racial hierarchy and White supremacy cannot be attributed to the existence and circulation of these works in Chile alone, their availability helps to contextualize Chilean racial thought that incorporated these "foreign" racial concepts with more "traditional" Latin American ideas regarding racial mixture and tolerance.

Transnational Influences and Conceptual Imprecision in Eugenics as a Discipline

Some of the most obvious international contributors to the Chilean eugenic milieu were eugenicists from other Spanish-speaking countries because of the ease with which texts could circulate when translation was unnecessary. But it should not be assumed that eugenics was a uniform intellectual pursuit or movement throughout the Spanish-speaking world. Rather, the mobility of Spanish-language texts demonstrates the functional reality of how certain eugenic concepts came to be associated with an identifiably Latin scientific community. An example of this mobility of ideas in the Spanish-speaking world is the 1911 text *Homicultura* written by Cuban eugenicists Eusebio Hernández Pérez and Domingo F. Ramos.[2] Hernández and Ramos were both physicians with specializations in gynecology and obstetrics. Ramos in particular rose to prominence within the Cuban medical community because of his interest in eugenics.[3] Speaking to the connections within the Latin world of eugenics, their book begins with an homage to the French obstetrician and creator of homiculture Adolphe Pinard.[4] Further attesting to connections among Latin eugenicists, they included a French translation of their work in an appendix. However, perhaps speaking to their proximity to the United States and its own influence on scientific developments on the island, they also included an English one.[5]

Homicultura is important not just in terms of its demonstration of potential linkages across the Latin eugenics community. It also illustrated the internal tensions operating within eugenic theory itself. The very term "homiculture," or the cultivation of the entire person, asserted the importance of both nature and nurture in an individual's development. As Hernández and Ramos put it, homiculture incorporated various disciplines associated with pre- and postnatal health care such as "patrimatriculture . . . puericulture and postgenitoculture."[6] Essentially, Hernández and Ramos supported Pinard's claim that puericulture, or the care given to pregnant women, would be most successful if extended across the life of the individual. This entailed not only regular physical examinations but the oversight of people's everyday lives so as to ensure the most complete realization of their natural abilities. Showing just how important environment and access to resources were to this burgeoning medical field, in the remainder of *Homicultura* the authors went on to discuss the types of care that physicians should attempt to provide to their patients both before and after a child's birth such as home visits, milk inspections, and oral health instruction.

One of the earliest English-language eugenic texts to reach Chile was the work of the British eugenicists and married couple William Cecil Dampier Whetham and Catherine Durning Whetham entitled *An Introduction to Eugenics* (1912).[7] Dampier, who preferred to use his mother's family name in his professional writing, was born in 1867 and studied physics at the University of Cambridge in the 1880s.[8] His wife, Catherine, was born in 1871 and is now best known for her 1917 monograph, *The Up-*

bringing of Daughters, which described the couple's experiences raising five daughters.[9] It was the Whethams' mutual interest in family, specifically genealogy, that brought them to the field of eugenics. Their early forays into the fields of heredity and genetics resulted in their first coauthored book, *The Family and the Nation: A Study in Natural Inheritance and Social Responsibility*, in 1909. *An Introduction to Eugenics* was one of four books on the subject that the pair would write together over the course of their respective careers.[10] Although a number of Dampier's other works related to the history of science eventually made their way to Chile, *An Introduction to Eugenics* seems to be the couple's only work related to heredity and genetics that was available to a Chilean audience.

The Whethams were especially interested in using eugenics to address a perceived "extinction of the upper classes," a concept regularly discussed in Chilean eugenic texts particularly when critiquing the use of birth control.[11] Supporting the idea that the upper classes were also the most eugenically fit, *An Introduction to Eugenics* at first glance seems to maintain a hard-line hereditarian approach to social problems that one would expect from British eugenicists who tended to favor biological determinism over environmentalism. For example, the Whethams argued that "[Francis] Galton satisfied himself that heredity was far more powerful than environment. . . . Hence Eugenics is concerned chiefly, though not exclusively, with the study of heredity and its bearing on social problems."[12] However, demonstrating the conceptual and ethical difficulties in maintaining such a position in all circumstances, they also offered support for those eugenicists who preferred environmental efforts at racial improvement. On the very first page, they also quoted Galton as saying that eugenics was "the study of agencies under social control that may improve or impair the racial qualities of future generations either physically or mentally."[13] Galton left unclear what these agencies might be, contributing to an intellectual climate in Chile that preferred to emphasize environment over biology as an important factor in racial health and eugenic fitness. Blurring between the importance of environment and that of biology was further encouraged when Whetham and Whetham went on to explain that Galton's quote indicated, "as thus defined, the subject [of eugenics] includes the study of all agencies which have racial importance, whether those agencies are concerned with nature or with nurture, that is, with the natural qualities and gifts implanted in mankind by heredity, or with the development or suppression of those qualities or gifts by the outward circumstances of the life either of the individual or his parents. In other words, it includes the study of the influence on race *both of heredity and environment*."[14] Their recognition of the environment as an essential element of racial fitness, in any context, demonstrates that eugenic theory itself was unclear regarding the significance of the environment. This imprecision, in turn, facilitated a "Latinization" of eugenic concepts when they arrived in Chile in terms of emphasizing the importance of the environment for racial health.

Accepting that people's environment did indeed play a role in their overall development also created space for Catholic eugenic supporters. The Whethams stipulated, for example, that some religious development was necessary for the "successful evolution of human society."[15] This statement demonstrates that religion and morality still mattered greatly, even among eugenicists committed to biological determinism. A society with no moral compass whatsoever gave the married couple and most other eugenicists pause. Not only that, but religious instruction encouraged a belief in the collective good that was vital to the success of any eugenic program in Chile or elsewhere.[16]

Another example of foreign eugenic texts available in Chile was *The Revolt against Civilization: The Menace of the Under Man* (1922) by Theodore Lothrop Stoddard, which arrived in a condensed form in Chile as *La amenaza del sub-hombre* (The menace of the Under Man) in 1923.[17] Stoddard was one of the best-known American historians of his day and published numerous books and articles over the course of his career. He was also a member of the Ku Klux Klan, and his belief in White supremacy permeated his writing on both eugenics and history. Stoddard dedicated his professional and personal life to demonstrating how European races represented the peak of human achievement and how non-European races consistently threatened to undermine those achievements.[18] So notable a presence was he in the international eugenics community that his concept of the Under Man as explored in this text went on to inspire the concept of the *Untermensch* in the work of the Nazi racial theorist Alfred Rosenberg.[19] If Latin American racial thought was less focused on White racial purity, then one might expect this type of writing to be unwelcome in Chile because of its emphasis on the separation of the races and insistence on biological determinism.

Yet, this text was available in Chile precisely because someone took special steps to ensure it reached a Chilean audience. *La amenaza del sub-hombre* was translated by Chilean physician and government functionary Lucas Sierra.[20] To be clear, Sierra was not a man working at the fringes of the Chilean medical or eugenic community. In his biography produced by the Museo Nacional de Medicina (National Museum of Medicine), Sierra is referred to as one of the "masters of modern Chilean surgery."[21] Graduating from the Universidad de Chile's Facultad de Medicina (Faculty of Medicine) in 1888, he rose to prominence within the Chilean medical community as a cutting-edge surgeon and for his work on venereal disease. He spent significant periods of his early adult life in Europe, serving as a field surgeon for the French during the First World War.[22] The year before the Stoddard translation was published, Sierra founded the Sociedad de Cirujanos de Chile (Chilean Society of Surgeons). He was also a prolific academic writer himself, and one of his most famous works was *Cien años de la enseñanza de la medicina en Chile* (One hundred years of medical instruction in Chile), which was published in 1934.

These biographical details make the combination of Stoddard and Sierra seem rather unexpected, yet Sierra played a central role in ensuring the publication of *La amenaza del sub-hombre*. It was originally published in serial format in *El Mercurio*, the national daily newspaper, making it available for widespread consumption by the average Chilean reader, not just the more erudite academic community.[23] Based on the strident racism and preference for biological explanations of events both past and present, one might expect that Stoddard's work would hardly be chosen by any Chilean to be translated and published for mass consumption. As many different historians of science, race, and eugenics have argued, strict Darwinian biological determinism of the variety favored by Stoddard was not popular in Latin America. However, the preference for neo-Lamarckian environmentalism that characterized Latin American racial thought did not preclude concepts such as racial hierarchy, White supremacy, and biological determinism. Indeed, the very existence of this monograph is indicative of how many of these elements flourished in Chilean racial thought, even as it was founded on the principle of racial mixture. It was not until the early-to-mid 1930s—when the Nazi government promulgated a series of racial purity laws in Germany—that Chilean racial theorists began to meaningfully object to those racist elements operating in their own work.[24]

The fact that Stoddard and Sierra combined to produce this translation becomes all the more striking because of their disparate views regarding biological determinism. Stoddard wrote, for example, "the new *biological* revelation has taught us the supreme importance of heredity and the error in which Humanity has tended to believe that the biggest influence on human existence has been the environment which surrounds it, [in other words] the humanitarian factor."[25] Statements like this fit very well with Stoddard's overall belief that racial differences were innate and fundamental, protecting the concepts of racial hierarchy and White supremacy. Yet, only five years before, in 1918, Sierra had written in his own work *Bases de higiene moderna: papel que en la difusión de sus principios debe desempeñar la mujer* (Basis of modern hygiene: The role that women should play in the diffusion of its principles): "Experimental science has shown that illnesses have nothing to do with the feared 'punishments from God' but rather they grow from the carelessness [and] ignorance of men . . . and it is a duty of every citizen who loves his homeland . . . to contribute to the fight against

venereal diseases that mine and destroy the flower of our race, against alcoholism and tuberculosis that bring misery to the home, [such as] widow-
hood and orphanhood when not stupidity and insanity."[26] Clearly, based
on his own writing, Sierra's approach to racial thought was more informed
by the belief that racial threats were environmental rather than arising from
inherent racial qualities or conflicts between races. Whatever incongruities
existed between Sierra's other work and his translation of Stoddard, they
did not stop Sierra from wholeheartedly supporting the ideas put forth in
La amenaza del sub-hombre.[27] In his brief introduction to the text, he noted
that "the inconvenient [truth] with which we are now confronted, thanks
to the advancements and progress of modern medicine, is a social selection,
[made with] charity and piety—which does not permit nature to effect the
natural selection, as in the past—that often times drives us to preserve not
the most fit but the opposite."[28] Even beyond this affirmation of Stoddard's
book, the fact that Sierra translated this work and saw it published in the
daily Chilean newspaper of record suggests that Sierra and the editorial
staff at *El Mercurio* shared similar ideas regarding the concepts of racial
hierarchy and White supremacy. More to the point, they did not feel their
membership in the mixed race *raza chilena* was an obstacle to maintaining
such an opinion. Belief in the strength of their racial superiority afforded
this possibility.

It is impossible to know what inspired Sierra to translate a work such as
Stoddard's for public consumption, but it speaks to the intellectual openness of the Chilean eugenic community and the availability of foreign texts
to form part of local racial thought. This openness was reflected in the
conceptual malleability of eugenics itself. A seemingly innocuous comment
included in Stoddard's work bears scrutiny to show how this worked in
practice. He wrote: "The environment has much less importance to man
than it does to inferior animals. This fact is of enormous importance."[29]

Presumably unbeknownst to him, this comment could have been interpreted in a much more friendly way to those who preferred an environmentalist approach to racial hygiene. As a strict Darwinist, Stoddard
should have posited that the environment affected animals and humans
in the same way. Natural selection should, conceivably, affect all life on
Earth to the same degree. Instead, this statement suggests that he believed
human beings were special animals because they were sentient and had
the ability to change their own circumstances. This behavioral awareness
was the foundation upon which eugenic theory and practice were built, as
people could be trained to select eugenically desirable marriage partners
and implement eugenic policies. Yet, all these opportunities for choice also
implied that the environment was of at least some importance, as humans
could manipulate that as well.

Unfortunately for Stoddard, he could not escape this reality. "The fundamental difference between both ideas and methods resides in the false and exaggerated influence that is attributed to the environment as a factor in changing and improving humanity—*from without*—[by changing] the existing *individual*, while that which eugenics maintains [is most important] is *heredity*, and it seeks to improve the race by *internal methods*, determining which individuals of those available should perpetuate the race or not, having always in mind the perfecting of the race."[30] Thus Stoddard recognized that some were more interested in the changes that humans could effect upon themselves from the outside, even as he preferred to focus on "internal" changes achieved through the choice of a eugenically fit sexual partner and state-mandated efforts to limit the reproductive rights of unfit individuals. It was this conceptual ambiguity and professional deference evident even in the most racist of eugenic theory that opened the door for Catholic eugenic supporters eager to play a role in the development of Chilean racial thought.

Another monograph available to eugenicists in Chile was Leonard Darwin's *¿Qué es la eugenesia?* (*What Is Eugenics?*), a text he wrote expressly to combat the perceived failings in Latin eugenic theories, and specifically the lack of emphasis on biological determinism.[31] The son of Charles Darwin, Leonard Darwin spent his early life as a soldier and became a Liberal Unionist member of the British parliament in the 1890s. By 1911 he had succeeded his cousin Francis Galton as chairman of the British Eugenics Society and remained in that position until 1928.[32] *What Is Eugenics?* was originally published in London in 1928, and its Spanish translation was published in Madrid in 1930. The Swiss anthropologist Eugene Pittard, professor of anthropology at the University of Geneva, wrote the introduction to the Spanish version. Having risen to prominence in the 1920s for his study of skulls from a variety of European cultures, Pittard was probably chosen to write this introduction because of his seeming position between the Anglo and Latin intellectual communities. As he put it: "This little book by Darwin is simple, clear and well organized, therefore, accessible to everyone, even the least informed reader. My wish would be that it amply spread among Latin peoples, where eugenic concerns have been less established."[33] Notably, Pittard and Darwin attributed these differences between Latin and mainstream eugenic camps to the fact that Latin eugenicists suffered from less institutional support. Although it is true that the financial resources in Latin American nations were significantly less and there was virtually no success in terms of negative eugenic legislation, the amount of press coverage, academic writing, lectures, books, private groups, and government interest dedicated to implementing positive eugenic measures such as public health campaigns to improve racial hygiene belies this claim.[34] The real issue was the disagreement within the international eugenic community itself regarding how much emphasis to place on biology versus environment.

Rather than discussing this underlying conceptual division within the discipline in his book, however, Darwin insisted that the reason Latin eugenic policies did not adequately restrict the lives and choices of unfit individuals was because of a faulty understanding of evolution.[35] To address this misunderstanding, he first discussed one of the primary means of discrediting evolutionary theory at the time, the lack of proof. Even the most enthusiastic supporters of Darwinian evolutionary theory in the interwar period recognized that the fossil record—while giving every indication that species did evolve—was not complete, and particularly not when dealing with human beings.[36] In response, Darwin wrote: "We accept the facts [of evolution] as evident, though doubts and difficulties constantly present themselves when one tries to apply to man the knowledge we possess about animals."[37] Although Darwin recognized it was difficult to accept the fact that the laws governing animal evolution applied equally to humans (something Stoddard had struggled with), he insisted this was the truth. The growing evidentiary base that did exist and the undeniable logic of Darwinian evolutionary theory were enough to counteract any doubts one might have regarding the validity of a eugenic program based exclusively on biological inheritance as the most important determining factor for fitness.

In this light, Darwin contended, eugenic programs aimed at environmental issues to improve racial traits were useless. "If we accept the scientific truth we cannot agree with the opinion that care and education given to man constitute a practical method of improving the race."[38] Although advocates of biological determinism often stated that people needed education to truly understand eugenics and apply it to their own lives, Darwin's argument overlooked this to create a straw man. For the purposes of his book, which was aimed at the Latin eugenic community, he had to insist that allowing undesirables to continue to survive on government handouts and Christian charity did nothing to help them nor did it prevent racial degeneration. Rather, it allowed unfit individuals to thrive, ultimately weakening the race as a whole. Darwin went on to recommend two methods of discouraging the unfit from having children: the first was moral suasion, and the second was legislation. He argued that persuasion was always preferable to legally imposing on the rights of individuals: "There are two ways to work toward obtaining small families among individuals of this class: persuasion and imposition; the first is always preferable to the second in terms of achieving the desired result."[39] However, he was not completely opposed to the use of legal force if it became necessary.

This raised concerns about what the appropriate amount of legal intervention might be into the private lives and reproductive decisions of individuals. Darwin wrote: "It is clear that locking up a human is repugnant to us at an instinctive level, because of the fact that all of us aspire to be free; but, in reality can we really call a mental defective *free*?"[40] Although he was writing about the potential incarceration and reproductive restriction of individuals with mental illness or developmental delays, this premise could be expanded to apply to any person identified as eugenically unfit. Being unfit, Darwin argued, meant the individual was not truly free to make their own decisions. In these cases, then, it should not be a concern when medical experts or government functionaries compelled individuals to accept eugenic intervention into their lives typically in the form of state-mandated sterilization. After all, stipulated Darwin, "each and every one of us suffers the consequences that derive from the presence of *incapables* and *inferiors*."[41] And, though he did not say so, every individual is expected to sacrifice some of their personal liberty in order to live as part of a larger society. Eugenic interventions, both positive and negative, could be construed as logical extensions of that sacrifice.

Despite both Darwin's and Pittard's lamentations about Latin sympathy or scientific misunderstanding, these biologically based approaches to eugenic theory and practice did indeed have their supporters in the Latin world. In fact, Latin eugenic writers often blamed the relative failure to institute or legislate eugenic programs on Catholic obstructionism just as North Atlantic eugenic writers did. Luis Hernández Alfonso's 1933 monograph *Eugenesia y derecho a vivir* (Eugenics and the right to life) was one such example.[42] Hernández was a Spanish journalist who studied both medicine and law. Speaking to his intellectual expansiveness, the same year *Eugenesia y derecho a vivir* was published he also had another book come out, entitled *Verdad y mentira de la República española* (Truth and lies of the Spanish Republic).[43] In *Eugenesia y derecho a vivir*, Hernández argued against what he perceived to be Catholic opposition to eugenic legislation while simultaneously lauding his own career and colleagues: "[Lawyers] are not, nor can we be enemies of Eugenics; but we are supporters of justice; and as both are compatible . . . [w]e believe the Church's (or better said its ministers) opposition to the eugenic campaign is stupid."[44] Hernández clearly believed that Catholic clergy members were actively blocking eugenic legislation efforts, though it is unclear which specific programs he was referring to. His statement also demonstrates how secular intellectuals used Catholic objections to negative eugenic practices as a heuristic tool to claim that Catholics objected to eugenics as a whole.

Eugenesia y derecho a vivir also recognized the difficulties involved in the application of eugenic practices. One of the biggest challenges was to control sexual contact between men and women. Hernández argued that the main issue was that eugenicists typically discussed sex only in terms of reproduction and offspring, whereas progressives of various political stripes discussed sex as a purely pleasurable physical encounter. "Both interpretations are unacceptable," he wrote. "To suggest that the sexual act is, simply, a function to perpetuate the species, is to negate the quality that distinguishes man from beast; to affirm that the only objective of sex is pleasure, is to consider man a being apart, without being subject to the biological principles of reproduction."[45] For Hernández eugenic science, which often essentialized sex to the point of breeding, did not recognize the complexity of human interaction and behavior. Similarly, treating sex as only a means to pleasure freed humans from their eugenic reproductive responsibilities. He insisted that there were factors involved in human sexual behavior other than the need for procreation or the desire for pleasure. Only an awareness of both emotional and physical sexual impulses could hope to inform a responsible eugenic program.

He argued that when eugenicists occasionally did address the issue of sexual impulses, they discussed them in terms of trying to stamp out the spontaneity of the sexual encounter so as to encourage responsible reproduction. Hernández had a very dim view of this approach: "It is a fatal error to proceed as though instincts and desires do not exist. . . . It is and will always be stupid to think that suppressing the symptoms suppresses the disease. If instinct exists, the natural thing [to do] is to adequately satisfy it."[46] Instead of simply stamping out sexual desire, Hernández advocated for better understanding the sexual impulses so that they could be properly and eugenically controlled. Discussing sex only in terms of reproduction ignored the fact that most human beings engaged in sexual activities for a myriad of reasons. For Hernández, the outsized focus on reproduction that characterized most eugenic texts made eugenicists no better than religious figures, whose arguments he similarly disregarded and who seemed equally obsessed with sex only as a means of reproduction.

Emphasizing Environment over Heredity in Secular Eugenics

The fear that Latin American physicians and scientists were not fully aware of international developments in the field of eugenics, though widespread outside Latin America, was discredited by the fact that the biggest names in the field were regularly discussed. An article entitled "Puericultura e hijiene antenatal" (Puericulture and prenatal hygiene), for example, appeared in the *RMC* in September 1915, which mentioned both Pinard and Darwin. Showing just how famous their ideas were, the article began on the first page of the issue. Referring to the pervasive dread that infant mortality was one of the primary threats to the Chilean race, the author began by stating figures about how many children died in the earliest moments of life. The anxiety that resulted from this reality led to a growing interest in puericulture, and eugenics more broadly, within the Chilean medical community: "This cultivation of healthy children constitutes one of the factors that 'Eugenics' contemplates, that is, the science that studies the causes of racial decadence [*decadencia de la raza*], and that which might contribute to its improvement. This science of vast reach encompasses in it the great problem of heredity."[47] The connection between healthy children and heredity was not unusual among eugenicists anywhere in the world, but the obvious blending of biological determinism and environmentalism in Chilean eugenic writing often contrasted with that of North America and northern Europe.

The conceptual blending becomes more apparent in this particular article, as the author, in the second paragraph, went on to discuss puericulture and eugenics as working together. Portraying the relationship between these two disciplines as quite close, he or she wrote: "After many years, Pinard has become in Paris the most enthusiastic and convincing scientific paladin of puericulture; the first notions and practical ideas of eugenics have arisen in France, but it is in England where they have found a descendant of the great C. Darwin—Leonard Darwin—*The right man in the right place.*"[48] So, despite Darwin's laments to the contrary in *¿Que es la eugenesia?*, it is clear that Chilean scientists and physicians were aware of his ideas as well as those of other influential foreign eugenicists. What would have concerned Darwin, however, was the fact that the remainder of this article went on to discuss efforts to improve prenatal health care following Pinard's recommendations.

Although it is unlikely Darwin would have objected to improving conditions for pregnant women, he probably would have disagreed vehemently with the notion that these kinds of improvements would meaningfully affect the eugenic fitness of unborn children. Since the article's author focused more on how education would result in the prevention of the most serious threats to the Chilean race, Darwin most likely would have considered this to be evidence of Latin misunderstanding of evolution.[49] Possibly even more upsetting to Darwin and others of his persuasion, the emphasis on education led to the statement: "We are profoundly convinced that in this country where religion and priests play such a powerful role, the ecclesiastical authorities could participate in an eminently humanitarian and patriotic work by cooperating from the pulpit to popularize the fundamentals of hygiene."[50] Although relatively few secular eugenic texts so openly invited priests to join in the effort to improve the race, the idea was not unheard of in the Latin American context, which distinguishes it from the type of eugenic writing happening in the North Atlantic.[51]

Although most of these internationally produced texts portrayed Latin and Latin American eugenics as being in favor of environmentally based eugenic programs and, correspondingly, against the application of negative eugenics, this was not entirely the case in Chile. In his 1936 thesis to receive his bachelor's degree in law and social science from the Universidad de Chile, *Eugenesia y derecho* (Eugenics and the the law), Guillermo Millas Parada was quite open to the use of negative eugenic measures. Millas argued that there were a variety of historical examples of negative eugenics, proving that these types of ideas and practices had existed for thousands of years in a variety of cultures. As an example to demonstrate that eugenics was not a new phenomenon and should not be considered amoral, he specifically mentioned an ancient Spartan tradition of exposing young children to the elements to see which would survive.[52] He argued: "Eugenics is the rational application of the principles of selection, derived from the doctrine of evolution formulated by Darwin and Lamarck, to the human species."[53] His combination of Darwin and Lamarck as equivalent contributors to the understanding of evolution is illustrative of the way in which Chilean eugenic writers avoided the issue of hard-line biological determinism by subsuming it into a more flexible narrative of "improvement."

Millas also insisted that negative eugenic measures should not be the first line of racial hygiene defense, though he did support their use in specific cases. These were tools for the purpose of racial improvement that, unfortunately, sometimes had to be used: "Reality also imposes on one the negative action of Eugenics . . . having to then employ energetic and cruel measures, like sterilization. On this point, without fortunate Eugenics, one easily runs the risk of failure, but one cannot reject its general aim."[54] He argued that the future promised by implementing various eugenic practices was too good to shy away from potentially uncomfortable, or vaguely unethical, actions in the present. Nonetheless, he considered it a failure of eugenic policy if negative eugenic measures were the only defense against racial degeneration. This was because "unhealthy heredity is not only the factor of the individual and the race. Defective natural and social environments also play a similar role. Economic misery, fruit of irresponsible procreation, carries with it physical misery that is also a cause of racial degeneration."[55] Millas believed "economic misery" was also threatening to racial health, so environmental solutions were of equal import.

In his thesis, grounded in law, Millas spent quite a bit of time considering the balance between individual rights and eugenic policies. He argued that negative eugenic practices were tools that ought to be used only when all other positive eugenic measures had failed. The utility of negative eugenic measures could not be denied, but it appears Millas found them distasteful because of their obvious disregard for an individual's legal rights and physical well-being. He felt that the most effective eugenic programs relied on individuals integrating into their daily lives responsible behaviors that improved their environments. In this context he advocated for sex education for young adults, which would render the most objectionable negative eugenic practices unnecessary because people would know how to properly select eugenic partners. "The fundamental teaching of Eugenics, as a new science, brings difficulties. Before everything it is necessary to destroy the occultism that always has presided in issues related to the sexual education of young people."[56]

It is notable that, for all his concern about negative eugenic interventions, Millas was not as concerned about unsolicited state interventions into citizens' private lives when it came to environmentally oriented, positive eugenic programs. Chilean writers discussing positive eugenic practices aimed at improving the environment generally considered them to be physically noninvasive and therefore ethically sound and unproblematic.[57] In the case of positive eugenic practice and policy, Millas was less concerned about an individual's right to noninterference by the state. He contended that the potential of eugenics to affect all people outweighed the occasional objections of specific individuals. "It is a juridical axiom that in all Legal conflicts that which represents the most general interest must triumph. It is therefore evident that the interests of society in this case, must take precedence over the interests of each defective individual."[58] According to this version of philosophical utilitarianism (where what benefits the most people is the best course of action), the threat posed to the rest of society by a eugenically unfit individual made positive eugenic intervention into his or her life in the name of racial improvement a legitimate course of action.[59]

This created a situation in which institutional intervention and oversight of the private sphere to monitor the reproductive health and choices of all people became, for Millas, the ideal goal of a Chilean eugenic program. He stated that marriage was not just between a man and a woman but was also about the children they would one day produce.[60] To this end, he argued, the best way to ensure offspring would be protected was by requiring a medical examination for both parties prior to getting married.[61] "It is evident that the State has the obligation to intervene in the act of a human pair unifying to procreate in order to guarantee the future citizen, and the society that he represents, the right to a healthy life."[62] Millas was hesitant to support reforms that depended on negative eugenics alone, but his acceptance and encouragement of government oversight of domestic life and sexuality demonstrated that differences between Chilean and North Atlantic eugenics was not as extensive as might be imagined. State intervention into the private sphere in the name of racial health was acceptable, even in Latin America. The issue was more about just how far that intervention would be permitted to go.

As the 1930s continued, Chilean eugenic discourse regularly vacillated between biological determinism and environmentalism. In his 1937 monograph, *La eugenesia* (Eugenics), Julio León Palma exemplified this conceptual blurring and blending. León began his text by synthesizing Galton's decades of work on eugenic theory into four principles. "First: the influential part of parentage in the reproduction of a race or variety is rigorously defined (laws of ancestral heredity and filial regression); second: the probable influence of a generation on the traits of that which follows can be determined; third: social factors work on human nature, some to make it regress and others to improve it, and; fourth: the majority of those individuals considered to be gifted constitutes an essential condition for the enduring progress of the human species."[63] The first two principles enshrined not only the ideas of Galton but also those of Mendel and August Weismann, all three associated with the more hard-line approach to biological determinism.[64] But the second two principles foregrounded the more important environmental aspects of eugenics associated with Latin racial thought, influenced by the work of men such as Lamarck and Pinard, which insisted that an organism's environment could affect its overall health. Additionally, León continued that the most gifted among human beings must be allowed to flourish under all circumstances tacitly accepting that those individuals may come from backgrounds and families that would be considered dysgenic or unfit.

León's monograph is especially illuminating because it mostly reflected on the difficulties faced by working families when it came to improving the race while also affirming the existence of strict laws of heredity. On the one hand, five pages were dedicated to discussing Mendel's experiments and how traits were passed from parent to offspring. León wrote: "He observed these occurrences in animals, mice, coming to the conclusion that inheritance after various crosses, presented its combined traits in one way or another, and in a specific way, a phenomenon that he captured very well in what he called his natural law."[65] The idea that crosses between variations would result in clear and predictable ways was perhaps especially important in a Chilean context, where racial homogeneity arising from racial mixture was the presumed racial type for all people. It is suggestive of the inherent racism and White supremacy operating in Chilean eugenic thought that, only a few paragraphs later, León insisted on the importance of Mendel's laws, stating: "It is not unusual to notice in some families after various generations . . . the presence of a descendant with African blood when it was believed that that atavistic trait had been forever extinguished."[66]

On the other hand, in *La eugenesia* León also reflected repeatedly on how poor Chileans struggled to provide the kind of environments necessary for proper eugenic development and growth. "The phenomenon of procreation, intersects with Eugenics from the economic point of view, as much as selection may allow, by extending to cover the conditions of life that the proletariat should maintain, conditions that Eugenics desires to improve."[67] León argued that, although it might seem that eugenics encouraged unlimited procreation of the fit, the economic realities facing the lower classes were an essential component to the application of eugenics in Chile. People could not hope to raise truly eugenic offspring if they were unable to provide enough healthy food, a clean home, or proper clothing. In a surprisingly circular bit of writing, León reflected: "The food, clothing, and housing of the worst quality constitute the major economic factor of consequence that has not allowed families to feed and clothe themselves better, let alone live in more hygienic and comfortable homes."[68] León's reliance on both environmentalism and biological determinism to explain the problems facing *la raza chilena* was indicative of the prevalence of this discursive blurring of those elements throughout eugenic writing of the period.

However, not all Chilean eugenic literature combined these schools of thought. There were always those who favored a more exclusively biological understanding of eugenic theory, explaining the existence and popularity of works like that of Stoddard and other foreign writers. Hans Betzhold Hess's *Eugenesia*, published in 1939, is a standout among biological determinist eugenic texts in Chile. Historians have attributed Betzhold a special place among Chilean eugenicists, based on his professed interests in creating the "Chilean superman" through negative eugenic measures.[69] *Eugenesia* was a comprehensive work of over two hundred pages that covered a variety of subjects, but the main focus was always on how to address racial problems Betzhold considered specific to the Chilean national context: alcoholism, tuberculosis, and syphilis. His focus on these three conditions fits with the wider scope of eugenic writing in Chile. Yet, a stricter belief in biological determinism set Betzhold's writing and ideas apart from those of most of his colleagues. For example, when discussing how to limit the potential impact of criminality, he wrote: "We should not interpret mandatory castration [for sexual offenders] by judicial sentence as a punitive action: it is a curative action in an individual that is gravely ill and who, after the intervention, is returned to liberty."[70] This statement was specifically in reference to the use of castration on male inmates in the United States, but it suggests that Betzhold would have been in favor of a variety of negative eugenic measures being applied to the Chilean populace as well.

Emphasizing Environment over Heredity in Catholic Texts

Unlike the texts written by individuals outside the Catholic eugenic community in Chile, Catholic eugenic texts almost always explicitly mentioned the relationship between science and religion (sometimes specifically Catholicism) as an essential part of the ethical application of eugenic policies. Another difference (and this was relatively slight) between secular and Catholic eugenic literature in Chile was in how each group characterized their acceptance of biological determinism. Although a preference for biological determinism should not be mistaken for a predisposition to negative eugenic practices, most eugenic texts (in Chile and elsewhere) seemed to make this assumption over and over. Conceptually, Darwinian biological determinism and negative eugenics were linked, and most arguments against negative eugenics operated on this discursive pattern. Catholic eugenic writers—who particularly disapproved of negative eugenic measures such as coerced sterilization and birth control because they were direct, physical interventions that disrupted God's plan—were especially prone to this approach. As a result, one of the common ways in which Catholic eugenic writers engaged with eugenic discourse was by insisting that negative eugenic practices based solely on heredity were not the best means of improving racial fitness.

In his 1924 *LRC* article "El evolucionismo frente a la existencia de Dios demostrada por el origen de la vida" (Evolutionism before the existence of God demonstrated by the origin of life), Julio Restat Cortés outlined a typical Catholic approach to discrediting Darwinism and all eugenic concepts and practices associated with it. He wrote: "Lamarckism considers the organism as active; Darwinism, merely passive."[71] Restat's opinion on the matter grew from his own involvement in a variety of different Catholic organizations aimed at improving life for average Chileans. A Jesuit priest, he worked with other clergy members to found the Federación de Obras Católicas (Federation of Catholic Works) as well as the Asociación de Estudiantes Católicos (Association of Catholic Students) for both the Universidad de Chile and the Pontificia Universidad Católica de Chile. These organizations eventually connected him to the larger efforts aimed at social rejuvenation and reform that fell under the remit of the international Catholic social reform movement Acción Católica (Catholic Action).[72] Appearing as a series of articles, Restat's work shows that he did not object to evolutionary ideas outright. Instead, he believed that the primary factor in evolutionary development was an individual organism's environment and, importantly, its free will. His emphasis on the environment demanded the existence of charitable social institutions and supported the idea that they were essential to the advancement and perfection of the race.

To support his claim Restat wrote that the study of heredity was not really about the evolution of traits but, rather, about the means by which traits were transmitted from parent to offspring. "The law of inheritance is not reliable proof of the acquisition of the same traits that have been transmitted [from parent to offspring], but rather simply a means of transmission."[73] Correspondingly, the environment was much more important to the evolution and progress of all species including humans. What distinguished Restat's ideas from those of secular writers was his contention that human efforts to change their environment through the exercise of free will would always be superseded by the divine. "But to no one is it hidden that the environment alone is not enough and it is not capable of developing existing aptitudes and far from producing them. It is to exaggerate the influence of the environment to believe them capable of creating species."[74] Evoking the debate with materialists that other Catholic writers continued to have, Restat contended that any eugenic effort (positive or negative) could only go so far as to improve the human species. These improvements would never result in an entirely new type of humanoid, such as Betzhold might have imagined. For Restat, while the environment played an important role in human evolution, it was God that ultimately controlled this process. To support this view, he argued that an organ as complex as the human eye could not develop from the random process of use and disuse of organs proposed by Lamarck.[75] Nor could Darwin's process of natural selection be truly applied to human beings to create a new species. To prove this, Restat used the example of developing a new breed of horse. "The selection or choosing of breeders and other differing factors have produced a new variety or race; but they will never manage to create a new species."[76] No matter how hard breeders worked, they would never create something other than an ideal version of a horse. These developments and the apparent perfection of organisms in nature proved for Restat the existence of a divine creator.

Restat supported his claims regarding the role of the divine in the creation of the natural world by questioning the logic of some of the most popular and central tenets of Darwinian evolutionary theory. He argued against the idea that the strongest were those better suited for survival. As an example, he pointed out that dinosaurs, certainly quite strong animals, had not survived. "In the struggle for life the most gifted or strongest individual or species do not always survive. Is there any chance that the great monsters of the Mesozoic era have survived? The ichthyosaurus with its thirty feet of length and its armored jaws of 100 powerful teeth . . . were they unable to resist the battle with other species? If the battle for life is at the base of natural selection, it is very strange that animals much weaker than they have survived."[77] This indicated that natural selection, as Restat interpreted it, did not function the way other scholars insisted it did.

The second critique he made related to the means by which traits were passed on. According to Restat, Darwin stated that variations in any given individual trait were very small. If they were so small, then how could they be said to offer any advantage at all? How could nature select them? As he put it: "[Advantageous traits] should appear *suddenly* and in all their perfection, to be able to affect selection. . . . I have here, then, [demonstrated] the role of natural selection becoming absolutely null if one considers, as the theory peremptorily establishes, that traits develop gradually by small unnoticeable [*insensible*] variations . . . and if that is how it is, how can we give [these traits] value in the battle for existence if they are not useful before they reach their complete development?"[78] In this light, natural selection as theorized by Darwin could not possibly occur because there was no meaningfully new or distinct trait to select. Finally, Restat mentioned that there was still no observable proof of natural selection at work.[79] He argued that those who did believe in Darwinian evolution had misinterpreted the evidence available to them. "The important thing, as Lamarck, the father of Evolutionism, said is not to confuse the watch with the watchmaker, nature with its author, the effect with its cause."[80] The apparent perfection of nature did not prove the existence of a set of natural laws, according to Restat, but rather, the existence of a divine order created by a supernatural force or being.

One of the most striking aspects about Chilean Catholic eugenic texts was how often they combined science, social reform, and religious ideology into a narrative of national racial progress. Roberto Barahona Silva's 1936 *Estudios* article, "Los católicos ante el problema científico de la eugenesia," demonstrates how these concepts were best combined for maximum effect. The article was one of at least nine pieces Barahona wrote for *Estudios* between 1935 and 1946, and they all dealt with issues related to Darwinism or the application of eugenics to the Chilean population. Like many of these authors, Barahona had studied medicine, and this ultimately led him to the study of biology. He completed his studies in the early 1930s, and his interest in eugenics was a sign of the times.[81] Particularly notable about "Los católicos" was Barahona's effort to show how Catholic interest in eugenics had been demeaned in the Chilean media. "I do not believe I err if I maintain that in more than 95 percent of the books, magazines and conferences that exist in Santiago on eugenics, the Catholic Church appears as the receptacle of obscurity, stubbornness and wickedness."[82] Clearly, he was displeased with secular portrayals of Catholicism's response to eugenics as universally obstructionist, and he was in an especially appropriate position to decry these claims. Though not a clergy member, he was a devout Catholic activist and a physician while simultaneously contributing to the wider world of Chilean medicine through his work in pathology.[83]

Barahona used his expertise as a medical doctor to object to the notion that Catholicism was an obstacle to the acceptance of eugenic science. He argued that Catholics objected to their exclusion from the eugenics movement and insisted that Catholicism was a necessary component to ethical eugenic theory and practice. "The Church is the best help to Eugenics, in that it defends the familial institution, it oversees the economic-social rights of the lower classes and it consecrates the activity of many of its best men for the healthy education of the youth, it makes Eugenics true, solid and disinterested."[84] For Barahona, the Catholic Church was the only institution capable of effectively managing eugenic social welfare programs in Chile as it already had centuries of experience dealing with the private lives of its parishioners and running the necessary social welfare programming. Most important, eugenics was a science that required a moral guide to properly apply its principles.

The idea that eugenic practices could be open to the manipulation of extremists became an increasingly common argument among eugenicists in the Latin world—both Catholic and secular—over the course of the 1930s, as news of what German eugenicists were inflicting upon marginalized communities, particularly German Jews, became widespread.[85] Unsurprisingly, Catholic eugenic supporters in Latin America used this as a reason to insist on their involvement in the development and application of social programs aimed at racial improvement. The racial purity laws passed in Germany between 1933 and 1938, and the international news coverage of their promulgation, possibly informed Barahona's belief that eugenics needed to be guided by a moral force.[86] Whether he was writing directly in response to these laws or not, in his article he shows how Catholic eugenic writers sought to distinguish themselves by discussing the potential adverse ramifications and ethical pitfalls of eugenic programs focused solely on negative eugenic practices. Yet these objections to the implementation of negative eugenics should be understood as saying more about Catholics' role in the national eugenic movement in Chile than as an objection to eugenics outright.[87]

Barahona argued that the primary duty of Catholic eugenic supporters was to ensure the morality of eugenic practice by preventing the use of negative eugenic measures. He insisted, however, that this should not be considered a critique of eugenics as a whole: "Instead, the Church intervenes and is obligated to do so, when certain eugenic methods try to be applied, that signify a loss of human freedom. And this does not mean that [the Church] negates the foundations of Eugenics nor its utility." Barahona stipulated that it was up to the Catholic Church to protect the free will and bodily integrity of its followers above all else and even, or perhaps especially, in the context of eugenics. He spoke out against abortion, birth control, and coerced sterilization because they were artificial interventions into natural, God-given bodily processes.[88] He asserted that if an individual wanted to have a child, then he or she, regardless of eugenic fitness, should be permitted to pursue that goal. It was their God-given right. No force, particularly the force of the state, could change this:

> I believe, instead, that robust Eugenics is born from a conscientious nation, patriotic and Christian; from a nation that has renewed internally, by the perfecting of each individual. I believe in Eugenics that results in the millionaire that complies with his duties, not just of charity, but of social justice also. . . . I believe in Eugenics of honorable governments, whose sobriety and justice make the people believe in the existence of virtue; finally, I believe in priestly Eugenics, which upon drawing the sign of the Cross in absolution, uplifts the fallen man and launches to the world a New son of God.[89]

This was Barahona's summation of what the Catholic approach to eugenics should be in Chile. Eugenics was a valid science that complemented Catholic doctrine in order to restore mankind from its fallen position. Neither could function without the other. Both were necessary so that the Catholic Church could administer to the fallen both responsibly and effectively.

By the early 1940s, Catholic eugenic writers had not drastically changed in their bleak assessments of negative eugenic practices. What had changed, however, was the increasing association of eugenics as a whole with the negative eugenic methods used in Nazi Germany.[90] In the wake of revelations of Nazi eugenic extremism, Catholic eugenic writers actively sought to distinguish and disaggregate unethical negative eugenic practices from the wider discipline of eugenics as a tool for racial improvement. Despite the growing popular belief that eugenics led to extremism in the name of racial hygiene and purity, Catholic eugenic writers in Chile still argued that some eugenic theories and practices had merit and should be maintained. In the monograph *Eugenesia y su legislación* (Eugenics and its legislation), published in 1941, Amanda Grossi Aninat argued against the idea that eugenics was exclusively about negative eugenic practices. "For many Eugenics is just about the elimination of the unfit (negative eugenics), but it is not like that, even in its eagerness for perfection of the race, it tries to encourage unions under the prism of the species, seeking to protect the physical integrity of the fruit to benefit the collective by a conscious and directed selection (positive eugenics)."[91] Grossi saw eugenics as a discipline that was far more committed to environmental interventions such as the selection of fit marriage partners. That was the most reliable pathway to success. Overreliance on biological determinism and negative eugenics led to deep ethical problems and did not guarantee the eugenic improvements its supporters claimed it did, particularly when applied to human beings. "In no case does heredity [alone] determine the ideal, mathematical outcome, [and it becomes increasingly] complicated as one ascends from the most simple beings to the most complex such as man."[92] Similar to Restat, who argued that sophisticated body parts could not develop without divine intervention, and Stoddard, who insisted that humans were a unique type of animal, Grossi contended that biological inheritance was not enough to explain all the developments of an individual human being.

When it came to discussing eugenic theory and practice, most Chilean eugenic literature said much the same thing. Negative eugenic practices such as coerced sterilization, abortion, or birth control were considered too physically invasive and ethically problematic to be reasonably considered. Even though there were indeed some eugenicists such as Millas or Betzhold who advocated for these measures, they were in the minority. To be clear, this was not because state- or church-sponsored intervention into the private lives of individuals for the good of the race was considered inappropriate. A significant number of eugenic writers in Chile supported that principle to at least some degree. Positive eugenic interventions grounded in environmentalism—such as prenatal health care, mothers' centers, or education initiatives—were popular because they were perceived as being humane and noninvasive. Intriguingly, this narrative of positive eugenics being mostly altruistic has resulted in the widespread belief in the present that these social welfare programs were not connected to the overall popularity of the eugenics movement through the first half of the twentieth century.

There was, in fact, a significant amount of agreement across a wide breadth of historical actors. Politicians from different ends of the political spectrum, clergy members and anticlerical intellectuals, liberals and conservatives agreed that the arrival of the twentieth century had brought new types of problems with the potential to damage Chileans permanently at the biological level (even if environmental solutions were the cure). Luckily, as the prodigious amount of writing about these issues from the era indicates, there was a new tool that would address these racial threats: eugenics. And in a striking moment of convergence, a diverse array of Chileans agreed to some kind of application of that tool to the populace. This possibility for agreement was predicated on the widespread belief that there was, in fact, a specifically Chilean race that deserved protection.

Chapter 4

"One of the Most Uniform Races of the Entire World"

Raza chilena and the Construction of
Chilean Racial Homogeneity

Even more than their overall preference for positive eugenic interventions, Chilean eugenic advocates were characterized by an overarching conviction that the national populace represented a specific and unique racial type rather uncreatively, identified as *la raza chilena* (the Chilean race). While the first half of this book addressed how Catholicism and eugenics as intellectual frameworks overlapped and interacted, the second half will examine how eugenic literature contributed to developing racial thought in early twentieth-century Chile. The predominant narrative in Chilean eugenic literature of the early twentieth century—both Catholic and secular—was that the national population was comprised of an idealized racial type. This contention served to mark Chileans not only as racially exceptional but also as superior in comparison to other Latin American nations. One of the earliest works to elaborate a distinctive Chilean racial origin story was Nicolás Palacios Navarro's *Raza chilena: libro escrito por un chileno i para los chilenos* (Chilean race: A book written by a Chilean and for Chileans) published in 1904.

Originally written as a series of anti-immigration newspaper articles, Palacios's *Raza chilena* celebrated the Chilean population's racial profile in by documenting how the nation's history of racial mixture had created a mestizo racial type that was biologically superior to other Latin Americans.[1] The text was astonishing in its comprehensiveness. At 706 pages, it contained seven parts that argued for Chilean racial exceptionalism using linguistic, ethnographic, geographic, demographic, psychological, cultural, and historical methodologies. The monograph was peerless within Latin American racial theory literature in its insistence upon contemporary Chilean racial homogeneity as evidence of racial superiority. Unlike scholars such as Mexican anthropologist José Vasconcelos and Brazilian anthropologist Gilberto Freyre (whose work *Raza chilena* anticipated by at least two decades), Palacios insisted that the time of active racial mixture in Chile was over by the turn of the twentieth century.[2] For him, Chile had become a racially homogeneous nation while countries such as Mexico and Brazil still had much to do in this regard, and this was evidence of Chile's special racial character. Yet, despite *Raza chilena*'s early appearance and novel insistence on racial homogeneity, there is relatively little scholarship dedicated to Palacios or the impact of *Raza chilena* on Chilean racial thought. There is even less in terms of contextualizing it into the wider landscape of Latin American ideas about race. Only a handful of articles, book chapters, and essays mention the man or his monograph. This is especially true in English language sources.[3] However, a thorough examination of *Raza chilena*'s myth of racial homogeneity reveals how Palacios combined eugenic concepts premised on biologically determined racial hierarchy with the supposedly more Latin American contention that race mixing was not inherently problematic. It was this combination of ideas that paved the way for the construction of a racial ideology in which Chilean racial homogeneity functioned much as White supremacy did in other places, especially those with similar histories of colonial expansion, indigenous dispossession, and foreign migration.

Palacios demonstrates one of the many ways in which Latin American writers approached eugenic science. Based neither on pure neo-Lamarckian environmental concepts nor on Darwinian notions of heredity, *Raza chilena* is an important example of how the blending of scientific theories worked in practice. The book shows how Chilean eugenics and racial thought were profoundly connected to sociocultural developments such as growing nationalism in the wake of the War of the Pacific (1879–1883), a corresponding growth in anti-immigration sentiment (particularly aimed at southern Europeans), and the increasing visibility and influence of labor activists at the end of the nineteenth century. Palacios's membership in the Chilean medical, eugenic, and nationalist communities placed him in the position to reflect upon what distinguished one nation from another at the biological level. The myth of racial homogeneity that he laid out in *Raza chilena* demonstrates how eugenics served to link national populations to biological racial identities not only in Chile but elsewhere at the beginning of the twentieth century.

Palacios's familiarity with biological, eugenic, and evolutionary debates both inside and outside Latin America allowed him to select, reject, and synthesize various eugenic concepts in order to create a distinctly Chilean racial origin story. The myth of Chilean racial homogeneity also incorporated elements of Darwinian and neo-Lamarckian eugenic theory to insist that Chileans had, simultaneously, both pure and mixed racial heritage. This is evident in Palacios's use of the terms "White" and "mestizo" as interchangeable throughout the text when referring to the Chilean people. Like other Latin American eugenicists at the turn of the twentieth century, Palacios was most concerned with proving Chile's civility and modernity compared to North Atlantic nations, and he linked these claims to Chileans' ability to claim Whiteness.[4] In *Raza chilena* he conflated mixed-race identity with Whiteness to connect Chileans to other White, European-descended peoples living outside Europe in the so-called New World. His work contributed to the construction of a new type of White person, one who had mixed-race origins but, for all intents and purposes, was effectively White. Palacios's blending of hereditarian and environmental eugenic theoretical concepts undermined the boundaries between racial categories, inviting a more thoughtful consideration of the meaning of Whiteness both in Latin America and in settler societies generally. His ability in *Raza chilena* to blur the line between White and mixed-race people also allowed the myth of Chilean racial homogeneity to persist long after both nationalism and eugenics had lost their appeal for the general public.

The Man behind the Myth

The myth of Chilean racial homogeneity and corresponding racial superiority created by Palacios in *Raza chilena* was informed by his burgeoning nationalism and educational experience at the end of the nineteenth century. The eldest of three brothers, he was born in 1854 in the small town of Santa Cruz, about 110 miles south of Santiago, in the pastoral O'Higgins Region. At the age of twenty, he moved to the capital to enroll in the Universidad de Chile's Facultad de Medicina.[5] In the introduction to the second edition of *Raza chilena* (published posthumously in 1918), his brother Senén stated that medicine never fulfilled Palacios's passion for empiricism and exactitude. However, studying medicine in the 1870s did allow him to be in contact with a number of important Chilean intellectuals. The introduction lists the likes of Manuel Antonio Matta Goyenechea, cofounder of Chile's Partido Radical; Diego Barros Arana, author of the sixteen-volume *Historia general de Chile* (General history of Chile), published between 1884 and 1902; and José Victorino Lastarria Santander, leftist revolutionary and author of *Don Guillermo: historia contemporánea* (Don William: Contemporary history), published in 1860.[6] Senén stated that these men, progressives and nationalists all, profoundly influenced Palacios's worldview with respect to medicine, politics, and most notably, the importance of Chile's indigenous past as fundamental to its national character and racial singularity.

It was also at "La Chile" that Palacios read the work of both Charles Darwin and Herbert Spencer, men who most shaped his subsequent understanding of eugenics and racial thought.[7] This should not come as a surprise. Alex Levine and Adriana Novoa state that, in Argentina, Darwinism was specifically linked to nationalism because "[Ernst Haeckel] and Herbert Spencer were the main intellectual reference points for those interested in Darwinian evolution. Unlike Darwin himself, both had constructed totalizing systems within which Darwin's ideas could be harnessed in service to nation building."[8] It was this second point that eventually became the most important for Palacios. Darwinian evolution, as applied via Spencer, was a tool for the construction of a Chilean national identity and future.[9] Clearly, Palacios's time in medical school was a critical period for his intellectual development, which informed the racial vision of Chile's past, present, and future he later expressed in *Raza chilena*.

Palacios's ideas about race were also influenced by his military service during the War of the Pacific, a conflict in which Chile was victorious against the combined military forces of Peru and Bolivia. Swept up in the wave of patriotism, he postponed his medical studies in order to work as a field medic. His brother described this period as essential to the creation of a Chilean national identity: "The year 1879 arrived, and soon the War of the Pacific broke out, shaking Chile in its entirety in an explosion of patriotism that ran from one extreme [of the country] to the other like a trail of fire, enflaming the national soul in a bellicose ardor."[10] Senén was injured at the battle of Tacna, but Palacios went on to the battles of Chorrillos and Miraflores, both known for their brutality and high death toll.[11] Palacios's service in the Chilean military further developed his racial ideas, particularly in light of his contact with Peruvians upon his arrival in Lima after these two famous battles.[12] Military service fomented his belief in Chilean racial difference, especially relative to the supposedly more indigenous neighbors to the north.

After the war, Palacios returned to Santiago and finished his medical studies in 1887. He then went north to work as a doctor in the Tarapacá

Region, where the local economy was dominated by the mining industry. While there he began writing the series of newspaper articles that would eventually become *Raza chilena*. These articles were inspired by his belief that the mining industry represented a significant threat to Chilean racial integrity. Specifically, he felt that the growth of foreign-owned mines and the corresponding increase in foreign-born workers willing to work for less were fundamentally changing Chilean society.[13] After watching these changes over a period of seventeen years in Tarapacá, he first published *Raza chilena* anonymously in 1904 in order to draw attention to government programs that favored foreign investment and subsidized the immigration of "cheap" foreign laborers. To Palacios, both of these practices exploited Chilean workers in different ways. From above, they were employed to do back-breaking labor that physically compromised their racial health. They were also laterally squeezed by the arrival of immigrants who threatened their racial distinctiveness. The best protection against these kinds of indignities, he contended, was to demonstrate beyond any shadow of a doubt that Chileans were a unique and superior race.[14] *Raza chilena* was written to prove this contention so that politicians would have no choice but to put a stop to these kinds of government programs privileging foreigners over superior Chilean stock. The country could then be left to the task of improving its racial homogeneity, which would further encourage national progress. However, Palacios feared that many Chileans were unaware of their singular national racial character and its value.

Chilean Racial Homogeneity and Foreign Immigration

At its core, *Raza chilena* was about acquainting Chileans with their inherent civilized nature and providing a historical narrative of Chilean racial exceptionalism compared to other Latin Americans. Palacios wrote that his book was meant to counteract "that campaign of disgrace brought about by the Government . . . which is bringing to the lands of the Nation families of races different from our own."[15] He evoked Chilean racial difference from—if not superiority over—immigrants to question the Chilean government's understanding of racial hierarchy and difference. Much like similar programs elsewhere in Latin America, Chilean politicians had instituted a number of programs and policies to encourage European immigration in the second half of the nineteenth century. These programs were often aimed at Spanish, Italian, and French migrants to encourage them to populate regions of the country that were considered vacant to prevent encroachment by nearby rival Argentina.[16] Chilean politicians supported these programs because they were also influenced by eugenic theory and therefore believed in the racial similarity of southern Europeans to themselves and hoped to further civilize the Chilean population by injecting European blood in large quantities.

Illustrating the complexity of racial thought operating in Chile at the time, Palacios disagreed with these programs because he felt southern Europeans were racially inferior. Instead, he agreed with eugenic thought emanating primarily from North America and northern Europe and insisted that southern Europeans were not desirable immigrants because of their racial failings.[17] It should be no surprise then that he categorically rejected these plans and made every effort to block their approval—visiting politicians and writing opinion pieces in various newspapers.[18]

Yet Palacios was not the only Chilean to express a dim view of southern Europeans' racial quality. In a 1902 article in the workers' daily newspaper *El Diario Popular*, entitled "La superioridad de los anglo-sajones" (The superiority of Anglo-Saxons), the anonymous author wrote: "It is well known that the most civilized peoples of the world are divided into two groups that are differentiated by the conditions of their character, by their education, by their better or worse initiative, by their more or less noble ideas and by the robustness of their physical constitution. These groups are the Anglo-Saxon peoples and the Latin peoples. Germany, England and the United States of North America, among others, belong to the first tier, and among the second are Italy, France, Spain, Portugal and all the American peoples of Spanish or Portuguese origin."[19] This writer clearly did not believe that encouraging southern European immigration to Chile would improve the Chilean race. Much like Palacios, he or she believed that southern European nations were slowly crumbling under the weight of modernity.[20] Although Palacios considered this an issue of racial compatibility, according to the author of this piece the problem was that Latin-descended peoples were too susceptible to religious influence, primarily from the Catholic Church.[21]

This author believed that the ultimate conflict between Latin- and Anglo-Saxon-descended peoples was a religious one, something Palacios generally avoided discussing. Further distinguishing this article from *Raza chilena*, the author considered Chileans as no different from other Latin Americans, clearly lumping all people in Central and South America together if they had Spanish or Portuguese ancestry. The apparent ignorance of Chilean racial exceptionalism as illustrated in this article would have been of profound concern for Palacios. To him, protecting the Chilean racial legacy presented an extraordinary opportunity to study how race mixing could result in the creation of a racially homogeneous and therefore superior population. Palacios claimed: "Two or three generations more and Chile will be able to count as one of the most uniform races of the entire world."[22]

In this context it is not surprising that Palacios took strong exception to government efforts aimed at attracting southern Europeans to Chile as they threatened the potential contributions of Chileans as a mixed-race, European-descended people to the future of humanity. Annoyed by Chilean government support for southern European immigration, Palacios pointed out that foreign scholars substantiated his claims that the Chilean race was special and in need of preservation: "This fact of great importance for us, and which has been verified by all of the observers who have met us, from Darwin to Hancock, the leading men of Chile seem to ignore."[23] Novoa and Levine argue that Latin American intellectuals often suffered with insecurity having to refer to European experts in order to substantiate their claims.[24] Yet Palacios's reference to North Atlantic scholars does not appear as a lament about the poor state of the human sciences in Latin America but, rather, as a demonstration of his prowess in navigating the relationship between local and transnational eugenics and racial theory. At no time did he question his own expertise. Rather, he doubted that local politicians were aware of the latest scientific developments regarding racial types and the place of the Chilean race within the wider scope of human progress. As the local expert in Chilean racial thought, he considered it his responsibility to familiarize all Chileans with the important information of their racial singularity.

Patriarchal Chilean Racial Origins in Araucanian Visigoths

Both Palacios and foreign eugenicists interested in the topic based their arguments in favor of Chilean racial uniqueness on indigenous heritage specific to the Southern Cone. And yet, though this indigenous ancestry was essential to the existence of Chilean racial distinctiveness, in *Raza chilena* Palacios depicted contemporary indigenous groups as both backward and disappearing.[25] He explained their disappearance as part of a larger evolutionary process that began when European and indigenous peoples first encountered each other during the colonial period, a theory known as the "vanishing race theory" in other settler societies. Social scientists at the beginning of the twentieth century increasingly wrote about how indigenous peoples were disappearing.[26] While there were many theories as to why this was happening, the overall consensus was that indigenous peoples were exceptionally suited to racial and cultural assimilation into White society. The vanishing race narrative was especially powerful in Chile, where indigeneity was associated more with maintaining certain cultural and spiritual practices than with phenotypic traits, and only cemented the notional existence of a singular Chilean race despite the reality of indigenous peoples' continued existence.

In *Raza chilena* Palacios portrayed Chile's national racial profile as the result of sexual encounters of European men with women from a specific indigenous group that supposedly no longer existed. "The Chilean race, as everyone knows, is a mestizo race of the Spanish conqueror and the Araucanian, and it came to the world in great numbers from the first years of the conquest, thanks to the extensive polygamy that the European conqueror adopted in our country."[27] The various conceptual leaps Palacios would make to claim Chilean racial exceptionalism were already at work in this statement. First, he identified the Araucanian peoples as the only indigenous group to contribute to the indigenous half of Chile's racial profile, despite the fact that there were many different indigenous groups in the region when Europeans arrived. Similarly, his use of the term "Araucanian" is notable. It was a term used to describe the ancestors of the contemporary Mapuche peoples, who very much still existed at the turn of the twentieth century (and still do today). However, racial theorists and eugenicists regularly identified the Mapuche as particularly backward, making the use of their name or lineage problematic for a man committed to proving his country's superior racial character. He opted for the more archaic term "Araucanian" instead. Additionally, Palacios had already begun the process of blurring the lines between "Spaniard" and "European," a choice that would have interesting implications when it came to Chilean racial identity.

Palacios's description of sexual relationships between these groups was specific. He stated that they were polygamous and racially exclusive, with individual European men having multiple Araucanian women as sexual partners. Protracted warfare in the region for a substantial portion of the early colonial period made the settlement of European women virtually impossible, he claimed. This engendered a closed environment in which European men and Araucanian women continued to procreate, ensuring that the race-mixing process that occurred was uninterrupted and therefore more complete making it "pure" in its own right, separating Chilean race mixing from other forms of racial mixture that happened elsewhere in Latin America. As he put it: "In our case, the conditions of production of the intermediate offspring have been the best possible. The distance between the country of origin of the conquistadors and our own, and the difficulties the journey presented at that time, obliged [the men] to come without their wives [*mujeres*], and the indefinite length [*prolongación*] of the battle, with the corresponding insecurity and scarcity of goods, [meant that] this state of affairs lasted for many years."[28] The fact that this mixture happened—and, according to *Raza chilena*, was completed—by the time of independence (or before) was essential to Palacios's claim of Chile's racial superiority relative to other Latin American nations, but there were some major issues that he did not address. He neglected to discuss how indigenous men fit into the story. He also overlooked the fact that the reason warfare continued during the colonial period was precisely because indigenous peoples were willing neither to give up their communal lands nor to humbly submit to Spanish sovereignty.[29] Palacios selected certain aspects of the Spanish-Araucanian colonial encounter in order to rationalize sexual relationships between indigenous women and European men to bolster the myth of Chilean racial homogeneity and exceptionalism.

The choice of the Araucanians over other indigenous peoples also buttressed these contentions. Although there were multiple indigenous communities in the region at the time of European arrival, Palacios selected the Araucanians as the exclusive indigenous progenitors of the Chilean race. Additionally, he stipulated that the Araucanians were racially pure themselves prior to European contact because their racial characteristics were stable and long-standing.[30] This, then, ensured that the offspring of this racial pairing would be "pure" in its own, new way. In *Picturing Tropical Nature*, Stepan discusses a similar belief held by the Swiss geologist and biologist Louis Agassiz, regarding Brazilians of mixed indigenous and European heritage. "These 'in-between types' were grounded, theoretically, in the supposed stability of the 'pure' parental types themselves."[31] It is unclear whether Palacios ever read any of Agassiz's work, but it is notable that he supported similar views of how racial mixture might also include elements of racial purity.

Characterizing the colonial past in this way allowed Palacios to create a present in which "pure" indigenous Chileans like the Mapuche were disappearing, an idea that was essential to racial progress and that was reiterated in the popular Chilean press. In a 1907 article in *Zig-Zag* entitled "Razas que mueren" (Dying Races), the author contended: "In the United States and Mexico, the Redskins have already passed on to occupy their place in museums and tales. . . . In all of the countries of South America the same has happened. The Indians leave or have left; the same Araucanians that during three centuries had the veteran conquerors of Europe on the run have given up discretion for the flattering treason of alcohol."[32] As in *Raza chilena*, the author of this article also distinguished between the noble Araucanians of the past and their contemporary descendants, the notorious Mapuche. Although the Mapuche remained visible in the early twentieth century, as a problem to be solved by public health advocates and politicians, their discursive erasure was essential to the construction of the myth of Chilean racial homogeneity and exceptionalism.

Differing from Palacios, who believed that indigenous peoples were simply being absorbed into the larger population, this writer cast the disappearance of indigenous people in a more sinister light. The arrival of European and, later, Chilean colonists to parts of Patagonia and Tierra del Fuego had brought commercial alcohol with them, and indigenous people were ill prepared to deal with the consequences. Although sympathetic, the author ultimately saw this as the cost of progress, capturing a version of the dying race theory in writing: "I have here something painfully fatal but inevitable."[33] Approaching indigenous alcohol consumption like this shows how the notion of the disappearing indigenous peoples described as pure-blooded pervaded popular consciousness. The author of this article seemed somewhat nostalgic, but Palacios hardly lamented the disappearance of Araucanians because they represented Chile's past. Only one race, *la chilena*, represented the nation's future and the future depended on cultivating Chileans' European heritage.

However, this was not the European ancestry one might expect of people living in South America. Rather than treating Spain as the racial homeland, Palacios contended that Chileans' European heritage came from northern Europe. He argued that the Spanish subjects who came to Chile during the colonial period were from a specific ethnic subgroup living in early modern Spain. In his view, the Europeans that came to Chile were "the direct descendants of those blonde barbarians, warriors and conquerors, that in their exodus to the south of the European continent destroyed the Roman Empire of the west."[34] In short, Palacios claimed that the Europeans who arrived in Chile in the sixteenth and seventeenth centuries were direct descendants of the Visigoths who had spread throughout Europe a millennium before.[35] Claiming this lineage was no coincidence. It tied Chileans to the supposedly more productive northern European races and ensured their racial superiority over both potential immigrants from southern European countries and residents of other Latin American nations, particularly those nations that attracted far more European migrants such as Argentina and Brazil. This demonstrates how much racial hierarchy mattered to Palacios, even in a mythical racial origin story that valorized race mixing.

Palacios's contention that the Chilean race demonstrated a particularly desirable example of racial mixture highlights his belief in racial hierarchy as biological fact. Not every mixed-race person was as suited to modern life as Chileans were. In his opinion, racial mixtures present in some Latin American countries would only hasten the racial degeneration of the whole, because the parent races were too psychologically divergent. "When two races of divergent psychologies, I am not speaking of different levels of culture, cross [they] bring with them the imbalance of the peripheral nerve system with the central one and [its] cerebral moderators."[36] While a group's "level of culture" was not necessarily indicative of their racial value, the best racial mixtures arose from pairings that were biologically suited to each other in other ways. If this important element were overlooked, then the ramifications would be both quick and severe. Palacios implied that nations founded on unstable racial mixtures would ultimately see massive amounts of undesirable traits—such as mental illness, alcoholism, and delinquency—develop across the entire population.

Happily for Chileans, though Araucanians and Visigoths were quite different in many ways, Palacios argued that they shared one very important psychosocial trait that fostered the ideal type of race mixing: patriarchy. "Effectively, the Goths and the Araucanians, so different in physical appearance, both had, with the same clarity and stability, all the characteristic traits of that which the knowledgeable call masculine or patriarchal psychology, in which the criterion is that the man comes first absolutely over the woman in all spheres of mental activity."[37] For Palacios, patriarchal social structures indicated the overall level of civilization of both groups prior to their mixture.[38] However, his assessment of Araucanian society's patriarchal character was questionable at best because, even though he discussed Visigoth cultural psychology at length in *Raza chilena*, he never bothered to include a psychological profile of Araucanians.[39] Nonetheless, though Araucanians were considered to be at a lower level of cultural development in comparison to the Visigoths, their similar patriarchal social structures mitigated any damage that might have otherwise resulted from race mixing.[40] By emphasizing the connection between patriarchy, civilization, and race throughout *Raza chilena*, Palacios confirmed that Chileans were biologically bound to each other through a cultural tradition of gender difference. It was this same emphasis on patriarchy and gender difference in the service of racial exceptionalism that fostered the connections between Catholic and secular eugenic texts.

Chilean Phenotypes and Creating Racial Homogeneity

Even presuming patriarchal societal similarities, claiming that all Chileans were racially homogeneous was no easy task. Palacios stipulated that there were stark differences between Araucanians and Visigoths, both physical and cultural. He was not terribly concerned about the cultural differences, mainly because the contribution of indigenous peoples to *la raza chilena* was almost entirely biological. Additionally, indigenous culture was in the process of disappearing, rendering it a problem that would be solved simply by the passing of time. Yet the physical differences between Visigoths and Araucanians presented a challenge to the myth of Chilean racial homogeneity as Palacios sought to construct it. He had to explain how a wide variety of phenotypes existed in a population that he claimed came from the same racially mixed heritage. One way he addressed this was by decoupling phenotype and race. Contending that all Chileans were racially the same, even when phenotypically different, effectively elided racial difference present in the Chilean populace at the turn of the twentieth century. Essentially, it made characteristics like hair, eye, and skin color irrelevant in the abstract. However, in concrete terms, *Raza chilena* clearly pointed to a racial hierarchy based on precisely those physical traits. Thus, while the Chilean race was defined as racially mixed, "typical" Chilean traits were also simultaneously linked to traditionally European phenotypic characteristics.

Palacios distinguished European characteristics from indigenous ones using fairly typical eugenic parameters of the period. He linked European ancestry with the physical features of blonde hair—and failing that, height. When discussing European heritage he wrote: "The conquerors of Chile were blonde in almost their totality, and those who were not showed their Germanic heritage in their elevated statures."[41] In addition to being blonde and tall, the following characteristics were indicative of Visigoth heritage according to Palacios: "fallen" eyebrows, wavy or curly hair, blue eyes, light skin, and (for men) marked amounts of body and facial hair.[42] It is unclear in this section of *Raza chilena* whether Palacios believed that these features were superior to indigenous ones, but it is clear that, for him, possessing even one of these supposedly Visigoth physical traits proved the existence of an individual's European ancestry. Thus, even if any individual Chilean appeared to have mostly indigenous physical features, having a large beard or light eyes served to obscure his or her indigenous heritage.

Blonde hair and blue eyes aside, Palacios still felt compelled to explain why Chileans manifested a wide variety of phenotypes if they were in fact a racially homogeneous population. He came up with the following: "From the countryman of Araucanian physiognomy, seeming almost pure, to the blonde countryman of well-marked Germanic aspect, the gradations are as numerous as one could imagine. However, there exists a very numerous intermediate type with the combined traits of its two progenitors, without it being easy to say which of the two is dominant."[43] He pointed out that the large number of Chileans who shared the same phenotype demonstrated the racial homogeneity of the race as a whole.

This seems a somewhat simplistic approach to the inheritance of traits, but it is important to remember that this phenomenon was not terribly well understood in this period even outside Chile. Weismann's germ plasm theory was compelling, but not especially attractive to Latin American scientists because of the seeming unimportance of environment.[44] Mendel's work with pea plants, which would greatly shape the understanding of biological inheritance later in the twentieth century, had only recently been rediscovered.[45] Thus, Palacios interpreted the large amount of Chileans who shared phenotypic traits that seemed to hover somewhere between European and indigenous as demonstrative of internal racial characteristics present in the entire population. In an exceptionally long passage, he explained how this worked and attempted to fix numerical figures to the different

Chilean phenotypes. He argued that 10.5 percent of Chileans had skin that was "white, though it does not have the transparency of the blondes of northern Europe":

> The origin of this group is owed to the cross of successive generations of Europeans with mestizos until the seed has been imprinted with these Germanic traits. The Second group comprises 19 percent of the race, and is made up of individuals with dark hair and eyes. . . . Their skin is completely opaque and of a reddish color that evokes the Araucanian, but lighter. The third group is the intermediate between the previous two; by its number and its [physical] features, it is the genuine representative of the Chilean race. It makes up around 70 percent of the country's population. Their hair is blonde or brownish in infancy, but it becomes darker even becoming black between seven and fifteen years of age. . . . The color of the skin of Chileans in this group runs an extensive gamut, going from the white of the blondes with blue eyes, to the mongoloid shade of the Second group.[46]

According to this metric, some Chileans might manifest more European or indigenous features, but despite their outward appearance, they still carried within them the same racial heritage as any Chilean. After all, even Chileans with the lightest skin tones were not actually Europeans: "The white Chilean is always more pink and with the characteristic tint of Araucanian pigment."[47] What made Chileans both unique and homogeneous, according to Palacios, was that they would always carry with them a marker of their Araucanian ancestry.

Race Mixing and Racism in *Raza chilena*

Although Palacios privileged European heritage and generally tried to obscure racism directed at indigenous Chileans, he manifested a number of racist tropes directed toward other groups. To further drive home the point that Chileans were racially different, and better, than other Latin Americans, in his monograph he specifically focused on other types of race mixing that occurred outside Chile. For him, a key aspect of Chilean racial exceptionalism in the Latin American context was the supposed absence of African heritage. He claimed that there were very few African-descended people in Chile at any point in time—so few as to make their influence on the racial composition of the overall population negligible. Echoing claims he made about the sexual relationships between European men and indigenous women, he attributed this to the fact that a relatively small number of enslaved people were brought to Chile during the colonial period because of their high cost. "I should also remind [the reader] that negro slaves were never employed in agricultural or mining tasks. The African slaves that were brought to the country remained in the cities, as buggy drivers and domestics in the rich homes. Only the Jesuits, just before their expulsion [in 1767], had begun to bring negros to have them work in the countryside. When they were required to leave the country, some hundreds of slaves of that race were found on their numerous plantations, who were then sold [to slaveowners] abroad."[48] This statement goes quite a long way in demonstrating the inherent racism operating in Palacios's racial theorizing. First and foremost, the idea that a person of African descent might arrive in Chile without being enslaved did not seem to cross his mind. Second, he mistakenly referred to the forced labor that enslaved people were expected to perform as being employed. It also seems he believed that racial mixing during the colonial period was occurring primarily in the Chilean countryside between people of European and indigenous ancestry while people of African descent were confined to either cities or plantations only to be sold to foreign owners later. This claim worked to substantiate Chilean racial superiority in two ways: by insisting that enslaved African-descended individuals in colonial Chile were unable to mix meaningfully into the population and that the vast majority of those individuals were ultimately removed from the country only to weaken the stock of neighboring Latin American nations.

Palacios not only claimed that those of African descent brought to the region were physically confined and therefore unable to participate in the race-mixing process, he also stated that enslaved people were severely chastised for any "genetic impulsiveness with punishments more terrible than the lynching that Americans use with the same purpose."[49] Referring to colonial legacies of African enslavement in Latin America served two purposes. First, it implied modern Chile's relative civility compared to other Latin American nations because it had a much smaller tradition of slave importation and was the second country in Latin America to abolish slavery.[50] Second, it served as evidence of relative racial superiority compared with the rest of the region, reaffirming Palacios's belief that European heritage was best. The fact that the limited size of the enslaved population could be explained by the Spanish Crown's disinterest in colonial Chile and its dependence on the forced labor of indigenous groups went unmentioned.

Palacios was exceptionally harsh in his criticism of people of African descent. "It is difficult to calculate the damage the introduction of one single negro could do to a country."[51] In *Raza chilena* he affirmed that African heritage was the least desirable and most alien to true Chileanness. Although he did not know exactly how traits were passed from parent to child, both Darwinian and neo-Lamarckian eugenic theories indicated that entire populations were threatened by the presence of undesirable individuals.[52] Further substantiating that African heritage formed no meaningful part of the Chilean racial composition, Palacios pointed out that "our climate is unfavorable for negroes [and] it is very well adapted for the races of northern Europe."[53] In Palacios's myth, there was simply no room for African-descended peoples in Chile's colonial past nor in its present.

This was partially the result of his belief that different types of blood had different abilities to be absorbed into the mixed-race populace. He argued that "black blood has a power of absorption that is much more than white. Thus, while not one trace of white [blood] remains at the fourth unilateral generation with black, in the mestizo 6.25 percent of white blood remains."[54] Palacios contended that, unlike indigenous blood, African blood was not as easily absorbed into the larger, predominantly European population.[55] African blood could only disappear when carefully mixed with European blood. If Afro-Chileans reproduced exclusively with each other or mostly indigenous Chileans, the stain of their blood would not be reduced but magnified as "the essence of the negro can be confirmed up to the sixth generation." This was especially concerning because of "the cerebral qualities of the negro: the lack of mental control, the predominance of the imagination and the relatively low elevation of principles, persist even longer."[56] Palacios therefore exhorted all Chileans with any African heritage to marry the lightest Chileans possible until they were no longer distinguishable from the mestizo majority.[57] The use of the terms "white," "light," and "mestizo" interchangeably throughout this passage in contrast to "black" and "negro" was notable, implying that Palacios saw the divide between White and mestizo as murky at best. His use of imprecise racial categories also lent itself to the myth of racial homogeneity in the face of phenotypic difference in particular. If "mestizo" also sometimes meant "White," it could be applied much more liberally to virtually any Chilean, culturally whitening any person who identified as such.

The myth of Chilean racial homogeneity was not only about anti-African racism and cultivating a White identity. Differentiating this myth from similar race-mixing theories popular in other Latin American nations, Palacios also spent a good deal of his time denigrating the so-called Latin races. In fact, his anti–southern European feelings grew directly from his antipathy for this racial group. "The Latin race really shows a singular predisposition to remain immobile in the old ways and a certain repugnance in appropriating the last step in the mental evolution of the human species."[58] Afro-descended peoples might threaten the ability of the Chilean race to achieve complete homogeneity, but Latin-descended peoples would cause mental stagnation in addition to racial degeneration. Palacios's statements regarding Latin-descended peoples were significantly different from those of the politicians he decried for facilitating immigration schemes for these groups based on cultural similarity and presumed racial superiority. His animosity toward the Latin race actually illuminates how his racial ideology shared important characteristics with racial theory developing outside Latin America.

Recalling Leonard Darwin's *¿Qué es la eugenesia?*, eugenic texts in the English-speaking world routinely panned the Latin race for its supposed indulgence and ineptitude. Palacios read English language texts, admired men such as Darwin and Spencer, and clearly developed similar opinions.[59] Eugenic texts written in the United Kingdom during this period were particularly negative in their depictions of the Spanish. For example, when explaining why Spain had lost its empire and fallen so far from its early modern imperial grandeur, in his book *Hereditary Genius* (1869) Galton argued: "The extent to which persecution must have affected European races is easily measured by a few well-known statistical facts. Thus, as regards martyrdom and imprisonment, the Spanish nation was drained of free-thinkers at the rate of 1,000 persons annually, for the three centuries between 1471 and 1781. . . . It is impossible that any nation could stand a policy like this, without paying a heavy penalty in the deterioration of its breed, as has notably been the result in the formation of the superstitious, unintelligent Spanish race of the present day."[60] Palacios never referred to Galton in *Raza chilena*, but it is likely he was aware of the anti-Spanish statements peppered throughout English-language eugenic texts, as he traveled to Europe in order to research the origins of what he liked to call "the Great Orphan [Race]."[61] Indeed, Stepan and Alejandra Bronfman demonstrate that Latin American intellectuals were painfully aware of negative images of the region based on its colonial relationship with the Iberian Peninsula.[62] Texts produced in North Atlantic nations pointed to Iberian colonial policies as the explanation for disordered and degenerate race mixing in the first place.[63] Anti-Spanish discourse in North Atlantic eugenics literature helps to explain why Palacios sought out an alternative European heritage for the Chilean race. It also demonstrates how racial hierarchy was maintained, and even celebrated, in a work that was ostensibly about racial mixture and the erasure of racial difference.

Palacios's treatment of African- and Latin-descended peoples demonstrates that race mixing was not free from racism in his national racial origin story. Rather, the entirety of the myth rested upon a very specific racial hierarchy, which placed a premium on European heritage and phenotypic Whiteness. European ancestry was always best, but Chileanness required the presence of indigenous ancestry as well. There was no way to avoid this, so the difference between White and mestizo was elided in order to accommodate that reality. But the accommodation did not extend to other racial groups. Mestizos resulting from other race crossings—Afro-Chileans, for example, and most immigrants of whatever persuasion—were racial others and therefore could not belong to the racially homogeneous Chilean nation as Palacios described it.

Raza chilena as an Enduring National Myth

Although many aspects of Chilean nationalism have changed since the turn of the twentieth century, the myth of mestizo racial homogeneity persists. Chileans today often point out that they are not like other Latin Americans because they lack the requisite African or Latin heritage that would racially link them to the rest of the region.[64] The longevity of Palacios's myth is partially due to the fact that it was written as a polemic. Polemics are inflammatory, malleable, and popular, and *Raza chilena* functioned brilliantly in all these capacities. Its contention that Chileans were their own distinct race provoked a strong reaction almost immediately, and the book received considerable press coverage, both positive and negative, upon its publication and in the years that followed.[65] As a result, even those Chileans who may not have actually read the book became aware of Palacios's racial origin story. Additionally, many of the ideas first discussed in *Raza chilena* were later referenced by subsequent public intellectuals and academics and were incorporated into national histories, resulting in the book's long shadow over Chilean racial thought in the twentieth century.

Press coverage was especially influential in popularizing the myth. A book review lauding the text appeared in the *LRC* a year after its publication. The reviewer wrote: "Very rarely, and perhaps never until today, has a work more scrupulous, suggestive and patriotic than this one been written in Chile, therefore it can be said that it produces an enormous good for the Chileans who love their country." This author contended that Palacios's book was a patriotic achievement because it established Chile as one of the modern nations of the world by virtue of its homogeneous and special racial character. His or her criticisms of the book were fairly mild. The reviewer felt that the argument regarding Chilean Visigoth heritage required more proof. However, it is unclear how much proof would have been required: "To the proofs of the author we could add for our part the nickname of *Goth*, which always and until today the Chilean has given to all Spaniards."[66] This evidence was anecdotal at best, but it shows the appeal of Palacios's myth of northern European ancestry, even when this reviewer doubted its credibility.

The perception of *Raza chilena* as a patriotic work only seemed to grow with time. Upon Palacios's death in 1911, the medical journalist and physician Arístides Aguirre Sayago praised the myth of Chilean racial exceptionalism in the medical periodical *RMC*. The obituary claimed that Palacios "gave us that which no one, not even the founding fathers, could give us, our rehabilitation as Chileans, as a homogeneous race and only engendered by the fusion of another two good and virile lineages: the Goth and the Araucanian."[67] Aguirre found solace, and possibly superiority, in believing that the Chilean past was characterized by racial mixture between two supposedly pure groups and that the nation's future would be purified by a commitment to maintaining racial homogeneity. Although the founding fathers created the national borders, according to this obituary they were unsuccessful in creating a Chilean national pathos. Palacios did so by creating a myth based upon racial belonging even as it excluded many people living within Chilean borders in the past and present. In this case, racial exceptionalism was tantamount to patriotism, showing the explicit links between nation and race in early twentieth-century Chile.

Palacios's esteem as a national figure continued to rise even after his death as a result of popular and media interest in *Raza chilena*. On New Year's Day 1926, a statue commemorating Palacios was erected on the Santa Lucia hilltop in the center of downtown Santiago. Then president Emiliano Figueroa Larraín and a number of state ministers attended the opening event, which became the next day's cover story for *El Mercurio*.[68] This type of coverage demonstrates that, by the mid-1920s, Palacios was recognized as one of the leading Chilean intellectuals of his age and that the myth of Chilean racial homogeneity was far from esoteric theoretical writing addressed to only a select few. The myth had ascended to such heights that its creator merited commemorative statues and celebrations attended by public officials more than a decade after his demise.

Not every Chilean agreed with this posthumous celebration of Palacios and his book, but after such a public endorsement by the president even those who disagreed with Palacios still felt they had to mention his work. For example, in his biographical entry appearing in Virgilio Figueroa's *Diccionario histórico, biográfico y bibliográfico de Chile* (Historical, biographical and bibliographic dictionary of Chile), published in 1931, the author stated: "There is more delivery than truth, more lyricism than science [in the book]. It deserved applause and diatribes. . . . And some admirers took it so seriously they did not back down in their commemorative offerings until they succeeded in the erection of a public monument in memory of the author of *Raza chilena*, which turned out anti-aesthetic."[69] Figueroa could not disguise his disdain for Palacios and the book, but he included him in the dictionary of important Chileans all the same. Soon after, the myth of Chilean racial homogeneity would move beyond the confines of the book and author to take on a life of its own.

In a 1939 article published in *Medicina Moderna*, physicians Luis Cubillos and Eduardo Brucher did not support the idea that indigenous peoples living in Chile shared similar characteristics of any sort with "normal"

Chileans. In a move that would have probably surprised Palacios, they made this claim by modifying his argument regarding the historical racial purity of Araucanians. "The Araucanian race has its own characteristics, analogous to the many peoples in states of semi-civilization. Its discrete mix with Chileans, their affection for alcohol and their scarce ability to assimilate to current culture, go on to produce their eventual extinction and have changed some of their traits also; but the fundamental traits are forever maintained."[70] The stable racial traits of the Araucanian peoples to which Palacios himself ascribed such value Cubillos and Brucher now used as indications of the insurmountable racial differences between indigenous and mestizo Chileans. In fact, in the rest of this article, they went on to demonize the Araucanian-descended Mapuche peoples by demonstrating how they were biologically and culturally predisposed to a life of crime. Cubillos and Brucher's article demonstrates that Palacios's myth could be interpreted in a number of different ways, which only further encouraged its persistence in national narratives regarding race in Chile.

Perhaps what best contributed to the longevity of the myth of racial homogeneity was its incorporation into the work of the historian and politician Francisco Antonio Encina Armanet. Too young to be Palacios's contemporary, he was one of Chile's most polarizing academic figures of the mid-twentieth century. He published the twenty-volume *Historia de Chile desde la prehistoria hasta 1891* (History of Chile from prehistory to 1891) in 1940. In this series, Encina repurposed the myth of Chilean racial homogeneity, linking racial exceptionalism to virtually every historical event in Chile's past.[71] In these volumes he also consistently affirmed the myth that Chileans were all equally mestizo.[72] In itself, Encina's work might not have endured. What ensured the perseverance of the myth of racial homogeneity well into the late twentieth century was the fact that a condensed version of Encina's history was printed and distributed by the national publishing house Editorial Zig-Zag for a mainstream audience from 1954 to 1984.[73] What began as a series of anti-immigration articles in a far-flung regional newspaper ended up having a significant impact on how average Chileans understood their racial identity for at least eighty years. With the passage of time, Palacios's argument, filtered through Encina and passed down over generations, acquired gravitas and respectability even though nowadays Palacios himself and his book no longer hold much of a place in the national memory.

Raza chilena, important as it was, was not the only text that contributed to the notion that there was such a thing as a unique Chilean race. It did, however, pioneer some of the ideas that would ultimately become standard tropes in Chilean eugenic literature and racial thought in the early twentieth century. Some of the most resilient arguments from *Raza chilena* that continued to appear in eugenic texts were that active racial mixture was confined exclusively to the historical past, that the difference between White and mestizo was minimal in the Chilean case, and that patriarchal social structures were evidence of racial superiority. The emphasis on patriarchy was a natural outgrowth of eugenic theories themselves. And much as in *Raza chilena*, Chilean eugenic writing was deeply concerned with how eugenic tools could be used to modernize patriarchy in order to address the gender confusion that eugenicists considered to be the largest threat to Chilean racial integrity.

Chapter 5

"Intimately Linked to the Issue of Sex"

Racial Health and the Modernization of Patriarchy

After Palacios helped to establish the conceptual existence and value of a unique Chilean race, eugenicists in Chile were eager to discuss how its best qualities might be cultivated. The desire to protect and promote *la raza chilena* as one of the most exceptional races, not only in the Americas but in the world, was a driving force behind the writing of many texts. It was the overarching belief in the importance of the Chilean racial type that united Catholics and materialists, liberal and radical politicians, priests and physicians. However, it was not only belief in racial exceptionalism and superiority that bridged these various differences. Another central component to the construction of a theory of racial exceptionalism in Chile was the pervasive sexism operating throughout Chilean society, which eugenic concepts seemed to support and naturalize. A significant number of writers who discussed racial improvement in the first half of the twentieth century in Chile argued that modernized patriarchal social structures were necessary foundations for a healthy race. This required that Chilean women and men behave themselves accordingly, particularly with regard to sexual encounters and romantic relationships.

The work of physician and government functionary Waldemar E. Coutts is illustrative of this trend. A prolific writer whose area of expertise was the study and treatment of venereal disease, Coutts had his largest impact through his work as director of the División de Higiene Pública (Division of Public Hygiene) within the Dirección General de Sanidad (General Directorate of Public Health).[1] It was in his role as director that Coutts wrote one of his longer works, *A los jóvenes* (To young men), published in 1929. Illustrating just how concerned Chilean eugenicists were with sexual contact between women and men as a central avenue by which racial health could be affected, he wrote: "step by step, the multitudes come to realize that the vast majority of social problems that are still to be resolved, are intimately linked to the issue of sex."[2] His opinion about the socially transcendent nature of sex explains why so many eugenic authors of the day debated how to best manage this aspect of private life. Since the purpose of eugenics was to encourage the improvement of the human race through controlled breeding, the profound clinical interest in sexual couplings should be seen as more than simple voyeurism or prudishness. What becomes apparent when analyzing the interest in sex in Chilean eugenic literature is that it was closely tied to larger concerns about an increasingly modern and secular society in which patriarchal traditions and social structures seemed to be drastically changing.

The solution, then, lay in convincing Chilean men and women to submit to a legitimate authority that would be able to monitor their sexual and social behavior for the good of the race. However, the struggle for control between Catholic and secular eugenicists evinced in these texts demonstrates that there was little consensus regarding who would represent that authority. In the Chilean case, just as in most of Latin America, this power struggle was one of the reasons negative eugenic legislation efforts never materialized.[3] Yet, a variety of laws were passed between 1925 and 1940 aimed at *la defensa de la raza* (the defense of the race) through positive eugenic measures, and these laws indicate that efforts to control average citizens' behavior in Chile were neither merely theoretical nor totally ineffective.[4] Although the proper implementation of eugenic policies was the source of extensive disagreement between Catholic and secular supporters of eugenics in Chile, beliefs regarding the purpose of eugenic social reform were much more uniform.

Both Catholic and secular writers contended that the primary purpose of eugenic social reform was the rationalization of patriarchal gender models aimed at protecting and improving the Chilean race. Eugenic literature served as a means of naturalizing gender difference with a particular focus on men characterized as sexually voracious and women portrayed as innately nurturing and whose purpose was exclusively reproductive. Experts of the time discussed this binary in terms of structuring male and female behavior around the workplace and home respectively. Catholic eugenic writers further stipulated that this supposedly natural and patriarchal social order was God-given, but, like their secular counterparts, they argued that gender difference was fundamental to the protection of Chilean racial integrity. Historians have pointed out that the modernization of patriarchy in Latin American countries depended on national and local characteristics; there was not one common formula, as patriarchal practices were different and specific.[5] Eugenic science played an integral role in the maintenance and modernization of patriarchal gender roles for both men and women in early twentieth century Chile, emphasizing the localized nature of how patriarchy is modernized to suit national concerns and debates and its deep connection to logics that often reinforce racial hierarchy in any context.

Male Sexuality as a Problem without Solution

The racial problems arising from sex deemed inappropriate or dysgenic and the failings of traditional patriarchy to ensure eugenic results were often considered together in Chilean eugenic literature. Most eugenic writers targeted specific concerns such as alcoholism, infertility, and birth control. These particular issues were used as evidence of the limitations of traditional patriarchal social structures that had not responded to the modernization of Chilean society and are therefore emblematic of how Chilean eugenic writers characterized the relationship between racial fitness and gender difference. Concerns about patriarchy also informed how eugenic writers discussed their proposed solutions to the various problems facing the Chilean race. Eugenic programs proposed for women and men were significantly different and focused on separate goals for each gender. Despite this separation, their ultimate purpose was to ensure that men remained breadwinners and women became eugenically educated homemakers.

Although the literature regarding the modernization of patriarchal social structures often focuses on the experiences of women in Latin America, some Chilean eugenic writers did spend at least a bit of time discussing men and the need to instruct them in eugenic concepts. Chilean men presented specific challenges for cultivating the race because of their supposed rampant sexual desire and propensity toward alcoholism, which traditional patriarchy had very much encouraged.[6] Regardless of their class, education, or potentially questionable racial identity, Chilean men were perceived to be free and sexually indiscriminate by nature (which is to say, biologically), and they had the power to object to state or religious intervention into their sexual lives. Catholic and secular eugenic proponents addressed this issue in their writing but typically responded to it in different ways.

Catholic writers tended to focus on the idea that men were responsible for more than mere economic support of their families and encouraged them to be more committed to their wives and to practice sexual fidelity in order to preserve racial health. For example, Father Samuel de Santa Teresa, in his August 1910 article for the *LRC*, wrote that a man's chief duties as a father included educating his children and encouraging them to live morally: "The duties of the father toward his children: he must educate his children . . . [as] the idea of good lies asleep in the heart, it is necessary to awaken it."[7] In order to do this, fathers needed strong religious convictions themselves so that they could encourage responsible behavior in their children. Of course, for de Santa Teresa, it was only Catholicism that could instill the ability to tell right from wrong. Accordingly, parental religious guidance would help young men make the proper sexual choices that would improve the racial character of the nation.

Unfortunately, however, religious instruction alone was not always a guarantee of appropriate sexual behavior in men. After all, de Santa Teresa recognized, "there are all sorts of Catholics, good Catholics and Catholics who practice little, very little." Therefore, parents, particularly fathers, had to take an active role in raising their children in the proper Catholic tradition. Even as de Santa Teresa recognized that there was a wide variety among Catholic practitioners, he argued that Catholicism was the only means of instructing men in their proper domestic roles: "The only way to make a man right, good, faithful, obedient, honorable and what he should be, is Catholicism."[8] Without the emotional and moral message of Catholic instruction, men would believe that their only responsibility to their families was a financial one, allowing them to continue their sexual indiscretions, with disastrous effects. In de Santa Teresa's scenario, however, men would have neither the time nor the inclination to give in to their less noble sexual desires. This was all part of his larger contention that men should participate more actively in religious life. By the turn of the twentieth century, active religious commitment was increasingly portrayed as the domain of women and professional clergy members. Men were presumed to be engaged with other pursuits such as politics and business.[9]

Bernardo Gentilini, another Catholic social commentator, shared de Santa Teresa's concerns. Born in Italy in 1875, Gentilini arrived in Chile twenty years later. Shortly after, he became a priest and member of the Pía Sociedad de San Francisco de Sales (Pious Society of Saint Francis de Sales; also known as the Salesians of Don Bosco).[10] The order, speaking to the concerns raised in the *Rerum novarum*, was designed to educate young men living in poverty. Ideally, these men would ultimately be groomed to join the priesthood themselves.[11] Gentilini was a prolific writer, and his 1929 biographical entry in the *Diccionario histórico, biográfico y bibliográfico de*

Chile stated that, between his books and pamphlets, eight hundred thousand examples of his work were in circulation across South America.[12] Like de Santa Teresa, Gentilini argued that men were the masters of the house. In his 1918 monograph *El libro del hombre varonil: como cristiano y caballero, esposo, padre y educador, hombre de profesión y de negocios, ciudadano y apóstol social* (The book for the adult man: As Christian and gentleman, husband, father and educator, professional, citizen and social apostle), he argued that men should be examples of Catholic devotion for their households.[13] However, he specifically noted that the problem of male sexual desire was a significant challenge to this endeavor: "[Without religion] passions will dominate reason, and man would practically become a beast."[14] Unlike de Santa Teresa, he believed that men were not able to use reason in the face of sexual desire and they therefore presented a grave risk to the future and integrity of the Chilean race. In a section of the book entitled "Las pasiones del hombre" (The passions of man) he described this threat in rather poetic terms: "The age of torment.—The man to whom we direct our writing, has now arrived at the turbulent age when [his] passions whine like indomitable stallions or howl like the sea in a tempest."[15]

Gentilini did not believe that men were capable of mastering their sexual desires. His solution, then, was not to try and change men's desire for sex or their inability to control themselves when the possibility of sex presented itself. Rather, he contended that combating this inherent weakness in men was actually the responsibility of women. Women had to make their homes pleasant and comfortable enough to keep their sons and husbands in them. As he put it: "Let the home be a type of oasis in the midst of the arid desert of existence. . . . An oasis where the desert palms, whose verdant plumes sway in the wind, refresh like a fan the sweat-covered brow of he who sits at its feet in search of respite." Then, men would not be compelled to seek out spaces like bars and clubs, which threatened their ability to maintain sexual continence. After all, "who would risk venturing through the long and fatiguing quicksands of the world, if he considered his home a delicious oasis?"[16]

One of the more intriguing aspects of Gentilini's *El libro del hombre varonil*, made even more so considering he was an immigrant himself, was that he identified bars and clubs as the inventions of foreigners designed to tempt naturally modest Chilean men. Echoing the anti-immigration sentiments peppered throughout *Raza chilena*, he indicated that the alcoholism so much discussed and feared in local eugenic literature was actually abetted and perpetuated by foreigners. In the section "Los enemigos del hogar" (The enemies of the home), he wrote: "On every corner a *bar* is constructed—a foreign word that masks the sordidness of our taverns. . . . Additionally we see the development of the *club*—another foreign word, which with its attempted pretensions of a social home come to destroy the family home." The creation of new spaces in which to drink and socialize, supposedly influenced by foreign sensibilities if not actual foreign business owners, threatened the very fabric of the Chilean family by encouraging overindulgence in alcohol and disregard for family responsibilities. As Gentilini wrote: "We will only say that a *clubman*—a frequent guest of clubs—will not be the best of husbands, nor the best of fathers."[17] The use of English words in the original Spanish text not only reinforces his point about foreigners but may also suggest that Gentilini considered these developments to be more troubling racial incursions because they represented Anglo-Saxon sensibilities.

Secular eugenic writers also argued that men were biologically compelled by their sexual urges and were virtually incapable of controlling them. Intriguingly, this argument was often made by foreign writers whose work was then incorporated into Chilean eugenic literature. Alfred Fournier's 1921 book *Para nuestros hijos cuando tengan 18 años* (For our sons when they reach 18) claimed just that. Translated by the Argentine physician Emilio R. Coni, the Spanish-language edition of Fournier's book was distributed by the Liga Argentina de Profilaxis Social (Argentine League of Social Prophylaxis). It is unclear how this book made its way to Chile, but the fact it did suggests that Latin American public hygiene leagues formed ties with each other across national borders, showing the inherently transnational nature of the eugenics movement as a whole and the particularly strong linkages within the Latin eugenic community. Immediately dispensing with the idea that interest in sex should be mitigated, as de Santa Teresa and Gentilini had hoped, Fournier stated: "From the instant that [puberty] arrives, a new preoccupation has taken over you. A hope agitates you: pure or impure, a desire solicits you. Let's be frank: the woman has been born for you."[18] As a French dermatologist specializing in the treatment of syphilis, Fournier did not discuss male sexual desire in moral terms, but he did note it was a biological fact that had to be addressed in order to protect the health of future generations.

From his writing it is also clear that he believed he had a different opinion regarding male sexual behavior than a religious figure might. He stated that his interest in discussing sex education for young men was born of a strictly medical concern: "The woman! How little I would have to discuss with you about her if I were a moralist, philosopher, religious educator, etc.! But I am no more than a doctor, and as such, I am in charge of talking with you."[19] Fournier saw the physician as a counselor whose opinion would be based on medical facts and not the moral judgments upon which writers such as de Santa Teresa or Gentilini might rely. For him, providing young men with the information they needed to control their lust was essential not only for their own future but for that of their children.

As a physician, Fournier advocated for more male responsibility when engaging in sexual behavior. In *Para nuestros hijos*, he contended that young men should have all the medically relevant facts about sexually transmitted diseases in order to avoid contracting them. He even went so far as to state that he was not interested in scaring young men from engaging in sexual activity prior to marriage. After all, their urges were biologically driven and therefore nothing to be ashamed of. However, they deserved to know the un-adulterated medical truths about the risks that sex outside marriage entailed. Without that information, then, "you will certainly ignore the *true dangers* of these [venereal] diseases, that is to say, their current and future consequences. There is, therefore, much interest in that you be informed in that respect, and *scientifically* informed, that is, in an exact, positive, and true manner. [The more i]nstructed in how to accept [*conviene sobre*] the *venereal danger*, the more you will understand how important it is to guard against it."[20] In the re-mainder of the text he provided readers with a variety of specific descriptions of sexually transmitted diseases, focusing mostly on syphilis.

Although produced in Argentina, *Para nuestros hijos* fits into Chilean eugenic literature because of its discussion of syphilis, perceived as one of the most dangerous health conditions arising from dysgenic sexual contact. Linked to concerns such as alcoholism, infertility, infant mortality as well as a wide variety of conditions considered to be congenital at the time, syphi-lis was by far the most popularly discussed sexually transmitted disease in Chilean eugenic texts. While other sexually transmitted diseases were un-fortunate, syphilis was considered to have the power to alter an individual so much that it was a threat to the future of the entire Chilean race. This was in part because syphilis was initially thought to have hereditary effects. While a child of a syphilitic parent might not be born with syphilis, Chil-ean doctors attributed certain birth defects such as blindness, rickets, and body sores to the fact that one or both parents suffered from syphilis. This was especially true if the mother had any syphilitic lesions on or around her vaginal canal at the time of birth.[21] As Fournier put it: "In sum, recent inves-tigations show that syphilis can constitute, due to hereditary consequences, a factor in the bastardization and degeneration of the species, giving birth to inferior, decadent, dystrophic, degenerate beings."[22] Syphilis had the power to transform an individual as well as his or her offspring, making it a serious public health issue and racial threat. Despite Fournier's general openness regarding sex education and young men exploring their sexuality, in *Para nuestros hijos* he still idealized patriarchal gender norms by insisting that sex within the confines of marriage was best and by rendering female sexuality invisible.

This was similar to the approach used by Barbet in *Preparación*. Like Fournier, Barbet believed sex education was essential. Yet his approach can best be understood as a combination of the religious ideals espoused by writers such as Gentilini and secular ideals discussed by Fournier. He contended that sexual education was a vital part of encouraging young men to maintain their chastity until marriage. He characterized this as moral education that would teach men to practice "self-renunciation, first in small things, later in big."[23] Barbet concluded his book by insisting that it was not enough just to provide scientific or medical information about sexuality. Young men also had to have moral instruction to encourage their best behavior. "Without chastity, the young man will start to become accustomed to birth control and, much later, being logical, legitimate abortion, divorce and free love; immorality will reign and depopulation will come with her."[24] If young men were able to receive the benefits of sex with none of the responsibilities, as claimed by many eugenic writers who argued against birth control, then the Chilean race would be threatened because families would not be formed. The rather depressing foundation of this logic was that pregnancy was the only means by which men could be "forced" into marriage.

Barbet also contended that men needed to learn how to control their sexual desires. He called for an end to the sexual double standard that allowed men to visit prostitutes while women were expected to remain faithful to their husbands. "For a man to be able to demand of she that will be his wife, a pure body and soul, he needs to be able to lead by example and give her the same."[25] A man could not expect sexual fidelity from his wife when he did not maintain his own. This idea matched with those of a variety of other social commentators, mostly women, who argued that the sexual double standard contributed to the existence of prostitution, rape, and "white slavery."[26] Barbet even went on to argue that every person, no matter what the circumstances, was capable of living a chaste life. "There is no sexual temperament that inevitably leads to [sexual] incontinence; there are [only] weak wills, whose education has been disregarded."[27] Although he recognized that chastity was not necessarily the ideal state for all people, he argued that it was possible for everyone for at least short periods of time. All people, regardless of gender, were capable of controlling their sexual urges and maintaining their chastity before marriage and this was essential to the proper development of the race.

Support for sex education for young men was a common trope in eugenic writing by Chilean authors as well. The juvenile court judge Samuel Gajardo published *La educación sexual del niño y del adolescente* (The sexual education of boys and adolescents) in 1940, in which he stated that embarrassment and morals had no place in sex education.[28] Like Fournier, Gajardo believed that preconceived notions about the immorality of sex education would result in disaster for young men in the form of sexually transmitted diseases. Additionally, he did not see the conflict between moral instruction and sex education: "Catholic dogma does not contain any principle that is incompatible with sexual education for boys, this is teaching natural laws."[29] Mirroring arguments made by Catholic eugenic writers, he argued that one of the primary goals of Catholicism was to teach how the natural world worked and to illustrate humanity's place in that world. Sex education was nothing more than acquainting young men with natural laws they ought to know anyway. This instruction was all the more important because "the form by which the sexual instinct should be satisfied, in accordance with social conventions, is marriage."[30] To be clear, Gajardo recognized that reality did not always work out this way. People did have sex outside the confines of marriage.[31] However, he still argued that marriage was the best expression of natural sexual desire in an orderly, patriarchal society.

The modernization of this patriarchal formula came in the form of Gajardo's acceptance that young men were likely to engage in risky sexual practices, making sex education an exclusively male concern in his estimation. Although he accepted the fact that men had a powerful sexual drive, he argued that they did not know how to properly consummate physical relationships with women.[32] Specifically, Gajardo meant that men improperly understood sex to be about seeking only their own physical pleasure: "The man does not seek the woman out of blind virtue, but rather because in her he will find satisfaction of *his* appetite. It is a conscious activity, in which his will acts. And if he lacks experience, he does not know how to behave."[33] Rather than encourage this to continue, he believed men needed to be acquainted with the corresponding responsibilities of sex early on. In fact, Gajardo argued against waiting until puberty to tell boys about sex.[34] By then, their sexual desires and urges would be too strong for them to be effectively educated in proper sexual behavior and the results could be disastrous. As he put it: "Sexual desire is able to apply a tyrannical pressure [on young men], [rendering them] oblivious to any notion of criminality."[35] If fathers waited until sexual interest was already present in their sons before they discussed appropriate sexual behavior, their efforts went unheard at best. At worst, their sons would perhaps embark on a life of crime. This rather bleak outcome was probably more a reflection of Gajardo's expertise as a judge in the juvenile court system than about the state of parenting in Chile at the time.

For all the empathy he showed toward boys and men, Gajardo did not believe girls and women suffered from the same difficulties regarding controlling their sexual desire. "In the woman, the problem [of puberty] is normally less serious because in her the sexual instinct is more attenuated and because social life does not offer her the tyrannical stimuli that surrounds men."[36] This statement is intriguing in its characterization of female sexuality for two reasons. First, and less surprising, it claimed that women were not as strongly compelled by their biological instincts to have sex. Second, and quite revealing, Gajardo recognized that women were not socially permitted, as men were, to have or enter the physical spaces that might afford them the opportunity for sexual temptation. This helps explain why the various solutions offered by eugenic supporters to address problems related to the health of the Chilean race had to speak to these differentiated concerns related to female and male sexuality. For example, Gajardo believed that boys and young men should be taught about sex without any fear or shame. And, though he stated that girls should also be given information in a similar manner, he seemed to feel that the most vital information was related to knowledge of the reproductive cycle, rather than sexuality.[37]

Although most Chilean eugenic writers discussed reproduction within marriage as the ideal sexual encounter, some admitted this did not match reality as often as one might hope. Coutts dealt with this issue in his 1926 book, *El instinto sexual y la vida contemporánea: Su influencia en los actos delictuosos* (The sexual instinct and contemporary life: Its influence in criminal acts). Seeming to channel Gajardo's expertise, he claimed that the crime rate in Chile was directly connected to male sexual frustration. Coutts was born in the affluent beach town of Viña del Mar in 1895 to Ernest Coutts and Eugenia Billwiller, both members of the small but significant community of foreign nationals who found themselves in the country because of business interests. Reflecting his international connections, Coutts studied medicine in Edinburgh for two years before completing his medical training at the Universidad de Chile's Facultad de Medicina, specializing in urology.[38] His interest also extended to the treatment of venereal diseases, which led him to discuss sexuality and its links to racial health. In *El instinto sexual*, Coutts reflected upon how primordial sexual instincts could be adapted to fit a modern world that demanded more care in selecting sexual partners when "all manifestations of human power are subordinated to sexual tyranny."[39]

Losing control in the face of sexual desire was something Coutts considered to be especially true for men. He attributed the ferocity of male sexual desire to the evolutionary purpose of perpetuating the species: "Thus in all cases, in all species, in differing degrees, we observe that their multiple activities, their very existence, is oriented toward the incessant battle for possessing the female."[40] Unfortunately, though, he also believed that this urge no longer properly aligned with the eugenic principles necessary to protect racial health in the modern age. Male sexual urges needed to be domesticated to fit the new social reality. Men could no longer simply engage in sexual intercourse with any woman they wanted, as older patriarchal traditions tolerated; this behavior spread disease and produced dysgenic individuals. The best way to ensure that sexual urges would be controlled was to strongly encourage marriage as the only viable outlet for male sexual desire and expression.[41] His insisting on marriage as the ideal space for male sexual expression aligned Coutts's work with that of his peers while also having the unintended effect of encouraging Catholic engagement with these debates about the health of the Chilean race.

Setting Coutts's book apart from almost all other eugenic literature of the period, he recognized that confining sexuality only to marriage would be difficult not just because of male promiscuity but also because of female sexual desire. *El instinto sexual* accepted that women might also have interest in sex and might also engage in risky behavior to slake their thirst. This, in part, Coutts attributed to the increasing sexualization of all people thanks to the new kinds of social interactions promised by modern society. "Men, women, young and old, receive from the external environment titillating emotions in high amounts, that will agitate their sexual senses. We have noted that the biographs, theatrical spectacles, lectures, dances, meetings, all of the mechanisms of modern life in a word, seem to push individuals to achieve as quickly as possible the demands of sex . . . to search out whatever means necessary to procure it, and thus to enter into competition for the possession of the opposite sex."[42] The new physical and social spaces that Coutts mentioned provided new ways for men and women to interact. This, it seemed, ate away at previous patriarchal ideas of chastity in both genders. Without that protection in place, the fate of the Chilean race was dubious at best. This is a rather surprising line of reasoning for any eugenicist, as competition for members of the opposite sex was a foundational tenet of how species arose and supposedly improved, yet Coutts seemed wary of this sort of competition.

This may explain why the supposed sexual insatiability of men continued to be discussed in eugenic texts. Gentilini's *¡Sed puros! Educación de la castidad: gobierno de las pasiones* (Be pure! An education in chastity: Governance of the passions) published in 1936 demonstrates that he believed, despite his earlier exhortations, that efforts to control male sexuality had not been successful. Much like Coutts, Gentilini recognized that male sexual desire could incite behaviors that were dangerous for the individual and the Chilean race as a whole. To combat this racial degeneration, he again argued that the best method was to advocate abstinence before marriage for both men and women: "Just as there is hygiene to protect the health of the body, there is just such a [hygiene] for the preservation of the soul. This hygiene consists in carefully avoiding the morbid influences of passions."[43] However, as Coutts had done ten years before, Gentilini contended that this was a particularly difficult proposition because contemporary social mores allowed for women and men to interact socially in potentially compromising ways. "One can never insist enough on the immorality in amassing a crowd in a dark room, men and women before whose eyes, parade films of a certain erotic flavor."[44] He chose the specific location of a movie theater to make his example, but the general point was more important. Men and women of all social classes were increasingly in each other's company without supervision, and this created situations in which they could closely interact. New patterns of socialization, such as women working in factories and shops, caused familiarity between the genders that too often resulted in sex outside the confines of marriage.

Although he discussed new places that women and men could interact as Coutts had, Gentilini attributed the changing attitudes regarding sex exclusively to male sexual desire. Riffing on his earlier work, he contended that "very few men exist that have not experienced the insolent rebellions of the beast."[45] Just as he had done in his previous work, he advocated for a new sexual standard for men that encouraged male chastity and fidelity as the new measures of masculinity. Fighting against one's natural sexual urges showed real strength and would allow men to better manage their sexual desires, keeping them healthy. As he put it on the final page of the monograph: "Sensual love makes the strong weak."[46] With this new sexual standard, venereal disease and illegitimacy (among other social problems) would resolve themselves. Male sexual continence would also prevent racial degeneration because "there are contagions that stigmatize not only individuals, but families and entire generations."[47] Gentilini's reference to heredity and degeneration demonstrates just how widespread belief in gender difference created intellectual links between eugenic and Catholic principles that originated in very different contexts.

Even Coutts agreed that a new sexual standard for men needed to be created. In *A los jóvenes*, he stated that he wanted to change what being "manly" meant. In contrast to the idea that manliness was measured by the number of sexual conquests, Coutts insisted that a real man was someone who was able to master all the passions with which nature had endowed him and not succumb. "No, young men, the most virile man, the 'most manly' is he who takes his true place in life, he who works most and best defeats the other men in the struggle for existence and not he who makes of life a field of pleasures, and especially not pleasures of a sexual nature."[48] Both Catholic and secular writers argued that sex within the confines of heterosexual marriage was the best way for both women and men to address their sexual needs. They were also more inclined to suggest that men had a biological need to express their sexuality in a way that women did not. This was especially true in terms of how many sexual partners men might seek out over the course of their lifetime and, of more concern for eugenicists, during their peak child-raising years. Despite all the calls for male sexual control, mostly coming from Catholic eugenic writers, eugenic literature that discussed male sexuality generally maintained the position that it was indiscriminate. It was typically Chilean women who were treated as those who had the most control when it came to eugenic sexual selection. What this meant was that, in terms of practical implementation of eugenic programs aimed at sexual selection, eugenic proponents focused almost exclusively on controlling women.

Reproducing the Race as Women's Responsibility and Biological Imperative

Highlighting the patriarchal and sexist underpinnings of Chilean racial thought in the early twentieth century, eugenic writers did not suggest that women needed to be taught to control their sexual urges. Rather, they asserted, Chilean women needed to pay better attention to the skills with which they had been naturally endowed that were inherently directed toward maintaining and improving racial health. Just as Palacios insisted that women's primary role was as the incubators of race, female sexuality was described and conceptualized as exclusively for the purpose of procreation. Following this logic, because all women would one day become mothers, eugenic proponents tended to believe that women subconsciously sought out the most eugenically fit mates with whom to have children. With these assumptions firmly in place, writers of eugenic discourse aimed at Chilean women focused mostly on further celebrating their supposedly natural abilities to nurture and raise children.

The brief article "María y la mujer chilena" (Mary and the Chilean woman) made these gendered expectations very clear. Written in 1905, "María" appeared in the *LRC* and asserted that women should use the Virgin Mary as their role model in all things: "We are going to begin this essay proposing the Virgin Saint as the perfect model of virtue, and a divine panacea, able to remedy the evils of all humanity."[49] It should be noted that the article's ostensible author, Sofía del Campo, was actually a pen name used by a Catholic priest, Juan Ramón Ramírez.[50] While writing as his female persona, Ramírez argued that women's natural qualities as mothers and nurturers were essential to the racial renewal and health of the Chilean populace. Although Chilean men were admonished to change their sexual behavior, supposedly natural masculine qualities were not discussed in this way.

This was, in part, because most Chilean eugenic writers portrayed women as having moved away from their biologically determined gender roles by working outside the home and playing a larger role in the male-dominated public sphere, thus contributing to the overall decay of the traditional patriarchal social order. The effort to modernize this order for its continued survival meant that Chilean women were the focus of much more eugenic concern regarding the potential negative impact their possibly dysgenic sexual or social behavior might have on *la raza chilena*. Although male sexuality was indeed a concern among Chilean eugenicists, the quantity of writing about men is minor compared to the number of items written about women's behavior and its corresponding eugenic or dysgenic effects on racial health.[51] The amount of writing about female behavior might suggest that there would be significant variation among authors, but opinions regarding female sexuality were strikingly uniform and traditional. Returning to the work of del Campo (Ramírez), for example, the link between female behavior and racial health becomes apparent. "She" argued that women and men were naturally dependent on each other: "Feminine weakness finds strength in masculine robustness, and, in exchange, she with her affability softens and tempers in him the roughness of his character and energy of his passions."[52]

Del Campo's article was emblematic of an overall trend in eugenic writing in Chile in which, perhaps surprisingly, Catholic writers were more adamant than their secular counterparts about the role women should play in the advancement of the race. In 1912, another article in the *LRC* went even further than "María y la mujer chilena." Entitled "La mujer de mañana" (The woman of tomorrow), it was written by the French intellectual Étienne Lamy (identified as Esteban Lamy in the Chilean text) in order to address the issue of women's education. Lamy argued that women had been systematically kept out of various educational institutions and generally denied the opportunity to develop their minds. The article insisted that this imbalance should be addressed.[53]

Perhaps the most striking part of Lamy's article was his insistence that the lack of educational opportunities for women was specifically encouraged when it came to scientific disciplines. He contended that women had been forced out of those fields in two ways. First, they had generally been discouraged from pursuing any sort of education at all, which he characterized as resulting from some Catholics fearing more education would lead women to leave the church.[54] Second, he claimed that, when unsuccessful in discouraging women from pursuing an education, secularists made it appear as though scientific disciplines were in conflict with religious practice. As a result, women were forced to choose between their interest in science and their faith. Lamy advocated for women to actively pursue scientific degrees and insisted there was no likelihood of their losing religious dedication. He argued for offering women "a scientific course of study [that] respects and fortifies faith."[55] The assumption that women placed their religious interests over educational development shows more about Lamy's own beliefs concerning the relationship between gender and Catholicism than the reality of women's educational opportunities in 1910s Chile.[56] The call for women to enter the sciences was probably more motivated by the Catholic intellectual renewal precipitated by the *Rerum novarum* and the generalized belief in more Catholic oversight of eugenic programming.

Lamy's and del Campo's articles in the *LRC* also illustrate a larger aspect of Catholic eugenic writing, which posited that racial health was a special duty of the Chilean Catholic woman. For example, *La Cruzada* (The crusade), a newspaper published by the conservative Liga de Damas Chilenas (Chilean Ladies' League), included an article in 1917 that claimed: "Keeping your children from evil and making them love virtue, that is a true science." Thus, not only were Catholic women expected to raise their children according to a high moral standard, but the concept of race science was linked to child rearing, making Catholic women central to the racial health of the nation. Even more important, this author went on to argue: "How serious is the mission of a mother! Terrible when we reflect on how the salvation of the souls of her children, and even the children of these, depends on her management."[57] Mixing a Catholic woman's religious duty to inculcate her children in Catholic tradition with a statement about the effects it will have on her offspring demonstrates just how intertwined Catholic and eugenic concepts had become by the 1910s.[58]

Catholic and secular eugenic discourse in early twentieth-century Chile overwhelmingly agreed that a woman's primary obligation was to bear and raise children who would contribute to the racial health of the nation. This duty was further naturalized by the fact that most eugenic writers discussed a woman's desire to conceive in the same way they discussed male sexual desire, as a biological inevitability that was virtually impossible to control. Catholic eugenic authors generally considered the most important aspect of this task, beyond the birth itself, to be the religious education of children. Gentilini addressed this in another of his numerous publications, *El libro de la mujer: como cristiana, esposa, madre, educadora y apóstol* (The book of the woman: as Christian, wife, mother, educator, and apostle), published in 1917. In *El libro de la mujer* he argued that a Christian woman's most important characteristic was her charitable nature and that racial renewal would be the result of Catholic charity.[59] He believed this because he considered women to be naturally designed to care deeply for their families. As he put it: "No being could lavish as much love throughout the course of their life as the woman."[60] Based on a series of lectures given at the Pontificia Universidad Católica de Chile for mothers and educators, this monograph was aimed at an audience Gentilini believed to be in sore need of help.

He contended that women had to be educated about how to properly fulfill their obligations to the race. Biological inclination and skill could carry them only so far. Unfortunately, echoing the sentiments of Lamy, he thought the state of women's education in Chile left a lot to be desired. Gentilini was disturbed by the apparent lack of interest in women's education, particularly because of their perceived responsibility for the future of the race: "This [ignorance] would be unspeakable for all Christians, but especially in the woman, destined by her mission to give the heat of her soul and the fire of her mind to the future generation."[61] Although Gentilini insisted that women were naturally inclined to the morality that ensured racial integrity, he thought this had to be nurtured with formal education both religious and secular. This education was especially important for women because they were the most directly responsible for the eugenic fitness of the nation. However, unlike Lamy, his understanding of what might constitute female education seems somewhat limited by his own patriarchal tendencies: "When saying that home economics is the true female science, we do not want to say that which in his time Molière believed, that the only obligation of women is to know how to make a good soup. But rather that home economics be part of the vast educational program for women."[62]

Belief in Chilean women's need for education and the power of the maternal drive often combined with efforts to curb the sexual double standard in Chilean eugenic literature. Both Catholic and secular eugenic proponents, though they respected and expected voracious male sexuality, lamented the fact that men seemed to be permitted to indulge in any sexual vice with limited or no consequences. This might appear a more progressive approach, but eugenic supporters who called for an end to the sexual double standard often blamed women for the current state of affairs. One example is a brief monograph by Mayers, *La mujer defensora de la raza* (The woman defender of the race). Mayers was one of the first women to receive a degree in medicine from the Universidad de Chile (in 1917). A top student she then received scholarships to study in Paris, London, and Berlin where she developed an expertise in public health and pediatrics.[63] In *La mujer defensora de la raza*, Mayers held women accountable for the poor state of the Chilean race by implying that they were a bit too free with their favors: "From birth, the woman must prepare to comply with the most sacred and delicate of missions; she should arrive to [her] marriage demanding the same conditions of purity of body and soul of he who will be her husband as she has observed."[64] While on the one hand offering a solution to the sexual double standard, in this statement she also tacitly held women responsible for its existence in the first place. They had not demanded proper sexual behavior from their partners.

In *La mujer defensora de la raza*, Mayers argued that, by refusing to marry impure men, women could quickly change this double standard. This approach to how to solve the eugenic problems facing the Chilean race did notionally empower women to some extent. It gave them more leverage to refuse marriage to unacceptable men. However, this solution was problematic at best. First, it assumed that men were equally interested in and dependent upon marriage as women were. Yet, we can surmise that men were not necessarily as interested, based on the previous analysis regarding male sexual desire as well as eugenicists' concerns surrounding the interwar marriage crisis. In fact, women may not have been as concerned about marriage either, since many eugenic writers simultaneously lamented rising rates of illegitimacy.[65] Second, Mayers assumed that women had the power to move beyond emotional attachment to their male partners and end relationships for strictly eugenic reasons.

Eugenic Efforts to Address "Inappropriate" Gender Behavior

The imbalance between Chilean eugenicists' concerns about male and female behavior becomes even more pronounced when they proposed eugenic public health programs. There seemed to be no concrete plans regarding instructing men in eugenic principles, such as targeting their inability to control sexual desires, but early twentieth-century eugenicists developed a number of programs aimed at cultivating and improving women's child-rearing skills. For example, in a series of articles about poverty that appeared in February and March 1910 editions of the *LRC*, Adela Edwards de Salas advocated for the construction of schools to instruct new mothers. Edwards de Salas was the founder of the Cruz Blanca (White Cross), a charitable organization aimed at helping Chilean women by offering job training, guidance when leaving sex work, support for single mothers, and aid for victims of domestic abuse. It was also responsible for unifying the group Acción Nacional de Mujeres (Women's National Action), which had eighteen thousand members by 1935.[66] In the articles, entitled "Nuestros pobres y sus hijos—escuelas maternales" (Our poor and their children—mothers' schools), she argued that poor women did not know the best child-rearing techniques and were incapable of providing the necessary eugenic resources for their children, so she proposed the creation and construction of mothers' schools. In her vision, these schools would "consist of giving practical lessons to poor women about how to wash, dress and feed their child, and on the first steps in caring for the sick before the doctor arrives."[67] This plan demonstrates her belief that poor women were unaware of proper hygiene and nutrition practices.[68]

The second article in Edwards de Salas's series addressed how to follow up on the work of the mothers' schools, which included a program of family supervision after the child was born. After all, it would be a waste of effort if the children who were saved by the early childhood mothering program ended up even worse off as young adults.[69] If conditions in a child's home were dangerous, Edwards de Salas advocated for the removal of the child from that environment. This was for the protection not only of the child but of the race as well: "To regenerate our country and so that the old and corrupted element does not ruin the rest, one has to do what one does with rotten fruit: to expel that which no longer serves and take the seed and let it fall in better soil so that a new healthy plant can emerge. The children [of the poor] are those seeds if we take them from their unhealthy environments and put them in better ones; that is the only way we will extinguish alcoholism."[70] This passage is in line with other eugenic texts in its recognition of environment as a major factor in an individual's eugenic development. But the passage is notable, however, in its rather casual discussion of taking children from their families. A poor child needed to be removed from his or her family for the good of the child, if that family could not provide the basic necessities required to maintain a hygienic environment. Child removal being treated as a primary means of eliminating alcoholism also evoked a myriad of stereotypes aimed at indigenous peoples.[71]

The need for educational programs for young mothers was a common theme in Chilean eugenic writing. Writing for *El Eco de las Damas Chilenas* (*EDC*; The echo of Chilean ladies), "Verónica" in her 1912 article "La enseñanza doméstica" (Domestic instruction) contended, as Edwards de Salas did, that women needed instruction to be good housewives. However, in her case, the recommendation was not just aimed at poor women. This was for all women and was to be limited to domestic training only: "This instruction is not professional instruction that specializes in a science so that with it she can earn a living; this is a general knowledge of all that she needs to know to be an excellent housewife." Verónica stipulated that domestic instruction for mothers should not be confused with professional education. She did not want to give the impression that a program of study regarding home economics should lead to women working outside the home. Rather, proper education would allow women to better serve in their roles as wives and mothers. Verónica also added: "Even more so; this instruction though it appears material, prosaic, and positive, may on the contrary spiritualize and become real moral and religious propaganda."[72] Verónica believed that teaching women to care for their homes and their bodies would result in spiritual growth and racial health for the whole country.

Eugenic writing in the early twentieth century regularly argued that appropriate behavior for women and men, sexual and social, was essential to modernizing and maintaining the patriarchal social structures that Palacios and others considered so important to racial health. Many of these writers believed that new social spaces such as movie theaters, clubs, and bars were making room for new ways for men and women to interact. More women than before were working outside the home. Some eugenic proponents believed it was uncontrolled male sexual urges that caused the most trouble, but seemingly many more believed that women were the ones who needed a stronger eugenic intervention. The vast majority of eugenic authors agreed that ideal sexual intercourse should be heterosexual and within the confines of marriage.

None of these beliefs was uncommon to the Latin American eugenics movement nor to the eugenics movement as whole. What was unique about the Chilean case was the role that Catholicism played in terms of both modernizing patriarchy and providing support for claims regarding the racial specificity and health of *la raza chilena*. A strong and widespread belief that Chileanness was a particular and knowable identity, different from other racial identities, set the eugenic theory developing in Chile apart.

Chapter 6

Picturing *la raza chilena*

Visual Imagery and the Creation of a Racial Type

Chilean eugenicists from a variety of ideological positions reached consensus based on underlying assumptions regarding the importance of patriarchy to modern society and to protecting racial health, based on the works of writers such as Palacios, which were dedicated to proving the existence of a unique Chilean race, a necessary starting point for all subsequent racial theory and eugenic practice. Writers who focused on racial history sought to differentiate the Chilean national population both from former Spanish colonizers and from other Latin American racial identities emerging at the turn of the twentieth century. One of the most popular ways to do so was to distinguish Chilean specificity, based on connections to particular indigenous groups, from the general Spanish or Portuguese heritage many born throughout Latin America could claim. This meant a rather fetishistic reverence for a specific indigenous group—in the Chilean case, the Araucanians. What set the Chilean racial narrative apart from similar stories developing throughout Latin America, however, was the claim that the racial mixture process that had resulted in their singular racial type had long since been completed. The phase of active racial mixture—regularly and exclusively associated with the colonial era in eugenic literature—was over. *La raza chilena* was not to be confused with the supposedly lesser racial mixtures emerging throughout the region in the early twentieth century.

Insisting on the racial homogeneity of the national populace in the present was a much more involved effort than one might imagine. The myth of Chilean racial homogeneity was built not only upon the work of nationalist writers such as Palacios but also upon large amounts of visual representations of Chileans. Studying a small sample of these images published in various medical journals during the interwar years will demonstrate how visual culture played a central role in the consolidation of—and belief in—the existence of a specific Chilean racial profile that public health professionals considered exemplary of the best type of racial mixture. The intersection of gendered and patriarchal assumptions in this racial narrative is apparent in images of Chilean women who were understood to be eugenically fit and "normal" and of those who were not. The first group of women in this sample were portrayed as White, while "abnormal" women were characterized as racially mixed. This set of visual tropes contributed to the larger body of racial discourse that worked toward Chilean racial exceptionalism and superiority because most Chileans were understood to be normal. It should be noted that images of "pure" indigenous women also appeared in the pages of these same medical periodicals, but they were not treated as examples of the national racial type. Similarly, although images of men and children were used to convey racial uniformity across the entire population as well, physical descriptions and depictions of Chilean women are especially demonstrative of the gendered and racialized tropes at play in early twentieth-century Latin American imagery.

Visual Culture in Latin American Ethnography and Medicine

Studying visual culture has more often been the realm of the anthropologist rather than that of the historian. In fact, since the advent of the camera, anthropologists in particular have made use of visual images for the purpose of better understanding and categorizing the differences, racial and otherwise, among human beings.[1] The relationship between racialization and visual imagery extends well before the invention of photography.[2] In the case of tropes appearing in Chilean eugenic literature, one of the most powerful ways that racial exceptionalism and homogeneity were conveyed was through visual images. Typically, those images portrayed "normal" Chileans as effectively White and "abnormal" Chileans as individuals of darker hues, who were then implicitly read as having more indigenous heritage but still retaining a mestizo identity.

One of the first historians to reflect upon the impact and importance of visual culture's relationship to national identity in Latin America, especially indigeneity's role in that identity, was Deborah Poole. In her monograph *Vision, Race, and Modernity: A Visual Economy of the Andean Image World* (1997), she examines how images of Andean indigenous peoples circulated internationally. She argues that photographs of these individuals depicted them according to a formulaic narrative of exoticism, which in turn created an international understanding of what a "Peruvian" looked like. In the case of Peru, this idealized image was coded as indigenous both abroad and at home.[3] Applying the concepts of theorists such as Susan Sontag regarding the power of the photograph, Poole showed how the choice of these images was not casual.[4] The process of selecting photos for an international visual market was done by Peruvians and foreigners alike, a process in which profit was by far the most important motivating factor. Thus, Peruvian visual culture became monetized in addition to serving as a visual template for what might constitute a normalized image of Peruvians both within Peru and abroad.

More recently, Hilda Lloréns has similarly used images to examine the development of the "Puerto Rican" racial type by both Puerto Ricans and by outsiders. Lloréns studies images from the twentieth century in order to understand "the power-laden cultural and historic junctures imbricated in the creation of representations of Puerto Rico and Puerto Ricans by Americans ('outsiders') and Puerto Ricans ('insiders') during an historical epoch marked by the twin concepts of 'modernization' and 'progress.'"[5] Just as Puerto Ricans and continental Americans used racial imagery to assess whether the island's people were progressing, so too did Chilean media create a space in which the eugenically fit Chilean body could be displayed and evaluated. Especially salient to this discussion of Chileanness and racial superiority, Lloréns's work was inspired by the discomfort felt by Puerto Ricans when it came to discussing explicit racial identities such as Black and White, racial identities that inform American society and culture at large, of which Puerto Rico forms a part. As she put it, she had to move away from what people felt comfortable saying about race to be able to examine the items *"they created* about race (such as novels, plays, paintings, photographs, and performances)."[6] Chileans did not struggle with the same difficulties as Puerto Ricans in terms of naming racial others or undesirable racial traits, but the desire to portray Chileanness as racially exceptional and superior required similar efforts at obfuscation and denial of certain aspects of racism and prejudice, and these were manifested in images they produced.

Better understanding the role that images play in the creation and construction of racial meanings also inspired the work of Gisela Cánepa Koch and Ingrid Kummels. In their 2016 work, *Photography in Latin America: Images and Identities across Time and Space*, they make use of different collections of anthropological photographs taken throughout Latin America. What emerges from their work is that the images captured by anthropologists in the past develop different meanings over time.[7] The power relationships operating at the time of a photograph's creation are not necessarily the same as will operate when the scholar views that photograph many years later. In the case of Chilean images, it is difficult to assess what an image might have meant in the past. In particular, my own Americanness perhaps predisposes me to see race in a way that Chileans would not. Nonetheless, what these images repeatedly illustrate is an increasing consensus among eugenic texts of the early twentieth century about what "average" or "normal" Chileans were supposed to look like. Conformity of appearance, after all, was an essential component in proving that the nation was indeed as racially homogeneous as was advertised and therefore superior relative to its Latin American neighbors.

Images of "Normal" Women and Claiming Whiteness for All Chileans

Textual descriptions of the physical features of the Chilean race were important, but they were not the only way to shore up the idea that Chileans were racially homogeneous and superior. Visual representations were equally important to these claims, regardless of the style or place of publication, and contributed to an overall visual culture that depicted the normal Chilean racial profile as White in comparison to other Latin American racial types. The bulk of the images examined below come from the interwar period. This means that, though image production had become relatively widespread and quite a bit cheaper, the choice to include an image along with text was not casual. Most periodicals in this era operated with small budgets, and the decision to include an image of any sort suggests it was considered essential to the purpose of the text.[8]

One of the magazines that regularly included images in its remit was the *Revista de la Salud Pública de la Cruz Roja Chilena* (*RSPCRC*; The Chilean Red Cross public health review). First released in 1922, *RSPCRC* remained in print for eighty-eight years. The establishment of a branch of the Red Cross in Chile, the Cruz Roja Chilena (CRC), was touted as an important development connecting the remote country to a prestigious international organization. According to the magazine's opening message, "Nuestra primera palabra" (Our first word), which appeared on the first two pages of the inaugural issue, the foundation of the CRC had resulted in "more than sixty [associations], distributed to even the most remote villages of Chile. Our new members surpass thirty thousand."[9] How reliable these numbers were is hard to gauge, but the notional existence of access to health care throughout the entire country was a powerful claim. The message also discussed the other important element of the *RSPCRC*'s mission. The magazine "would be the exponent of [the CRC's] efforts and, especially, of popular, hygienic, civic and moral education."[10] In the most basic terms, then, the *RSPCRC* was designed to be the means of popularizing important aspects of racial theory and eugenic practice, primarily among Chilean women who were either studying to be nurses or already working in that or a related field.

The claim to popular widespread coverage of both the magazine in particular and the CRC in general is vital to understanding how the images in this periodical were contextualized and understood by the people creating and viewing them. The figure of the female nurse was the type of person that the pages of the *RSPCRC* portrayed more than any other. The International Committee of the Red Cross was originally founded in Switzerland in 1863 precisely to address the need for more nurses on international battlefields, so it comes as little wonder that nurses were depicted so often in the pages of the *RSPCRC*.[11] What is more important to understanding the visual culture surrounding the Chilean racial type was how these nurses were depicted, particularly in light of the fact that the *RSPCRC* was meant to promote the work of the organization at the popular level.

The first article in the first issue, entitled "Antecedentes sobre la Cruz Roja Chilena" (Antecedents of the Chilean Red Cross), explained how certain legal developments had occurred over the previous two years to allow for the foundation of the Red Cross in Chile.[12] The article included photographs of individuals who were central to the organization's founding—such as the former Chilean president Jorge Montt Álvarez who was then serving as the organization's president, the physician Lucas Sierra, and the bishop Rafael Edwards. The article also included a list of members on the steering committee. Notably, although the organization was exclusively meant to train women in the field of nursing, there were no women serving on the committee.

According to the article the first time a Red Cross organization operated in Chile was during the War of the Pacific, one of the bloodier battles in recent national memory.[13] Dating the origins of the CRC to this moment in national history also had a particular resonance with racial theory at the time. Just as Senén Palacios had pointed to that conflict as the true awakening of his countrymen to their racial specificity, a number of scholars have pointed out that this military conflict with Peru and Bolivia served as a foundational moment for the concept of *chilenidad* or Chileanness.[14] Linking the emergence of the CRC to this historical moment then appears significant indeed.

In addition to outlining the origins of the CRC, "Antecedentes sobre la Cruz Roja Chilena" is interspersed with images of people who were important to the organization's foundation. These included the president of Chile, Arturo Alessandri; Archbishop of Santiago, Crescente Errázuriz; the Chief Medical Officer of the Sanitation Administration, Pedro Lautaro Ferrer; and Bishop Rafael Edwards. All these men exemplified the supposedly widespread Chilean physical features that Palacios contended existed across the national population. They all had light skin, dark hair, and facial features associated with European heritage. These men all belonged to the most elite levels of Chilean society, illustrating the power these physical attributes had within it, despite the importance of racial mixture to the existence of a supposedly unique Chilean racial phenotype.

It is unclear which of the various periodicals aimed at public health, medicine, and hygiene first began the trend of taking photos of nurses performing their duties, but portraying nurses as racial exemplars became a trope within medical photography of the interwar era in Chile. In addition to photos of groups of nurses, the first issue of the *RSPCRC* also included the photos of the immediate past and current presidents of the CRC—Sofía Eastman de Huneeus (see figure 1) and Carmela Prieto de Martínez respectively.[15] These women also had light skin, dark hair, and European-associated features. This especially reflected Eastman's family history. She was born in 1873 to Tomás Eastman Quiroga and Sofía Cox Bustillos, both with British fathers who had followed the shipping industry to Valparaíso and then married into prominent Chilean families.[16] Eastman and Prieto were members of the upper classes and were therefore more likely to have significant amounts of European heritage relative to the overall population, and their images conveyed the idealized Chilean racial type for all *RSPCRC*'s readers.

The racialized character of images of nurses becomes more apparent in an article that appeared in a 1923 edition of *RSPCRC*. A regularly appearing section of the magazine was entitled "La herencia de la salud" (The inheritance of health) and this edition included a treatise written by then president of the Royal College of Physicians of Edinburgh, Sir Robert William Philip (misspelled as "Phillip" in the text). The treatise, "El hombre debería avergonzarse de estar enfermo" (Man should be ashamed of being ill), was written for the International Committee of the Red Cross.[17] Despite the seeming contradiction with the section's emphasis on biological determinism, the general thrust of the text was to insist that men's general health was primarily the result of their own good or bad decisions. Unfortunately, Philip wrote, "only a fraction of humanity reaches the level of health and well-being that corresponds to hereditary potential, and that could be easily achieved following certain elementary rules." Although, in a general sense,

Figure 1. Immediate past president of the Cruz Roja Chilena, Sofía East-
man de Huneeus. Her lighter skin is the result of her parents both having
British heritage. As such, she represented an especially ideal model of the
Chilean racial type. Credit: Biblioteca Nacional de Chile

Philip seemed to avoid the concept of racial hierarchy as he indicated that environment and human will played a significant role in eugenic fitness, he also pathologized marginalized groups and held them responsible for their poor health. Philip went so far as to argue: "It is not an exaggeration to ensure that the majority of the weaknesses and infirmities of life, excluding that which results from age, result from ignorance or disregard of elementary physiological laws, and from individual and collective neglect to obey the fundamental principles of health." This statement makes Philip's position quite clear regarding personal responsibility and health. However, it went beyond this to contend that dysgenic defects affected not only the individual but the "welfare of the society" as a whole.[18] These words appeared on the same page as images of CRC doctors and nurses who matched the parameters of what Chilean eugenic literature described as fit.

Even stronger proof of how images and words combined to create a vision of the "normal" Chilean racial type appeared later in Philip's article. When explaining the practice and teaching of medicine, he wrote: "So important is the normal form to vital well-being, that it would be useful to draw the attention of medical students, heads of family, teachers, and tutors of children toward the perfection of the forms reproduced in the sculptures of the Greeks. The quality of childhood and adolescent development should increase in conformity with that model."[19] This concept of an ideal racial type was not unusual among physicians, eugenicists, and biotypologists of the period, but it bears a special importance when thinking about gendered and racialized bodies in the Chilean context.[20] The men and women pictured alongside Philip's words were implicitly portrayed as these types of ideal physical models.

The racialized implications of the images that appeared in the *RSP-CRC* in the 1920s did not rely on nurses alone. One of the most striking images included in the periodical was on its December 1928 cover. Not a photograph but an illustration, it depicted a woman holding a Chilean flag and supporting herself on a red cross. Beneath the image was text: "[The Red Cross] is complete abnegation and sacrifice and its work, universal and sublime, is the work of all for all, without distinction of race, nationality or religion" (see figure 2).[21] These kinds of statements are not exclusive to the CRC or to other Chilean volunteer-based public health organizations. But the woman holding the flag and representing the CRC is clearly meant to be viewed as a White woman. In an image that used only blue and red ink, her skin is made a tint of pink rather than leaving it free of color (a fairly common practice in images of this period when depicting white skin). The use of pink, rather than leaving the face blank, serves to emphasize the racial identity of the CRC's avatar. Portraying the CRC as a White woman reaffirmed the kinds of visual claims made throughout the *RSPCRC* when

Figure 2. It was somewhat unusual to depict White skin in this manner. Typically, magazines using illustrations chose to simply leave a person's skin blank to function as White regardless of the color of paper that it would be printed on. Credit: Biblioteca Nacional de Chile

including photographs of its members in its pages. It also evoked the claim that Palacios made almost a quarter of a century before regarding the pink hue that would always endure among White Chileans as a marker of their Araucanian ancestry.

The images in *RSPCRC* were not exclusive to that periodical. In fact, many different magazines aimed at practitioners of public health, social work, and medicine used similar visual tropes. For example, *Servicio Social* used comparable images in its pages, despite the fact that its target audience was made up of social workers rather than nurses. In the March–June 1927 issue, an article appeared about the founding of the Escuela de Servicio Social de Santiago de Chile (Santiago School of Social Work). The article emphasized that, as of 1927, Chile was the only country in the entire South American continent that could boast of such an institution. In fact, according to the article's anonymous author, Chile was the only Spanish-speaking country to have a school of social work at all, which indicates that the author was interested in highlighting Chilean exceptionalism, in this case as related to eugenic innovation and social reform, even before images were added to that same end.[22]

The first images in the article depicted the school building alongside a description of the founding of the school, which foregrounded the involvement of European social scientists. According to the author, the school was founded as a result of the physician Alejandro del Río Soto-Aguilar's 1924 trip to Belgium.[23] Del Río was one of the most prominent Chilean public health advocates in the first half of the twentieth century, and the school of social work now bears his name.[24] While in Belgium, del Río became acquainted with the physician and secretary of the International Committee of the Red Cross, René Sand, and various others from his circle.[25] Sand was making a name for himself throughout Europe as one of the first physicians to develop a program of study for social work.[26] Inspired, del Río decided to open a school of social work in Chile, and he contacted Sand in order to get a recommendation regarding who should head the school in its formative years. In fact, two different Belgian women directed the school during these early days.[27] In this context, when the image of the first class of the Escuela de Servicio Social de Santiago de Chile graduates appeared in *Servicio Social*, a significant amount of work had already been done relating to the racial character of the average Chilean woman. Their photograph, too, reaffirmed the belief that the Chilean racial type was a light-skinned person with dark hair and eyes.

The images of social workers—or *visitadoras* as they were typically called at this time—that appeared in the March 1928 *Servicio Social* article "Servicio médico y asistencia social en la escuela" (Medical service and social work in the school) cemented the idea that social workers and nurses were representative of the idealized Chilean physical appearance and corresponding racial heritage. The first photo to appear in the article was captioned: "When the case requires it, it is the Social Worker who comes to the child's home to do the necessary investigations and to teach the basic

Figure 3. The *visitadora* (social worker) became a staple of Chilean social welfare programs in the early twentieth century. The name indicates two major aspects of the job itself: only women were considered appropriate for this type of work because they would often visit families at home. Credit: Biblioteca Nacional de Chile

rules of Hygiene."[28] The caseworker, in her official uniform, sits just to the right of center (see figure 3). The reader is meant to understand that the family the visitadora has come to help, while seemingly not at the lowest scale of poverty, are beneath her in terms of both class and race. She sits while everyone else stands. The family depicted in the photo all appear to have skin that is noticeably darker than hers.

The racial difference the viewer is supposed to understand between the family and the visitadora is further supported by the article's text. Written by the social worker sisters Laura and Blanca San Cristóbal, the article is mostly about how schools should be the primary spaces for hygienic instruction. But there seems to be a particular reason for selecting this location, rather than another. As the San Cristóbals saw it: "With its population coming, in its majority, from the popular classes [who have] little care for personal hygiene and that of their homes and with the economic resources that in only certain cases reach basic comfort, [the school] offers a fertile field for contagion and the spreading of all types of epidemics and diseases, [and thus] should take advantage of this movement in favor of public health."[29] Much like Philip, who pathologized ill health as a personal failing, these authors also saw poor school children as a "fertile field" to practice their ministrations. The biggest threat to the overall racial health of the population was understood to be the lower classes, because they were presumed to be more likely to suffer from alcoholism, tuberculosis, and syphilis, all diseases associated with poverty that contributed to racial degeneration. Schools may well also have been one of the few places where lower-class Chileans might interact with those of the middle or upper classes, in the form of teachers, guests, or administrators, making them the point of transmission of "socially transcendent" illnesses and thus threatening the eugenic fitness of the nation as a whole.

Like Philip, the San Cristóbals argued that the physical condition of one's body was intimately linked to one's character. When advocating for a program of physical education in schools to further the goals of public health and hygiene, the sisters wrote: "The immediate and rapid repercussion is already well known, in the close relationship between cause and effect, that the tone and physical conditions determine the moral and intellectual personality of the human being, and vice versa."[30] While emphasizing the power that individuals had over their own fitness demonstrates the underlying belief in the power of human beings to manipulate their environmental conditions for the purpose of racial improvement, it also spoke to the racialized beliefs operating within Chilean eugenic writing. The lower classes were racialized because of their poverty and seeming inability to live according to eugenic demands. Therefore they presented a challenge to the racial health of the nation as a whole. The racial superiority and exceptionalism promised by eugenic scholarship could be realized only through the strict application of eugenic practices aimed at the lower classes.

Intriguingly, the San Cristóbal sisters seemed to recognize just how big a job this was. They insisted that remaining positive in the face of extreme difficulties was one of the main components of the visitadora's remit. This type of emotional labor was essential, according to the article: "It is difficult and one needs a good dose of optimism, of confidence in the future, to not feel discouraged in the face of so much anomaly, calamity, affecting the social portion of that which contains the future seed of the Nation, it involves a problem of incalculable transcendence and before which, despite knowing the means and the techniques to combat it, we remain inactive solely due to lack of economic resources and materials and allow it to complete its work of racial demolition."[31] Tracing a path that many subsequent social workers would tread, the San Cristóbals openly discussed how hard their job was. In the face of increasing pressure to maintain and improve the Chilean race, with minimal financial resources, how could an average visitadora maintain her confidence and professional dedication? The answer to this question is not clear from the article, but perhaps belief in the exceptionalism and superiority of the Chilean racial type was of such value as to make the effort worth it.

Just as images of visitadoras and nurses functioned as indicators of the ideal Chilean racial type, individuals from the lower classes were used as visual counterpoints typically combined with articles about creating public health and hygiene education programs for them. For example, an article entitled "Plan de Organización de la 'Liga de Madrecitas'" (Organizational plan of the 'Little Mothers League'), written by Mayers, operated on the assumption that poor women were desperately in need of instruction in mothering just as Edwards de Salas had. Her article in the September 1927 issue of the *Boletín Sanitario* (Sanitary bulletin) was about how to familiarize young women with the newest trends in puericulture in order to lower infant mortality. Mayers noted that the best way to engage these new students was to combine instruction with kindness: "Only then can we achieve the desired end: the cooperation of the young girls in the campaign against infant mortality."[32] Using kindness to gain the trust of young women would address the issue that most disturbed Mayers, along with other Chilean eugenicists and public health officials at the time, her contention that at least thirty infants for every one hundred born in Chile did not survive.[33]

The text of "Plan de organización de la 'Liga de Madrecitas'" was mostly dedicated to outlining how a course in mothering should be organized; one of the most salient points being that students should be at least twelve years old.[34] Starting girls as young as twelve in mothering classes not only spoke to the reality of working-class homes, where older siblings might often be responsible for the care of younger ones or elderly grandparents, but also implied that these girls might become mothers themselves at a very early age. Mayers also pointed out that public health and hygiene programs such as this had already been implemented in the United States to good effect: "The United States Department of Education has also [had cause to] influence Home Economics programs in the addition of Puericulture for girls in all grades."[35]

Linking her program of mothers' training to the expansion of home economics in the United States—much like alluding to the European training and identities of the directors of the Escuela de Servicio Social de Santiago—put Mayers into the wider conversation among Chilean eugenicists regarding the national population's relative racial exceptionalism within Latin America. The image that appeared along with this article only confirms this contention. The article includes a photo of the first class of students. The girls are dressed very similarly to the nurses and social workers depicted in other periodicals, but they are distinguished by their age, darker skin, and the long braids some of them wear. These braids, not the trendy bob that was popular among young women the world over in the late 1920s, served to identify these students as traditional and, perhaps, more indigenous than their instructors. This contention is also supported by the fact that the girls hail from the Peñaflor community just outside Santiago, which retains an association with indigenous identity well into the present.[36]

Another version of this visual trope regarding the Chilean lower classes appeared in an article in the periodical *Medicina Moderna* in March 1928 written by the pediatric physician Iván Prieto Nieto and entitled "El Patronato Nacional de la Infancia" (The national board of infancy). Prieto wrote the article to celebrate the opening of the new building dedicated to improving infant health. He began with a history of the foundation of the Patronato Nacional de la Infancia. By the time of the article's publication, the Patronato had grown as a health and welfare organization primarily dedicated to providing food for poor children.[37] Similar to other organizations, the Patronato had implemented a system of home visits for women who were unwilling or unable to participate in their inpatient programs: "Every candidate being attended by a Leche League is visited at home by a social worker, who initiates a meticulous family analysis."[38] Surveillance and monitoring of poor families in itself was not inherently racialized, but the images included at the end of the article are less benign. The photos depicting the Patronato's building and staff confirm the notion that average Chileans were effectively White, as doctors and nurses appeared to be. Yet the photo of the mothers with their young children using the Patronato's services shows a group of people with noticeably darker skin, implying that the reason they need these services in the first place is because of their racially dubious heritage and not just their poverty.

Images of "Abnormal" Women and Gender's Connection to Racialization

Images from the previous section illustrate how different medical periodicals sought to establish what constituted supposedly normal Chilean racial characteristics and to align these with a White racial identity. Other images illustrate individuals whom medical professionals perceived as potential threats to *la raza chilena*, leading to their appearance being described as non-White. Essentially, individuals who had any condition considered as racially degenerative were typically racialized as non-White by virtue of their diagnoses. This dynamic became more apparent when the medical condition in question disrupted the gender binary considered so essential to eugenic fitness and racial health. A notable article appeared in the June 1930 edition of *Medicina Moderna* showed how this worked in practice. Discussing individuals identified as intersex, this article illustrates how physical "defects" of a gendered nature were also read as threats to Chilean racial integrity. The connection between gender disorder and racial degeneration discussed here illustrates how belief in modernized patriarchy as biologically sound bridged gaps between religious and secular understandings of eugenics.

Entitled "Algunas observaciones clínicas de estados intersexuales en la especie humana" (Some clinical observations of intersexual states in the human species), the article was written by Romeo Cádiz Oyarzun. At the time of the article's publication, Cádiz was a practicing surgeon and gynecologist.[39] Working with physicians such as the Lithuanian Chilean Alejandro Lipschütz and Spanish Gregorio Marañón over the 1930s and 1940s, Cádiz would eventually become one of Chile's first prominent sexologists. He published his magnum opus, *Sexo anormal: hermafroditisimo-pseudohermafroditisimo, ginecomastia, homosexualidad y otros estados intersexuales y anomalías de sexo: estudio general, clínico y terapéutico* (Abnormal sex: Hermaphroditism-pseudohermaphroditism, gynecomasty, homosexuality, and other intersexual states and sexual anomalies; general, clinical and therapeutic study), in 1958. "Algunas observaciones" probably was one of his earliest forays into the topic of intersexuality.

The article was comprised of a series of case studies collected from patients whom Cádiz saw at the Hospital San Agustín and at the Policlínica de Ginecología del Seguro Obrero (Social Security Gynecological Clinic).[40] Both institutions were designed to serve primarily female patients and were dedicated to reproductive health.[41] The Hospital San Agustín was mostly dedicated to the practice of obstetrics. The *policlínica*, on the other hand, formed part of a larger state-run effort to provide health care to all Chilean citizens. This might explain the working-class backgrounds of the individuals who appeared in "Algunas observaciones." As a note, because the subjects in the article considered themselves to be women regardless of Cádiz's diagnoses (quite stridently in one case), in this chapter I refer to the subjects of this article as women and use female pronouns.

"Algunas observaciones" as a visual representation *la raza chilena* was notable in two ways. First, it included a striking number of photographs in comparison to other articles in the journal. In total it featured twenty large photographs, some occupying full pages. This was not only unusual for *Medicina Moderna*, which was often more modest in its use of images, it was a large amount for any comparable professional journal at the time. Cádiz's article was also notable because it began by featuring an individual who had already appeared in a number of domestic and international publications regarding intersexuality. Identified as O.B.B., the first patient discussed in "Algunas observaciones" was considered such an unusual case that she was studied in Oscar Hiriart Corvalan's thesis to become a physician, which both Lipschütz and Marañón later used to discuss intersexuality more generally.[42] Kurt MacMillan refers to the writing about O.B.B. to examine the transnational connections in Chilean theories regarding intersexuality in the 1930s. He argues that O.B.B.'s case and its circulation in the international community of sexologists, "reveal[s] Chile's participation in multiple and overlapping transnational knowledge networks during the first half of the twentieth century."[43] This is certainly true, but the article "Algunas observaciones" also illuminates how intersexuality was linked to ideas regarding racialization and gender difference inside Chile as well. This becomes especially apparent when her case appeared in conjunction with those of other women presumed to be of a similar type.

For the women who appeared in "Algunas observaciones," their supposedly aberrant gender states opened the door to their racialization and pathologization as unusual Chilean phenotypes. The unlucky and famous O.B.B., for instance, first visited Cádiz's father, Buenaventura Cádiz González, because she had never had her period but did get monthly pains in her abdomen.[44] Rather than taking the case himself because of his own poor health, Buenaventura referred the young woman to his son.[45] Cádiz's case study notes are striking in their capturing O.B.B.'s seeming normalcy at first glance. When describing her general constitution, he noted that it was "normal." He also described her subcutaneous fatty tissue as "of feminine development."[46] In fact, most of the descriptions that applied to O.B.B.'s outer appearance reinforced the idea that the subject's sexual and gender identity were in alignment as female (see figure 4). Her throat was "of feminine type, nothing special about it." Her musculature was normal, she had no edemas or swollen glands. When describing secondary sexual characteristics, Cádiz described her hairline as having "feminine implantation." He described her breasts, which he was sure to photograph, as "well developed, pear-shaped, normal." Her pelvic examination also gave no indication of her intersexuality. Cádiz described this part of her body as "of feminine type—wide. Pubic hair with feminine arrangement."[47] This area, too, he photographed for posterity and eventual publication. When examining and describing the patient's vulva and vagina, he wrote that these also appeared normal. Overall, O.B.B. had all of the primary and secondary sexual characteristics of a woman.

However, despite all outward appearances, internal examination revealed that "there was not even a vestige of a uterine canal nor of any deformed variation [of such an organ]." The revelation that O.B.B. lacked this female reproductive organ—and could therefore never contribute to the Chilean race in the only way expected of women—opened the door to her eventual diagnosis as an intersexual and a corresponding pathologization of her body as racially aberrant from the "normal" Chilean's relative Whiteness. On the same page that Cádiz noted her lack of vaginal canal, he

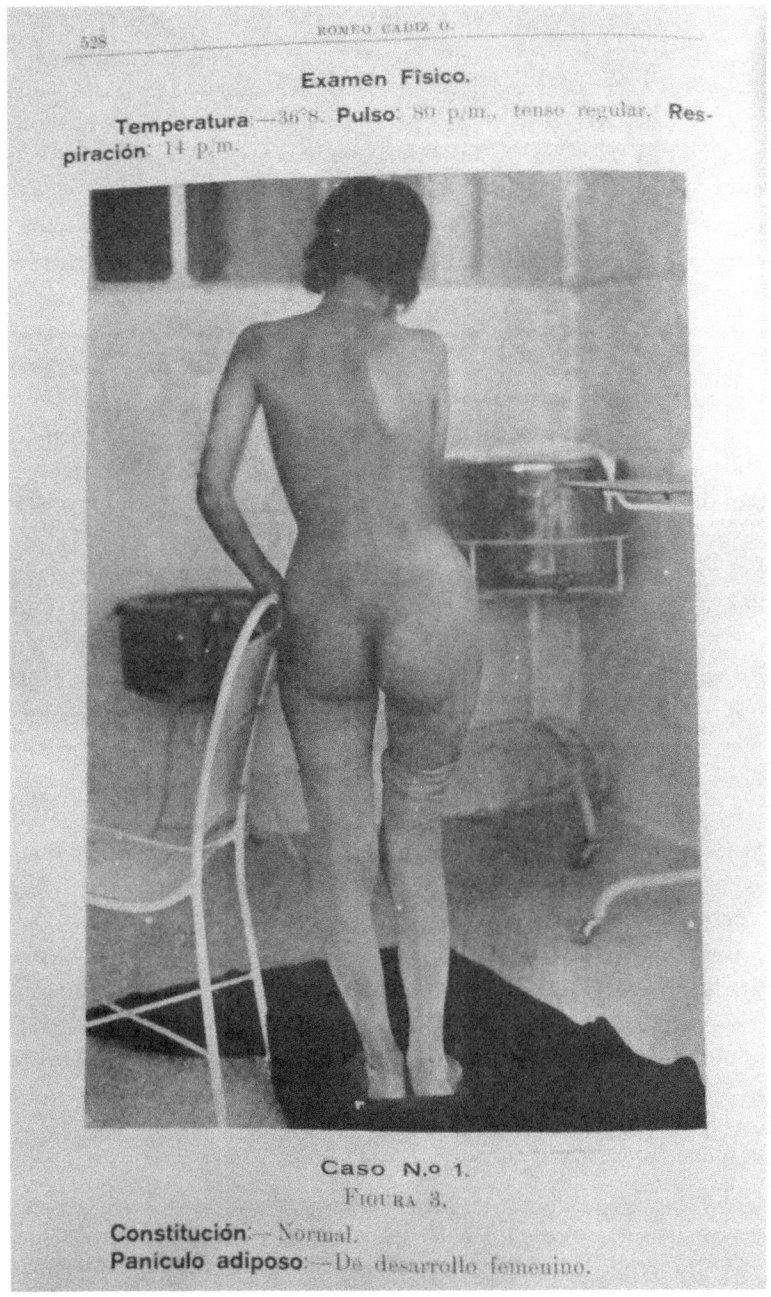

Figure 4. Based on this photo, where O.B.B.'s skin appears fairly light, it is suggestive that Cádiz described her as being "of dark color." When her gender identity became questionable by medical standards of the time, her racial identity then also seemed to have been up for debate. Credit: Biblioteca Nacional de Chile

also described her skin as "of dark color."[48] The more pathological elements of O.B.B.'s case were further outlined as Cádiz reported that someone had attempted to sexually assault her when she was only ten years old. After that incident, according to the case notes, she refused all types of sexual contact.[49] At the age of fourteen, however, this began to change as Cádiz noted that O.B.B. "has had a sexual inclination [libido] toward men and erotic dreams. She says that from that time she has masturbated (sometimes 3 and 4 times a day) to orgasm. Her maternal instinct has matured enormously over time."[50] This passage is intriguing in its combination of elements perceived as pathological by the medical community of the day—such as sexual assault, female masturbation, and dark skin—alongside idealized feminine traits such as sexual desire for men and motherhood.[51] From this perspective, it is no wonder that O.B.B.'s condition sparked the imagination of not only Cádiz but the wider world of sexologists writing during the 1930s.

It was the patient's own desire to have children, and the fact that she had found a partner she wanted to marry, that compelled her to seek out a doctor's help. She had had no success in getting pregnant on her own. Cádiz noted that her desire to be a mother had opened her up to medical scrutiny she would otherwise not have had to endure. The pursuit of motherhood had "obliged her to consult a doctor and to submit herself to the necessary tests and interrogations."[52] Cádiz's awareness that O.B.B. would feel embarrassed at best—and humiliated at worst—while undergoing these tests evinces the generalized reluctance felt by many Chilean women regarding gynecological procedures and exams at the time.[53] However, this did not stop Cádiz from photographing her genitals in an extreme close-up to help determine whether she was female.[54] After a series of examinations, Cádiz believed that the only way forward was to conduct a surgical procedure that would construct a vaginal canal in order to allow access to the ovaries he presumed she had. He came to this conclusion because his various external examinations had convinced him that O.B.B. was not an intersex individual, but a "real" woman.[55] During the surgery, however, Cádiz discovered that the patient had undescended testes in her abdomen. Surprising to both doctor and patient, the exploratory surgery brought to light the fact that O.B.B. had no female reproductive organs at all, "no uterus, no fallopian tubes, [and] no ovaries."[56]

As a result, despite his original opinion that O.B.B. was a woman, based on her outward characteristics, Cádiz's final diagnosis was that of intersexuality. MacMillan's work shows that arriving at this diagnosis was not an easy one.[57] After the surgery, the news that O.B.B. was not a "real" woman and would never be able to have children took its emotional toll. As Cádiz wrote: "I have continued to see this sick woman on repeated oc-

CASO N.º 2.

Figure 5. M.V.G.'s acrogmegalic condition set her apart from the other women included in Cádiz's study, but she originally came into his purview based on symptoms related to her reproductive health. This additional issue perhaps contributed to him describing her in some of the most insulting terms. Credit: Biblioteca Nacional de Chile

casions after she left the Hospital (June 1929) and I have noted during this time a complete change in her character, it seems that upon learning the truth of her sex she has suffered a psychic shock that has made her reject the testes which she carries within her, and she insistently asks me to remove them."[58] The shock that O.B.B. felt at being told that the medical establishment did not see her as a real woman as well as the revelation that she would never be able to realize her dream of having children most certainly would have affected her character, at least in the short term.[59] But her status as an intersex individual with dark skin and a dubious past meant that she became fodder for medical examination and speculation. It meant that her photographs would be used as examples of gender deviance and racial degeneracy. The images of her body that Cádiz included in this article contributed to a visual culture that sought to emphasize the importance of gender difference between women and men as essential to protecting the integrity of the Chilean race.

If O.B.B.'s intersex diagnosis was particularly notable among the burgeoning community of sexologists in Chile and abroad in the 1930s, as MacMillan argues, the remaining women in Cádiz's article did not enjoy that same privilege. They did, however, highlight the strong connection Cádiz made between intersexuality, pathology, and racialization even more than in O.B.B.'s case. The second case study in "Algunas observaciones" was of a woman identified as "M.V.G.," who sought medical treatment after her period had become extremely irregular. But this was not her only cause for concern. As Cádiz explained: "The patient [had] also noticed an enormous development of her facial features, hands and feet, so that now her face is completely disfigured as can be seen in the photographs" (see figure 5).[60] Using the term "disfigured" when referring to M.V.G.'s appearance set the tone for the rest of the case study, which discussed almost every aspect of her body and personal history as aberrant and racially compromised.

Unlike the previous patient, M.V.G.'s condition was noted as unusual from the start. Her constitution was described as "acromegalic," referring to an increase in the size of the bones in the face, hands, and feet because of hormonal changes.[61] While O.B.B.'s skin was dark, M.V.G.'s was described as "pigmented" and "infiltrated."[62] Her breasts were "atrophied."[63] Like O.B.B., Cádiz noted a moment in M.V.G.'s early childhood as being possibly relevant to her current condition. "Around ten years of age she had some kind of affliction that she did not know how to explain but whose principal symptom was a loss of visual acuity."[64] Although this was very different from O.B.B.'s sexual assault at the same age, Cádiz may have considered childhood trauma and intersexuality to be linked in some way.

Another important difference between O.B.B. and M.V.G. was that— despite the fact M.V.G. had female reproductive organs and O.B.B. did not—Cádiz seemed to be much more skeptical of her female gender identity.[65] When describing her extremities, he wrote: "Major development of hands and feet, almost double normal size as can be seen in the photograph and x-ray of the hands compared to a normal hand. There is a masculine hirsute-ness on the legs." M.V.G.'s condition then, whatever it may have been, made Cádiz see her in a more masculine light. Her supposedly more masculine outward appearance may also explain why he tested her for syphilis (unlike O.B.B.), as men were typically considered to be carriers of venereal disease because of their more promiscuous sexual behavior.[66]

M.V.G.'s trajectory also differed from that of O.B.B. because she ultimately decided not to accept Cádiz's recommended course of treatment.

After her examination, the physician determined that the problem was a pituitary tumor, which caused the hormonal disorder that led to her acromegaly and her corresponding "masculinization."[67] Cádiz therefore recommended that she undergo radiation treatments to shrink the tumor in order to alleviate her symptoms. For whatever reason, though, she decided not to undergo the procedure. Her images were used nonetheless in *Medicina Moderna* as instructional tools regarding intersexuality, its diagnosis, and treatment, despite the fact that Cádiz's own examination indicated she had no male reproductive organs and that her hormonal condition was the result of a tumor. Her inclusion in this study of intersexual individuals seems questionable at best and suggests that her "pigmented" skin perhaps played a role. Although her case differed in significant and important ways from that of O.B.B., the photographs of both women contributed to a growing visual archive of what constituted abnormal and racialized Chilean bodies.

The next case study featured in "Algunas observaciones," of a subject identified as "B.J.M.," similarly linked intersexuality with pathological threats to the Chilean race. According to the case notes, B.J.M. had her first period when she was fourteen years old, but it was always a painful and irregular experience. She had come to Cádiz because the pains associated with her period now persisted whether she was menstruating or not. Despite this sign of biological femininity, like M.V.G. before her, Cádiz from the start of his diagnostic notes described B.J.M. as masculine. His initial description stated that she was a "sick woman of regular height and with masculine aspect and gestures. The attention is primarily called to the little development of the transverse processes of the pelvis and of the gluteal region." In contrast to the descriptions Cádiz used for O.B.B., he considered B.J.M. to have very few traits of traditional femininity. For example, her subcutaneous fatty tissue layer was described as "masculine," and her hairline was also portrayed as of "masculine implantation." She did have breasts, which Cádiz stated had "well-formed nipples," but he also indicated that "what comes to one's attention is that the development of the anterior muscles of the abdomen have a masculine aspect."[68] Most apparent in this description was not how B.J.M. thought of herself but, rather, Cádiz's estimation of her looks as unattractive and not feminine enough to him. His description is even more brief than his description and case study of M.V.G., and it is unclear what happened to B.J.M. after Cádiz collected this information and made his evaluation.

"Algunas observaciones" is mostly illustrative of the imprecision related to diagnosing intersexuality in the 1930s. O.B.B. had no female reproductive organs, but she appeared to Cádiz to be the most feminine. Both M.V.G. and B.J.M. had their periods and presumably were able to have children (fertility issues were not reported in the case notes), but he included them in a study of intersexual individuals primarily because they were not as conventionally attractive as O.B.B. There were other individuals included in this study who appeared to be women but were categorized as intersex.[69] Most important, the photographs of these women became part of a growing visual record of abnormality within *la raza chilena*. Especially relevant is the fact that the images were combined with assessments related to their skin tone and aberrant or dysgenic environments in which they lived. In this way, their photos were used to demonstrate how blurring the boundaries between male and female also led to significant concerns about the racial implications of these conditions for the entire Chilean population, not just for those labeled as abnormal by the medical community.

These images and ideas are suggestive in a number of ways. First, images of Chilean women played an important role in how eugenic fitness and dysgenic deviance were depicted. In the context of periodicals aimed at a medical audience, a reader might expect to see women's and men's bodies captured in equal numbers. However, when discussing potentially dangerous threats to the racial integrity of the Chilean populace as a whole, images of women dominated the visual landscape. The image of the ideal Chilean woman—or its opposite—was essential to the overall construction of the idea of the Chilean race as a whole, particularly when it came to supporting the contention that Chileans were racially superior among Latin Americans because of their homogeneous physical features. In this light, it should be no surprise that individuals identified as intersex by the medical community would represent a conceptual obstacle to the notion of Chilean racial exceptionalism. The women in "Algunas observaciones" were pathologized because of their intersexuality, and this opened the door to describing their skin as "dark." Importantly, one of these women would be unable to threaten the Chilean race by virtue of her intersexuality. The others, however, represented an increased threat because of their non-White racial identities and their ability to have children.

Perhaps the most striking aspect of these images for the outside observer is the obvious racial divide at work in early twentieth-century Chilean society. Women described as poor also seemed to have darker skin. Those women needed help and support in a number of ways in order to protect the future of *la raza chilena*. This help was offered by women with lighter skin and, presumably, more money. And yet, according to the logic of the day, all of them were descendants of those same two noble races that Palacios wrote about years before. The work that he and many other eugenicists, Catholic and secular, managed to do over the first decades of the twentieth century created the conditions for most Chileans to see class difference as the primary issue affecting their lives. However, another equally important factor was staring them in the face.

Conclusion

On a warm and sunny day in early September 1952, the former dictator Carlos Ibáñez del Campo was named the new president of Chile, having won 47 percent of the popular vote. This moment was surely personally important to Ibáñez—to win the presidency legitimately, after taking the role by force almost thirty years earlier. It was also an important moment in Chile's political history. Ibañez was a political conservative, and his rise to the presidency marked the end of the coalition of center-left political parties that characterized the Frente Popular's era of political control of the previous two decades.[1] The years between Ibáñez's election and that of Salvador Allende in 1970 were shaped by the 1925 constitution, spearheaded by Ibáñez himself when he was dictator and which fomented radicalism at both ends of the political spectrum and an increasingly precarious economic situation. Much like the debates occurring in nations all over the world during the 1950s and 1960s, Chileans began to question the traditional social and economic rationales that structured their lives.

At their most liberal those rationales, though seemingly far from the discipline of eugenics, were deeply influenced by the belief that Latin

Americans had not been adequately able to adapt to modern life and its corresponding economic demands. By the 1950s, this inability to achieve economic success relative to nations such as the United States was often attributed to "cultures of poverty" or the legacy of colonial entanglement.[2] This supposition explained, for some, why socialist and communist political agendas were becoming so appealing in the region. Some economic philosophies recognized that Latin America had been used for the extraction of its natural resources and had suffered for its colonial past. These philosophies were often ostensibly antiracist but continued to infantilize and racialize Latin American peoples and nations, which were still left behind no matter what the cause.

The persistence of the belief that Chile—and Latin American nations more generally—were economically and politically behind other nations in the mid-twentieth century had profound ramifications. Racialized concepts of degeneracy and progress were deeply sublimated within a Chilean culture that already insisted on its racial exceptionalism and superiority. Throughout Latin America the 1950s marked the high point in generalized belief among scholars, both in Latin America and outside it, that the region had managed to solve racial conflict through race mixing. Correspondingly, economic troubles in the region were characterized as the result of a failure to modernize or to fully incorporate all citizens (particularly those who were mixed race) into the formal economy. Scholars did not take seriously the possibility that Latin American countries may not have been interested in pursuing the same economic trajectories as nations in North America and northern Europe. Those avenues toward economic development were not possible anyway, as the wealth of those nations was built on modes of production that by the middle of the twentieth century were no longer considered morally acceptable, such as the enslavement of people of African and indigenous descent. Mid-century interests in addressing both racial conflict and extreme poverty combined to make Latin America a data mine for scholars interested in studying racial democracy and the efficacy of humanitarian development programs aimed at non-White, especially indigenous, peoples.[3]

Two individuals came to prominence during this mid-century period of Chile's history, Salvador Allende and Augusto Pinochet who have not appeared anywhere in this book. This may come as a bit of a surprise. Chilean historiography has been very much oriented around tracing the rise of *la vía chilena* (Chilean road) to socialism, its demise, and the role that both men played in that process.[4] However, historical examinations of Allende's rise to become the first democratically elected socialist president in 1970 and of Pinochet's September 11, 1973, coup were not only informed by the sociopolitical developments of the 1960s and early 1970s. Both men spent their formative years in the same eugenically driven atmosphere as the writers discussed here. Both Allende's and Pinochet's biographies reflect the racialized logics that informed their lives as well as their ultimate political goals and aspirations.

The two men were born within seven years of each other; Allende in 1908 and Pinochet in 1915. They both attended prestigious high schools in Valparaíso, one of the strongest markers of belonging to the Chilean elite both then and now.[5] They belonged to families that were perceived as Chilean, rather than indigenous. This meant they not only were comfortable economically, they were also perceived as White. Allende attended the Universidad de Chile, and Pinochet received his higher education at the Escuela Militar (Military College).[6] If anything, it was probably Allende who was more exposed to racialized discourses because of his study of medicine. Nonetheless, both men grew up in a world where Chile was a nation comprised of Chileans: people characterized as mestizos who had no particular interest in their indigenous roots beyond the fact of their existence.

Allende's biography in particular illustrates how important debates about race, eugenics, and Catholicism were to his understanding of social reform and socialist governance. In his medical school thesis, *Higiene mental y delincuencia* (Mental hygiene and delinquency) published in 1933, he explored how to apply eugenics to Chilean society in order to decrease crime.[7] Much as Gajardo and Coutts, for example, Allende saw a direct connection between a lack of eugenic fitness and delinquency. This was in no way remarkable in 1933, but this text would go on to plague Allende's legacy and memory in the twenty-first century. Showing how much the existence of eugenic literature and racial theory has subsequently been obscured in Chilean culture and society, the Chilean historian Victor Farías in his own book *Salvador Allende: antisemitismo y eutanasia* (Salvador Allende: Antisemitism and euthanasia), published in 2005, used this text to claim that Allende was, in fact, vehemently antisemitic.[8] Unsurprisingly, Farías's publication led to a massive debate within the Chilean press about the veracity of his claims and the memory of a historical figure, a debate that is still more polarizing than might be expected almost half a century on from Allende's death.

The public outcry in response to a medical student's thesis written almost eighty years previously shows how automatic knee-jerk reactions to the mere word "eugenics" are, not only in Chile but all over the world. So far has the word been buried—perhaps especially in Latin American nations that pride themselves on their supposed color blindness—that when it comes to the surface it is associated with only the most vile racist extremism. However, Allende's eugenic past, rather than being seen as an embarrassing misstep of a great leader, should be understood as the first framework through which he attempted to grapple with Chilean social problems that he felt were the result of class disparity. He ultimately chose to address those problems through political (and not eugenic) means, but early twentieth-century Chilean eugenic writers certainly identified the social problems that dominated debates about Chilean social welfare for the remainder of the twentieth century—health care, access to education, and the vast disparities between rich and poor.

These issues were always central to Allende's political career from its inception. The same year he graduated and wrote his thesis, he cofounded the Partido Socialista de Chile (Socialist Party of Chile). Five years later, in 1938, he led the Frente Popular's successful campaign to elect the reformist politician Pedro Aguirre Cerda as president.[9] In recompense for his hard work, Allende was made Minister of Health. It was in this office that he wrote his first major monograph, *La realidad médico-social chilena* (The Chilean medical-social reality), published in 1939.[10] Although he had mostly moved away from eugenic theory and racial logics as the means of explaining the poor health of the Chilean populace, in this book he still emphasized state-sponsored medical intervention into citizens' lives as the best means to address issues such as tuberculosis, infant mortality, venereal disease, and alcoholism. He linked these diseases to high rates of poverty among Chilean citizens. Thus, while his explanation for these conditions had shifted toward the necessity of alleviating poverty, it seems that, in his opinion, what constituted social ills was not meaningfully different from what eugenicists were proposing at this same historical moment.

Pinochet's young adult life was similarly filled with professional accomplishments. Upon graduating from the Escuela Militar in 1935, he was posted to a variety of locations throughout Chile. Later, he continued his studies at the Academia de Guerra (War Academy). By 1951 he was teaching classes at both institutions and he, too, began to generate texts that reflected his experience and point of view as editor for the institutional magazine *Cien Águilas* (One hundred eagles).[11] This formative period of Pinochet's life was influenced by eugenic discourse and the construction of a Chilean racial identity. The eventual dictator's insistence on a strong Chile—paired with Catholic extremism and the use of state violence to repress citizens, especially indigenous citizens—seems a logical progression from the racial ideologies circulating in various institutions during his early life. The continuities within Chilean society and culture precede the more obvious political rupture of the 1973 coup, then, and contribute to the persistence of cultural conservatism in Chilean society in the latter half of the twentieth century.

Allende and Pinochet's respective agendas for the Chilean people in the 1970s were not only born of political conflict. Rather, both men were equally impacted by the gendered and racialized notions first explored in Chilean eugenic texts, both Catholic and secular. Allende's interpretation of ideas regarding the racial integrity of the population ultimately led him away from the training of his youth, focused on biological realities, to a more politicized vision of Chilean society, considering how the state might be able to mitigate the inequalities that had arisen among fellow citizens. Even so, his belief that the state had a responsibility to the health and well-being of its citizens was cultivated in his earlier eugenically informed training as a physician.

If these impulses in Allende's political career can be characterized mostly as benign, or even beneficial, the impact that eugenic concepts regarding race and gender had on Pinochet was far more troubling. Both Pinochet's emphasis on Catholicism as the state religion and his insistence that the country had moved away from traditional patriarchal values resonate with some of the arguments made by Catholic eugenic writers. More disturbing, the disproportionate amount of state violence experienced by indigenous Chileans and foreigners under the Pinochet regime speaks to the lasting idea that Chilean nationalism was, to some degree, associated with the idea that national belonging was based on biological heritage.

The similarities in the lives and experiences of Allende and Pinochet highlights not only their being from the same generation and privileged upbringing but also the intellectual similarities across the Chilean elite in the early twentieth century. Concern for the Chilean race and a desire to modernize patriarchal social structures united historical actors who were often more comfortable pointing out their differences. The eugenic, racialized discourse created by Catholic and secular writers in the first half of the twentieth century was based on gendered concepts believed to be stable, natural, and scientifically proved. Women and men were different, both in terms of their complementary abilities and talents. Their differences were not the result of politics, education, or culture but, rather, were the direct result of inherent biological differences between the genders that were essential to the continued existence and improvement of the Chilean race. Emphasis on patriarchal gender roles for women and men allowed Catholics to play a central role in popularizing eugenic concepts that would later come to be more closely identified with social welfare programs proposed by the Frente Popular and in ultimately setting the stage for *la vía chilena*, allowing for an even fuller understanding of the rise of Chilean socialism in the 1960s.

An overwhelming uniformity of opinion regarding gender difference meant that the line between Catholic and secular eugenic theory and practice was not nearly as defined as members of each group claimed it was. What is most striking about the concerns that both groups shared is that they demonstrate how secularism and Catholicism were conceptually constructed by some historical actors to appear as diametrically opposing forces, rather than actually being so. The supposed opposition between Catholicism and science became an even more difficult position to maintain after 1950, when the Catholic Church as an institution in the papal encyclical *Humani generis* recognized that evolution was scientific fact.[12] Eugenic theories that suggested human beings could be organized into a racial hierarchy were not actually the issue for most Catholics. Rather, the supposed disagreements arose from debates regarding the *application* of eugenics—not its fundamental premises. In other words, according to most Catholic writers discussed here, eugenic practices were only suspect when Catholics were not included.

These moments of agreement, and their perceived impact on and connection to Chilean racial integrity, can be seen in a variety of different concerns repeatedly discussed in Chilean eugenic writing: alcoholism, birth control, and infertility. The synthesis of all these problems was identified in the so-called marriage crisis of the 1920s and 1930s. Eugenic writers seemed to agree about the problem, its scope, and its solution, but they did not agree on the role Catholics should play in the resolution of the marriage crisis or in the larger national debates regarding threats to the health of the Chilean race. Secular eugenic writers insisted that Catholics were more interested in retaining an antiquated system of charitable institutions, which dealt with problems only as they arose, instead of attempting to prevent racial degeneration before it began. Typically, this approach was characterized as a strategic choice on the part of the Catholic Church in order to keep the most desperate people dependent upon the minimal amounts of support the institution could offer. In response, Catholic eugenic writers countered that they were deeply committed to eugenic principles and were better fitted to apply modern eugenic practices than their secular colleagues, as they had previous experience in managing and monitoring family life as well as a moral compass to guide their work.

This power struggle inspired a prodigious number of articles in Catholic periodicals by writers who sought to legitimize their interest in eugenics by linking the science to the larger, concurrent debate regarding the relationship between religion and science. Although a few Catholic authors believed that religion and science had no relationship whatsoever, most contended that Catholicism and science were different ways of arriving at the same point. Most Catholic writers considered both science and religion, specifically Catholicism, to be concerned with revealing a divine plan. They argued that both Catholicism and science were about the revelation of the workings of a universal natural order that organized all life. Catholic writers often argued that the natural world and its laws were created by

God, but they still characterized science and religion as working in tandem. Some writers may have felt that religious truths outweighed scientific ones, but even so, Catholicism and science were characterized as mutually reinforcing. By extension, Catholic authors stressed that the involvement of Catholics in eugenics would only strengthen that scientific discipline.

A surprise from this research was the recognition that fitting eugenic and Catholic intellectual frameworks together was not as difficult as might be imagined. Standard eugenic practice was often considered to include procedures such as coerced sterilization, birth control, or abortion, but these methods were anathema to Catholic belief. This suggests that the response to eugenics would be one of Catholic disgust at both institutional and individual levels. This was not the case. Chilean Catholic eugenic discourse indicates that large parts of eugenic theory were treated as unproblematic; some proponents even suggested new types of interventions such as mothers' schools that could be used to protect the Chilean race while avoiding ethically dubious medical procedures that were popular elsewhere. Over the 1930s, this tactic was increasingly described in Chilean periodicals as a "Latin" style of eugenics, and it tended to be the more common means of explaining differences from eugenic movements outside Latin America rather than attributing those differences to religious influence. The emphasis on free will and the dignity of the individual as part of the collective good was so noticeable in Latin eugenic writing that eugenicists from outside that intellectual community commented on—and often derided—it as Leonard Darwin did. Within Chile, however, even secular writers were critical of overly zealous applications, or interpretations, of eugenic theory based exclusively on biological determinism.

The merging of Catholic and secular ideas regarding eugenic theory and practice was facilitated by two major factors: the belief in gender difference as being natural and immutable and the belief in the existence of a racially unique and homogeneous Chilean race. These shared beliefs regarding the Chilean race are apparent in the monograph *Raza chilena* by Nicolás Palacios. What is most striking about Palacios's work, ultimately, was not its claim regarding the origins of the Chilean race being built from the sexual encounters between a superior indigenous group and hardy Europeans; almost all Latin American nations have a similar racial origin story. *Raza chilena* was important because it used this origin myth to attest to Chilean racial homogeneity and superiority in the present. Packaged in this way, being Chilean meant being effectively White and therefore racially superior in comparison to other Latin Americans. This, in turn, allowed for the erasure of racial and ethnic minorities from the Chilean national imaginary.

An essential component to this racial myth was the strong emphasis on patriarchal social structure and gender difference as being essential for a modern and superior race. Chilean eugenic writers regularly discussed gender and the corresponding fears surrounding their belief that patriarchal social structures needed to be modernized. Both Catholic and secular authors reflected on male and female behavior in the modern age. Male promiscuity was seen as one of the most serious and, unfortunately, uncontrollable threats to the Chilean race. Men were considered by their very nature to be sexually indiscriminate, and it was thought that no amount of legislation or shame would truly change this. As a result, any female sexuality not connected to reproduction was labeled as both deviant and in need of eugenic intervention. Here, too, the differences were minimal between secular and Catholic eugenic writers. Most agreed that women's value to the race was strictly reproductive, and therefore their sexuality needed to be even more controlled than it might have been in traditional patriarchal societies. One of the ways in which eugenicists sought to control female sexuality was by creating eugenic education programs focused on reproduction.

Visual images also played an important role in supporting the claims to racial exceptionalism and Whiteness made by eugenic writers. One way the connection between White identity and Chileanness was made was by using images of women considered "normal" and "abnormal" by medical professionals. Normal women had various traits associated with European heritage; abnormal women were described as having a variety of non-White traits. If normal Chilean women were White, then this could further be extrapolated to apply to the national population as a whole. Medical abnormalities were just that—aberrations not indicative of widespread trends.

Unearthing the history of eugenics in Chile, and its connections to Catholicism, is not only important for better understanding racial thought and the persistence of racism. It also contextualizes late-twentieth-century responses to the Pinochet regime. For example, the Catholic reaction to Pinochet in the early 1970s was mixed: some individual Catholics staunchly supported him, but Catholic institutions relatively quickly began denouncing human rights violations carried out in his name. Parties such as the Partido Demócrata Cristiana (PDC; Christian Democratic Party) initially supported Pinochet because they perceived Allende as a communist threat, but eventually they came to be some of the most vociferous in their objections to Pinochet's authoritarianism.[13] This reaction grew out of the almost immediate realization that Pinochet's promise of a return to democratic rule was illusory. The Christian Democrats had objected to Allende's economic plan, not his overall message of revolution through social welfare. In fact, the PDC had actually been advocating for this type of social revolution since its inception in the late 1950s, in part because of its previous involvement in organizations connected to Acción Católica.[14] When the

Christian Democrat candidate Eduardo Frei Montalva was elected president in 1964, he made it clear that his political conservatism would not affect the social revolution he also planned.[15] Examining how Chilean Catholic texts approached eugenics—primarily as a scientific rationalization of charitable practices that would prevent racial degeneration—helps to explain these later events. The story told here is not a prologue that relates only tangentially to the 1973 coup, possibly the most important moment of twentieth-century Chilean history. Instead, this story demonstrates how concepts such as national progress or social revolutions in the second half of the twentieth century carried with them longer histories that depended upon shared ideas about what might be the most threatening or the most beneficial to Chile's future as a nation and as a people.

Carefully examining how eugenic discourse developed in Chile during the first decades of the twentieth century also shines light on the importance and popularity of race science in Latin America. On the one hand, the history of race in the region and its social, economic, cultural, and political ramifications has been studied extensively. Yet, study of the role played by science and medicine in the construction of racial and ethnic identities is still a relatively new field, in part because scholars of Latin America have often accepted the idea that race is mostly evidenced in sociocultural contexts. The study of race in Latin American science and medicine has increasingly shown that the notion that "race" is less influenced by biological or phenotypical factors there is a remarkably productive fantasy. So motivated have average Latin Americans been to demonstrate their lack of racial conflict and prejudice, they have often worked harder than people in any other region to erase and obscure the very real racial and ethnic divides operating within their societies. This is particularly true when it comes to the persistence of systemic racism and White supremacy.

Better highlighting these localized developments regarding racial identities and discrimination helps us move beyond characterizing Latin American science as merely a reconstitution of European or North American ideas and practices. The conceptual synthesis between Catholicism and eugenics—facilitated by ideas regarding gender difference and racial exceptionalism—shows a unique intellectual landscape in Chile that was both transnational and navel-gazing. Highlighting the complexity and vibrance of local intellectual communities like this is especially important in a Latin American context where the United States often looms large, particularly regarding the sciences. It is also helpful to further demystify the United States as hemispheric hegemon, as it is clear it was not the primary producer of foreign eugenic information arriving in Chile. In fact, for the first half of the twentieth century, France, Belgium, Germany, and the United Kingdom appear far more important influencers on Chilean scientific developments.

Finally, reifying gender difference in twentieth-century Latin America adds to the sizable amount of information on the modernization and rearticulation of patriarchy. Chilean eugenicists found fault with many aspects of their society, but a variety of so-called inappropriate gender behaviors were the most commonly discussed, perceived to be the most pervasive, and therefore the most threatening to racial health. These concerning behaviors included but were not limited to disinterest in marriage and children, female sexual promiscuity, and the abuse of alcohol. Although shoring up gender difference could have been achieved in many ways, Chilean eugenic writing focused almost exclusively on controlling female sexuality. This was not a new tactic, but the emphasis on female sexuality made women the guardians not only of their own modesty and bodily integrity but of the morality of men as well. They also became the primary contributors to racial health or degeneration.

This study of Chilean eugenics and racial thought prompts some further questions. There is a need for more careful study of the role played by the Catholic Church throughout the twentieth century in Chile, especially in relation to social modernization. More often than not, scholars portray the national church as an increasingly intransigent advocate for traditionalism and an obstacle to secularization in any national context. Indeed, the modernization of all societies is typically measured in the movement away from religious influence to secularism. It would be intriguing to see renewed historical interest in the precursors to liberation theology and their development leading up to the Cold War in Latin America. In a related vein, Chile is sometimes considered one of the more secular nations in Latin America, based on its relatively unblemished history of democracy. However, the lived experiences of many Chileans belie this reputation. Of the eighteen federal holidays recognized by the Chilean government, for example, half are religious. Divorce only became legal in 2004. Abortion remains illegal except in cases of rape, inviability of the fetus, or risk of death for the mother despite increasingly bitter public debates. This might be attributed to tradition, but this assumption overlooks a wealth of historical reasons as to why a supposedly secular post-dictatorial government struggles to dislodge Catholic ideals from its system of governance.

There is also a need for a more comprehensive reckoning with ideas related to racial hierarchy and White supremacy in Chile and Latin America. One of the most fascinating aspects of this research has been to see how the supposed racial homogeneity of the Chilean populace, along with the superiority of their progenitors, functioned as White supremacy does elsewhere. The fact that Latin Americans, regardless of their skin tone or accent, struggle to be seen as White when they leave the region and do not always react well to racialized categories such as "Latinx" or "Hispanic" demonstrates that there is much more to be examined when it comes to White racial identity in Latin America. This is especially true within the walls of the academy in White-majority countries such as the United States, where scholars themselves might have trouble accepting that "real" White people can be from Latin America at all.

Thinking through what it meant to Chileans to claim an indigenous heritage and an authentically White identity is especially pressing now for a number of reasons. Like many other White-majority countries in the past two decades, particularly after the global financial crisis of 2008, Chile has seen an uptick in anti-immigration rhetoric both in daily newspapers and from political leaders. The most vitriolic and disturbing has been directed at the small but significant Haitian community who began moving to the country in the wake of the 2010 earthquake, but migrants with African heritage from everywhere regularly discuss the racism they experience upon arrival in Chile. Indigenous Chileans such as the Mapuche remain a permanent underclass whose efforts to seek redress are routinely overlooked because their indigeneity is not seen as authentic enough or meaningfully different from any average Chilean. Despite recognition and even (to an extent) celebration of racial mixture, White supremacy remains a fundamental and under-recognized component of Chilean society. Catholic and secular eugenic literature of the early twentieth century played a critical role in this state of affairs.

Ultimately, better understanding the construction of racial thought and its relationship to eugenics in Latin America serves to demystify the notion of racial tolerance that pervades much of the contemporary Western world. Pragmatism regarding race mixing or the celebration of non-White ethnic groups as founders of a national culture do not preclude a belief in racial hierarchy and exceptionalism. In fact, examining the connections between Catholicism and eugenics in Chile shows how beliefs about racial difference and privilege can be maintained and institutionalized despite condemnations of the most extreme forms of discrimination and prejudice. In other words, early twentieth-century Chilean eugenic literature demonstrated one way to make racialization appear both rational and humane while simultaneously obscuring the existence of those who might say otherwise.

Notes

Introduction

Epigraph: Palacios, *Raza chilena* (1904), 21. All translations are my own unless otherwise noted.

1. A small sampling of the more recent scholarship includes Alberto and Elena, *Rethinking Race in Modern Argentina*; Cunin and Hoffman, *Blackness and Mestizaje*; de la Cadena, *Indigenous Mestizos*; Dueñas, *Indians and Mestizos in the "Lettered City"*; Eakin, *Becoming Brazilians*; Eiss and Rappaport, *Politics and Performance of Mestizaje*; Foote, *Military Struggle and Identity Formation*; Hooker, *Theorizing Race*; Lund, *Mestizo State*; Miller, *Rise and Fall of the Cosmic Race*; Rappaport, *Disappearing Mestizo*; Rosemblatt, *Science and Politics of Race*; Schwaller, *Géneros de gente*; Telles, *Pigmentocracies*; Vinson, *Before Mestizaje*; Weinstein, *The Color of Modernity*.

2. Kellogg, *Weaving the Past*; Vieira Powers, *Women in the Crucible*; von Germeten, *Violent Delights, Violent Ends*; Wade, *Race and Sex*.

3. For further discussion of *la raza chilena*, see Subercaseaux, "Raza y nación."

4. In histories of eugenics that are considered canonical, the focus is primarily on the United States and Europe, where these measures were more popular. Some examples of this canon include Blacker, *Eugenics*; Currell and Codgell, *Popular Eugenics*; Kevles, *In the Name of Eugenics*; Mazumdar, *Eugenics Movement*.

5. Resting beneath this contention is the corollary that eugenics was exclusively about protecting White racial purity, rather than a more generalized concept of racial improvement available to any race. Again, this is because of privileging eugenics as practiced and conceptualized in North America and Europe as mainstream and treating all other forms as alternative. This also demonstrates one of the fundamental differences between racial thought in the United States, where there is quite a lot of scholarship about eugenics, and that in Latin America. Hypodescent—or "the one-drop rule"—is the dominant way racial identity is ascribed in the United States. This means that any non-White heritage precludes an individual from legitimately accessing a White racial identity. An excellent starting place for

discussions regarding hypodescent in the United States is Jordan, "Historical Origins of the One-Drop Racial Rule."

6. Durst, *Eugenics and Protestant Social Reform*; Leon, *An Image of God*; Stern, *Eugenic Nation*.

7. Stepan, *Hour of Eugenics*. Biological determinism is the belief that an individual's behavior is not affected by one's environment but is entirely determined by their genetic heritage or physiology.

8. Lamarck, *Philosophie Zoologique*.

9. For a deeper discussion of positivism and Comte, see Pickering's three-volume work, *Auguste Comte*.

10. Sarmiento, *Facundo*.

11. Stepan, *Hour of Eugenics*, 11. Stern has noted that this approach "latinized" the study of eugenics. See Stern, "Hour of Eugenics," 432. The notion of a Latin race began to emerge in France in the 1830s, alongside the work of Comte, to identify Europeans who spoke Romance languages and preferred Catholicism. It was actually French writers who began to popularize the concepts of "Latin Europe" and "Latin America." For a longer discussion of the implications of these developments, see Gobat, "Invention of Latin America."

12. Stepan, *Hour of Eugenics*, 65. Levine and Novoa make a similar argument, stating that scientists in Argentina, "considered all of them to be strands in the larger 'civilized' lineage they sought to join. Consequently, they felt compelled to connect, and where possible reconcile all the diverse ideas coming from Europe, without any particular respect for their various pedigrees." Levine and Novoa, *¡Darwinistas!*, 29. This statement was made specifically in reference to the work of Ernst Haeckel, Jean-Baptiste Lamarck, and Charles Darwin.

13. Turda and Gillette, *Latin Eugenics*, 29.

14. Bowler, *Eclipse of Darwinism*.

15. Gayon, *Darwinism's Struggle for Survival*, 3.

16. Gayon, *Darwinism's Struggle for Survival*, 397. The meaning here is that Darwinism became a shorthand for biological determinism, which Gayon argued was inaccurate. Rather, Darwinism was an extreme form of the previous theory of species differentiation called Lamarckism.

17. Turda and Gillette, *Latin Eugenics*, 3.

18. Turda and Gillette, *Latin Eugenics*, 1–6.

19. Connelly, *Fatal Misconception*, 8. See also García González and Álvarez Peláez, "Eugenesia e imperialismo"; Palma, "Consideraciones historiográficas."

20. As an example, there are only a handful of texts related to the study of African American interest in eugenics: Chresfield, "To Improve the Race"; Dorr, *Segregation's Science*; Dorr and Logan, "Quality, Not Mere Quantity, Counts"; English, *Unnatural Selections*; Sherman, *In Search of Purity*.

21. Stepan, *Hour of Eugenics*, 111.

22. The entire encyclical is 130 paragraphs.

23. Pius XI, *Casti connubi*, December 31, 1930, https://w2.vatican.va/content/pius-xi/en/encyclicals/documents/hf_p-xi_enc_19301231_casti-connubii.html.

24. Negative eugenic practices were those that sought to limit supposedly unfit individuals from continuing to reproduce, often through the implementation of legislation that allowed them to be sterilized by the state without their knowledge or consent. In contrast, positive eugenic practices aimed to improve individuals through a variety of different types of biological and environmental intervention organized by a diverse array of state and private institutions with the ultimate goal of encouraging increased reproduction among those identified as fit.

25. Turda and Gillette, *Latin Eugenics*, 11.

26. Turda and Gillette define the Latin world as "a synthesis of ancient Roman civilization, linguistic and cultural commonality, and Roman Catholicism." Turda and Gillette, *Latin Eugenics*, 1.

27. Thompson, *Between Science and Religion*, 20.

28. Thompson, *Between Science and Religion*, 144.

29. Historians of science and religion have written about this subject since at least the nineteenth century. John William Draper's *History of the Conflict between Religion and Science* (1874) and Andrew Dickson White's *A History of the Warfare of Science with Theology in Christendom* (1896), in particular, have contributed to the notion among American scholars that Catholicism is hostile to the practice of science.

30. Cañizares-Esguerra, *Nature, Empire, and Nation*, 23. A number of historians of science have shown that Catholicism in particular has been treated as an obstacle to scientific progress in the nineteenth and twentieth centuries. See Bowler, *Reconciling Science and Religion*; Haught, "Darwinism and Catholicism," 485–92; Numbers, *Galileo Goes to Jail*; Schell, *Sociable Sciences*.

31. Stewart-Gambino, "Redefining the Changes," 23.

32. Serrano, *Universidad y nación*, 90. Many Catholic intellectuals spent both time and energy demonstrating that science and religion were separate realms that did not interfere with each other. As early as 1893, Pope Leo XIII in the encyclical *Providentissimus deus* recognized that science and religion could coexist for the mutual glory of God. See Hess, "Evolution, Suffering, and the God of Hope," 242.

33. Holt, "Foreword," xii.

34. In this approach I take inspiration from works such as Besse, *Restructuring Patriarchy*; Guy, *Sex and Danger in Buenos Aires*; Rosemblatt, *Gendered Compromises*; Rosemblatt, "Sexuality and Biopower"; Vaughan, "Modernizing Patriarchy."

35. Díaz Avilez, *To Be Indio in Colonial Spanish America*; Earle, *Body of the Conquistador*; Fisher, O'Hara, and Silverblatt, *Imperial Subjects*; Hering Torres, Martínez, and Nirenberg, *Race and Blood*; Jouve Martín, *Black Doctors of Colonial Lima*; O'Toole, *Bound Lives*; Patton, *Envisioning Others*; Restall, *Beyond Black and*

Red; Silverblatt, *Modern Inquisitions*; Vieira Powers, *Women in the Crucible*; Vinson, *Before Mestizaje*; Walker, *Exquisite Slaves*.

36. Block, *Colonial Complexions*; Brace, *Race Is a Four-Letter Word*; Hogarth, *Medicalizing Blackness*; Seth, *Difference and Disease*; Sussman, *Myth of Race*.

37. Doyle and Villela Pamplona, *Nationalism in the New World*; Ferrer, *Insurgent Cuba*; Johnson, *Workshop of Revolution*; Langley, *Americas in the Age of Revolution*; Lasso, *Myths of Harmony*.

38. Brazil stands out as the exception to this particular narrative, not only because there was no war for independence but also because the vision of race mixing there is mostly about European men and African-descended women.

39. Ferrer, *Insurgent Cuba*; Johnson, *Workshop of Revolution*; Lasso, *Myths of Harmony*.

40. The concept of the color line in reference to racial separation was first elaborated by Frederick Douglass in his article "The Color Line," written about race relations in the United States. The concept came into further prominence when W. E. B. DuBois used the phrase throughout his book *The Souls of Black Folk*, published in 1903. More recently, Marilyn Lake and Henry Reynolds used this notion to talk about race relations and Whiteness more broadly. See Douglass, "Color Line," 567; DuBois, *Souls of Black Folk*; Lake and Reynolds, *Drawing the Global Colour Line*.

41. An example of this changing approach appears in Eakin's *Becoming Brazilians*.

42. Vasconcelos, *La raza cósmica*; Freyre, *Casa-grande & senzala*.

43. Elkins, *Slavery*; Tannenbaum, *Slave and Citizen*; Tannenbaum, *Ten Keys to Latin America*.

44. Dávila, *Diploma of Whiteness*; Hanchard, *Orpheus and Power*; Nogueira Joyce, *Brazilian Telenovelas*; Skidmore, *Black into White*; Widdance Twine, *Racism and Racial Democracy*.

45. Appelbaum, Macpherson, and Rosemblatt, *Race and Nation*; Caulfield, *In Defense of Honor*; Miller, *Rise and Fall of the Cosmic Race*.

46. Fitzgerald, *Face of the Nation*; Frye Jacobson, *Whiteness of a Different Color*; Painter, *History of White People*; Spickard, *Almost All Aliens*.

47. Kline, *Building a Better Race*; Maxwell, *Picture Imperfect*; Weikart, *From Darwin to Hitler*.

48. For national histories, see García González, *Las trampas del poder*; Miranda and Vallejo, *Darwinismo social y eugenesia*; Orbegoso, "Eugenesia, tests mentales y degeneración racial." For a discussion of the "middle way," see Rosental, "Eugenics and Social Security."

49. Gibbon, Sans, and Ventura Santos, *Racial Identities*; Wade, *Degrees of Mixture, Degrees of Freedom;* Wade et al., *Mestizo Genomics*.

50. Telles, *Pigmentocracies*.

51. Scholarship on immigration and migrant communities in Latin America has been far more developed than scholarship on Whiteness. For some examples

of recent scholarship about race and migration, see FitzGerald and Cook-Martin, *Culling the Masses*; Foote and Goebel, *Immigration and National Identities*. The work on Whiteness, however, is just beginning. See Twinam, *Purchasing Whiteness*; Weinstein, *Color of Modernity*.

52. For more extensive discussion of this belief, see Walsh, "One of the Most Uniform Races."

53. Literally, the word "mestizo" means an individual who is racially mixed. In most of Latin America, though, it has come to apply exclusively to those with European and indigenous heritage. Mixtures between other racial and ethnic groups have a variety of other names, some quite pejorative.

54. Wade Chambers, "Locality and Science;" Glick, "Cultural Issues in the Reception of Relativity"; Glick, "Relativity in Spain"; Glick, "Science in Twentieth-Century Latin America"; Lopes and Podgorny, "Shaping of Latin American Museums"; Schell, *Sociable Sciences*.

55. Collier and Sater, *History of Chile*; San Francisco, *La Guerra civil de 1891*; Zeitlin, *Civil Wars in Chile*.

56. Collier and Sater, *History of Chile*, 147–48.

57. Castillo Infante, *La flecha roja*; Milos Hurtado, *Frente Popular en Chile*; Rosemblatt, *Gendered Compromises*; Silva and Henríquez, "El Frente Popular"; Silva Bascuñán, *Una experiencia social cristiana*.

58. Hutchison, *Labors Appropriate to Their Sex*, 22.

59. Elsey, *Citizens and Sportsmen*; French and James, *Gendered Worlds*; Klubock, *Contested Communities*.

60. Collier and Sater, *History of Chile*, 177.

61. Fuenzalida Guzmán, *El deber electoral de los católicos*; Fuenzalida Guzmán, *Qué es la Acción Católica?*

62. For a careful discussion of the difficulties that faced the Partido Conservador in the early twentieth century, see León, "Crisis del Partido Conservador en Chile (1945–1953)"; León, "La crisis del Partido Conservador en Chile." For history of the Falange Nacional and Chilean conservative parties in general, see Castillo Infante, *La flecha roja*; Castillo Velasco, *Las fuentes de la democracia cristiana*; Díaz Nieva, *Chile*.

63. Smith, *Church and Politics*.

64. The coup, its antecedents, and its aftermath lie outside the scope of this monograph. The coup was headed by military leader Carlos Ibañez del Campo in an effort to end an oligarchic system of governance known as the Parliamentary Republic. See Castedo and Lagos Escobar, *Chile*.

65. Celis Brunet, Cortínez Castro S.J., and Pimstein Scroggie, "Religion and Law," 214–17.

66. Regarding the Parliamentary Republic, see Álvarez Hernández, "La república parlamentaria de Chile."

67. Serrano, *¿Que hacer con Dios en la República?*

68. Schell, "Eugenics Policy and Practice"; Suárez y Lopez-Guazo, "Mexican Eugenics Society," 150; Turda and Gillette, *Latin Eugenics*, 29.

69. Glick, "Relativity in Spain," 248.

70. Silva, *In the Name of Reason*; Tinsman, *Partners in Conflict*; Vergara, *Copper Workers*.

71. Collier and Sater, *History of Chile*; Silva, *In the Name of Reason*; Fernandez Abara, *El Ibañismo*. Demonstrating the lasting legacy of Ibáñez's political conservatism, he is also credited with founding the Chilean police force, the Carabineros, who were particularly connected with the torture and abuses that occurred as part of Augusto Pinochet's regime between 1973 and 1990. See Bonner, *Policing Protest*.

72. Congar, *Catholic Church*, 24.

73. Congar, *Catholic Church*, 22–23.

74. Congar, *Catholic Church*, 22.

Chapter 1. "The Girl Is Not Pursued"

I would like to thank Warwick Anderson, Karin Alejandra Rosemblatt, and Patience A. Schell for giving feedback on earlier versions of this chapter, which is an expanded version of my article "Restoring the Chilean Race: Catholicism and Latin Eugenics Chile" that appeared in the *Catholic Historical Review* 105, no. 1 (Winter 2019): 116–38.

1. "Guerra al alcoholismo," 458.

2. The literature on temperance movements and efforts to prohibit the sale and consumption of alcohol is extensive. A small selection includes Andersen, *Politics of Prohibition*; McGirr, *War on Alcohol*; Moore, *Bootleggers and Borders*; Rorabaugh, *Prohibition*; Worth, *Teetotalers and Saloon Smashers*.

3. This was not a fear that was unique to Chilean eugenicists, though they may have felt the problem was especially pronounced in Chile. The idea that the fittest members of society were too committed to the use of birth control was a common trope throughout the international eugenic community. One of the most vehement in their commitment to the notion of "race suicide" was the White supremacist historian Lothrop Stoddard.

4. de Tezanos-Pinto S., "Valparaíso y sus medicos," 129.

5. Van Lennep, "Esterilidad del matrimonio," 340.

6. Van Lennep, "Esterilidad del matrimonio," 343.

7. Bliss, *Compromised Positions*; Drinot, *Sexual Question*; Guy, *Sex and Danger in Buenos Aires*; Spongberg, *Feminizing Venereal Disease*.

8. Van Lennep, "Esterilidad del matrimonio," 343.

9. Universidad de Valparaíso, Escuela de Obstetricia y Puericultura, "Historia."

10. Ankelen H., "La esterilidad femenina," 209.

11. Hanlon, "Christ under the Microscope," 96. Barbet became most famous for his authentication of the Shroud of Turin. See Zugibe, *Crucifixion of Jesus*.

12. Barbet, *La passion de N.-S. Jésus-Christ*. For discussions of the Latin scientific community see Walsh, "Restoring the Chilean Race."

13. Barbet, *Preparación del joven al matrimonio*, 28.

14. Barbet, *Preparación del joven al matrimonio*, 30. This argument matches that of Allende, *La realidad medico-social chilena*, 117, and that of Besse, *Restructuring Patriarchy*, 39.

15. Biblioteca del Congreso Nacional de Chile, "Ricardo Cox Méndez."

16. Memoria chilena, "Jaime Eyzaguirre."

17. Huneeus Cox, "Birth-Control o la limitación de la Natalidad," 28.

18. Huneeus Cox, "Birth-Control o la limitación de la Natalidad," 28, 30. For more discussion of Latin American counterarguments concerning the concept of overpopulation, see Buckley, "Overpopulation Debates in Latin America."

19. Huneeus Cox, "Birth-Control o la limitación de la Natalidad," 31–32.

20. Guitarte, "Esterilidad fisiologica," 362.

21. Guitarte, "Esterilidad fisiologica," 361.

22. Guitarte, "Esterilidad fisiologica," 364.

23. Dorsaz, Rendu, and de Guchteneere, *Le contrôle rationnel des naissances*.

24. E. M. S., "La Iglesia católica acepta el birth control," 246.

25. E. M. S., "La Iglesia católica acepta el birth control," 249.

26. Keymer F., "Uso de anticoncepcionales," 241.

27. Keymer F., "Uso de anticoncepcionales," 240.

28. Keymer F., "Uso de anticoncepcionales," 242–43.

29. Keymer F., "Uso de anticoncepcionales," 245.

30. Keymer F., "Uso de anticoncepcionales," 246. A similar point was made in another chapter in the same volume by Juan Wilson, a physician in Viña del Mar. He wrote: "All these authors note that the same results present themselves in women, but also that the spermatic liquid is absorbed by the vagina and when she engages in sex without ejaculation, profound disorders arise, principally in the nervous system." See Wilson, "De los hijos, fin primario del matrimonio," 235–36.

31. Thonet Ingles, "Sobre patologia del fraude sexual," 203.

32. Thonet Ingles, "Sobre patologia del fraude sexual," 205.

33. Miranda T., "Clinica ginecológica," 43–44. See also "Current Comment," 1564.

34. Miranda T., "Clinica ginecológica," 44.

35. Castaño, "El alcoholismo aristocrático," 46.

36. Castaño, "El alcoholismo aristocrático," 46.

37. Castaño, "El alcoholismo aristocrático," 47.

38. Castaño, "El alcoholismo aristocrático," 46, 49.

39. Cifuentes Grez, "El Proyecto de Represión del Alcoholismo," 4.

40. There were various different efforts to limit alcohol sales and consumption in Chile throughout the late nineteenth and early twentieth centuries. See Fernández Labbé, *Bebidas alcohólicas en Chile*.

41. Cifuentes Grez, "El Proyecto de Represión del Alcoholismo," 6.

42. Cifuentes Grez, "El Proyecto de Represión del Alcoholismo," 5.

43. Bennett Leay, *El alcoholismo y las enfermedades mentales*, 21.

44. Bennett Leay, *El alcoholismo y las enfermedades mentales*, 25. Bennett was not the only one to believe that alcoholism was intimately connected with mental illness or developmental delays. Another example of this was an article in the *Boletín del Ministerio de Higiene, Asistencia y Previsión Social* (National eugenics), in October 1927. See "Eugenesia nacional," 5–6.

45. Collier and Sater, *History of Chile*, 150.

46. Collier and Sater, *History of Chile*, 171.

47. Merlin, "Un problema social," 3.

48. Out of a total of 387 documents with authors who discussed idealized gender norms and behaviors in this period, the majority (251) were about women.

49. Green, "Doctoring the National Body."

50. Olavarrieta, *Higiene del matrimonio*.

51. Merlin, "Un problema social," 3.

52. "La crisis matrimonial," 5.

53. "La crisis matrimonial," 5.

54. "La crisis matrimonial," 5. At its most basic, the plot of *Eugénie Grandet* revolves around the notion that the heroine's marriage options are severely impacted by the financial desires of the men around her because their fortunes are newly gained and corrupting in their acquisition.

55. "La crisis matrimonial," 5.

56. Htun, *Sexo y estado*; Lavrin, *Women, Feminism and Social Change*. The road to the legalization of divorce in Chile would be exceptionally long. It was not finally permitted until 2004. Ironically, the inability to get a divorce led many Chileans to determine that neither civil nor religious ceremonies were desirable, which only added to the concerns about the state of marriage in the country. Confirming the fears of eugenicists, marriage rates remained low throughout most of the twentieth century. Those who did choose to marry might also determine to separate later and treat that separation as akin to an official divorce.

57. Besa de Díaz, "Ideas que vivifican, ideas que matan," 7.

58. Lavrin, *Sexuality and Marriage*; Logan, "Each Sheep with Its Mate"; Poska, *Regulating the People*; Robins, *Of Love and Loathing*; Twinam, *Public Lives, Private Secrets*.

59. *La Revista Católica* is a widely circulated Catholic periodical founded in Santiago in 1843 and still published today.

60. Errázuriz et al., "Circular Colectiva del Episcopado Chileno," 5.

61. Errázuriz et al, "Circular Colectiva del Episcopado Chileno," 7.

62. Errázuriz et al, "Circular Colectiva del Episcopado Chileno," 9.

63. Heise Gonzalez, *Historia de Chile*, 243.

64. Fuenzalida Guzmán, "Deberes de los católicos," 692.

65. This change of heart may also be attributed to the fact that Errázuriz was considered an apologist by more conservative clergy members, of which Fuenzalida was one. For a longer discussion of the internal debates regarding how politically active Chilean clergy members should be, see Andes, *Vatican and Catholic Activism.*

66. Fuenzalida Guzmán, "Deberes de los católicos," 692.

67. Gorostarzu, "El problema social del matrimonio," 618.

68. Gorostarzu, "El problema social del matrimonio," 619.

69. Gorostarzu, "El problema social del matrimonio," 621.

70. De la Luz, *La mujer y la especie,* 20.

71. Mayers, "La educacion higiénica de la nacion," 199.

72. Aedo-Richmond, *La educación privada;* Barr-Melej, *Reforming Chile;* Collier and Sater, *History of Chile,* 180.

73. Mayers, "Educacion higiénica," 202 (original emphasis). All italics within quotations are from the original unless otherwise noted.

74. Cordemans, "De la caridad al servicio social," 7.

75. Illanes, *Cuerpo y sangre,* 281, 273–75.

76. Illanes, *Cuerpo y sangre,* 282.

77. Cordemans, "De la caridad al servicio social," 7.

78. Throughout his life Cox remained committed to advocating for the church. See Andes, *Vatican and Catholic Activism,* 122–23.

79. Cox Méndez, "Orientaciones contemporáneas del catolicismo," 5.

80. De Santa Teresa, "El católico de hoy," 836.

81. Aspe Armella, *La formación social y política;* Schell, "Honorable Vocation for Ladies"; Verba, *Catholic Feminism.*

82. Rucker S., "Orientaciones de acción social," 95.

83. Walsh, *Catholic Churchmen in Science.*

84. Jörinssen, "El concepto de caridad," 322. Her name is spelled Jörrisen in the article.

85. Illanes Oliva, *"En el nombre del pueblo,"* 289.

86. Schelkens, Dick, and Mettepenningen, *Aggiornamento?;* Jodock, *Catholicism Contending with Modernity;* Kelly, "Catholicisme ondoyant"; O'Leary, *Roman Catholicism and Modern Science.*

Chapter 2. The Two Truths

1. Andes, *Vatican and Catholic Activism,* 122–23.

2. Leo XIII, *Rerum novarum,* §6.

3. There are numerous monographs and articles dedicated to debunking the conflict thesis as originally conceptualized in the works of John William Draper and Andrew Dickson White. A small sample of these include Attridge and Numbers, *Religion and Science Debate;* Brooke, Osler, and van der Meer, "Science in Theistic Contexts"; Dawes, *Galileo;* Hess and Allen, *Catholicism and Science;* Ivey, *Radiance from Halcyon;* Jones, *For the Glory of God.*

4. Andes, *Vatican and Catholic Activism*; Collier, "Religious Freedom"; Curley, "Transnational Subaltern Voices"; Serrano, *¿Que hacer con Dios en la república?*; Turner, "Science and Religious Freedom"; Vaggione and Morán Faúndes, *Laicidad and Religious Diversity.*

5. Buchenau, *Plutarco Elías Calles*; McNamara, *Sons of the Sierra*; Vaamonde, *Oscuridad y confusión.*

6. Butler, *Popular Piety and Political Identity.*

7. Gazmuri, *El '48' chileno.* For the growth of secularism in Chile, see also Serrano, *¿Qué hacer con Dios en la república?*

8. Draper quoted from Numbers, *Galileo Goes to Jail*, 1. Numbers also speculates that Draper's anti-Catholic sentiment was especially strong because he had a personal dislike for his sister, who had converted to Catholicism (2–3).

9. Numbers, *Galileo Goes to Jail*, 1. The generations of scholars immediately following White and Draper were especially vitriolic in their estimation of religion and religious thinking and their opinions filtered into both common and academic thought with pervasive strength in the North Atlantic. See also Bowler and Rhys Morus, *Making Modern Science*; Gilbert, *Redeeming Culture*; Olson, "Series Forward," xiv.

10. Draper's work was published in Spanish in 1876 and White's in 1910. Draper, *Historia de los conflictos*; White, *Historia de la lucha entre la ciencia y la teología.* See also Alonso, "Ciencia y religion," 93–95.

11. Barabino and Besio Moreno, *Congreso Científico Internacional Americano*, 194.

12. Biblioteca del Congreso Nacional de Chile, "Paulino Alfonso del Barrio."

13. Eagleton, *Materialism*; Schofield, *Mechanism and Materialism*; Vitzthum, *Materialism.*

14. As rector, Vergara was head of the entire university from 1898 to 1914. In this position, he made decisions regarding faculty and curriculum. Thus, he represented an upper level not only of the Chilean clergy but also of the educational community. Pontificia Universidad Católica de Chile, "Monsignor Rodolfo Vergara Antúnez." See also Subercaseaux, *Historia de las ideas y de la cultura en Chile*, 162.

15. Regardless of its religious affiliation, the Universidad Católica was (and is) one of the two most prestigious universities in Chile. The other is the Universidad de Chile. Both still rank as some of the top universities in Latin America. See Serrano, *Universidad y nación.*

16. Vergara Antúnez, "El materialismo y la origen de las cosas," 639.

17. Vergara Antúnez, "El materialismo y la origen de las cosas," 639, 633.

18. When Vergara wrote this article, the predominant theory among astronomers and physicists was that the universe essentially had no beginning. This was referred to as the "steady-state model." So his critique is a bit misplaced, as most scientists did not necessarily think that there was a creation moment for the uni-

verse (though some may have). Even more intriguing, the Big Bang theory was originally met with skepticism when it was first proposed in the late 1920s because it suggested the possibility of divine creation. This was all the more problematic because the originator of the theory, Georges Lemaître, was a Roman Catholic priest. Definitive proof that the universe did emerge from a big bang came in 1964 when American astronomers Arno Penzias and Robert Wilson discovered cosmic microwave background radiation (CMB). For discussions of these various developments, see Holder and Mitton, *Georges Lemaître*; Kragh, *Cosmology and Controversy*; Kragh and Longair, *Oxford Handbook of Modern Cosmology*.

19. Vergara Antúnez, "El materialismo," 634.

20. Vergara Antúnez, "El materialismo," 635.

21. Debré, *Louis Pasteur*; Strick and Lederberg, *Sparks of Life*.

22. "Henry Charlton Bastian, M.A., M.d.lond., F.R.C.P., F.R.S."

23. Strick, "Darwinism and the Origin of Life."

24. Farley, *Spontaneous Generation Controversy*; Harris, *Things Come to Life*; Strick and Lederberg, *Sparks of Life*.

25. DeYoung, *Vision of Modern Science*.

26. "De nuevo la generación espontánea," 635.

27. "De nuevo la generación espontánea," 634–35.

28. Depassier, *La muerte del materialismo*, vi.

29. Depassier, *La muerte del materialismo*, vi.

30. Depassier, *La muerte del materialismo*, 4.

31. Campos Menendez, *Biblioteca nacional*, 63–65.

32. Vicuña, *Armonía de la ciencia y la fé*, 63. This is an opinion shared by Giovanni Noé as well: "It was an error of the liberal thinkers of the last century to believe that school could substitute for religion in the moralizing task of the masses." Noé, *La ciencia i los sentimientos humanitarios*, 25.

33. Vicuña, *Armonía de la ciencia y la fé*, 63.

34. Universidad de Chile, "Carlos Charlín Correa"; Sociedad Chilena de Oftamologia, "Historia"; Verdaguer Tarradella, "Reseña histórica del Departamento de Oftamologia."

35. Charlín, "Las dos verdades," 4.

36. Charlín, "Las dos verdades," 4.

37. Charlín, "Las dos verdades," 13.

38. Glick, Puig-Samper, and Ruiz, *Reception of Darwinism*; Miranda and Vallejo, *Darwinismo social y eugenesia*; Novoa and Levine, *From Man to Ape*; Palma, *Darwin y el darwinismo*; Ruiz Gutiérrez et al., *Darwin en (y desde) México*.

39. Gilson and Levinson, *Latin American Positivism*; Priego Martínez, *Positivism, Science, and "The Scientists."*

40. Pinto Duran, "Bernardino Quijada Burr," *Diccionario personal de Chile*, 210.

41. Muñoz Sougarret and Ther Ríos, "El pescador en el imaginario científico"; Tamayo Hurtado and González García, "La enseñanza de la evolución en Chile."

42. Tamayo Hurtado and González García, "La enseñanza de la evolución en Chile," 316.

43. Quijada B., *La teoría de la evolucion*, 9.

44. This position has come to be known as "day-age creationism," and its origin is often traced back to Saint Augustine of Hippo's *De genesi ad litteram* (*On the Literal Interpretation of Genesis*) written in the fifth century. In the modern era, one of its most visible early proponents was the Scottish geologist Charles Lyell who, in *Principles of Geology* (1830–1833), contended that geological change occurred over long periods of time. This interpretation is probably most associated with the American lawyer William Jennings Bryan. See Lyell, *Principles of Geology*; Numbers, *Creationists*; Saint Augustine, *On the Literal Interpretation of Genesis*.

45. Quijada B., *La teoría de la evolucion*, 10.

46. It should be noted that Darwinian evolution was not immediately popular in any scientific community, secular or religious, even in Darwin's home country of England. Especially at the turn of the twentieth century, scientists across the globe began to question natural selection and evolution. Bowler's work covers quite a lot of this ground for the Anglosphere. Glick, Novoa, Levine, Turda, and Gillette all discuss the reception of Darwinism across the Latin world. Official Catholic recognition of evolution was articulated in the 1950 papal encyclical *Humani generis* by Pope Pius XII.

47. Caro R., "Conferencia sobre el origen del hombre," 6.

48. The Hierarchy of the Catholic Church, "José María Caro Rodríguez."

49. Caro R., "Conferencia sobre el origen del hombre," 7.

50. Caro R., "Conferencia sobre el origen del hombre," 12. For a more thorough discussion of Latin American responses to coerced sterilization, see Walsh, "The Executioner's Shadow."

51. For an analysis of free will and marriage partners, see Seed, *To Love, Honor, and Obey*; Twinam, *Public Lives, Private Citizens*. For general discussions of how Catholicism conceptualized human agency in relationship to God's plan, see Chowning, *Rebellious Nuns*; Maritain, *Rights of Man and Natural Law*; Voekel, *Alone before God*.

52. Vergara, "El materialismo," 633.

53. Debré, *Louis Pasteur*.

54. "Estatua de Pasteur," *El Diario Popular*, 2.

55. "Estatua de Pasteur," *El Diario Popular*, 2.

56. In this same period in the United States, according to Larson, there was a similar debate about whether science was a realm of experts or something all intelligent people should be able to understand. In fact, general intelligibility across all disciplines was originally a central tenet of the scientific method popularized by thinkers such as René Descartes and Francis Bacon in the seventeenth century. Larson argues that the growing belief that science belonged to experts was part of the reason why, though William Jennings Bryan won the Scopes trial, evolution in-

creasingly became an accepted fact among average Americans in the mid-twentieth century. See Larson, *Summer for the Gods.*

57. Pasteur's interest in disproving the theory of spontaneous generation was motivated by his religious beliefs, but it has typically been discussed in terms of his work with fermentation. See Debré, *Louis Pasteur;* Geison, *Private Science of Louis Pasteur.*

58. A.F.L. "Crónica científica," 448.

59. Objections to monogenism for humans were fundamentally racist. Scientists in a variety of disciplines were committed to the idea that the different races of human beings indicated their different evolutionary trajectories and therefore proved the theory of polygenesis. For extended discussion of these theories, especially how they relate to race science between 1850 and 1950, see Brown, *Until Darwin;* Gould, *Mismeasure of Man.*

60. Barahona, "Los Católicos," 38.

61. The work of Gregor Mendel played an important role in the development of modern genetics, which has been discussed at length by a variety of scholars. Selected works include Bowler, *Mendelian Revolution;* Edelson, *Gregor Mendel;* Marantz Henig, *Monk in the Garden.*

Chapter 3. What Is Eugenics in Chile?

1. Astorquizo Sazzo, "Eugenesia," 416, 415.

2. Hernández and Ramos, *Homicultura;* González Quijano and Suárez Díaz, "Semblanza del General."

3. García González and Álvarez Peláez, *En busca de la raza perfecta,* 130; Rodriguez, "Dangers that Surround the Child."

4. Hernández and Ramos, *Homicultura,* front matter.

5. Hernández and Ramos, *Homicultura,* 95–203.

6. Hernández and Ramos, *Homicultura,* front matter.

7. Whetham and Whetham, *Introduction.* It appears this book was never translated into Spanish, so its readers would have had to be able to read English, which made it less accessible to average Chileans though probably not to most academics and physicians.

8. Taylor and Havelock, "William Cecil Dampier," 55.

9. Whetham, *Upbringing of Daughters;* Taylor and Havelock, "William Cecil Dampier," 56.

10. Taylor and Havelock, "William Cecil Dampier," 61.

11. Taylor and Havelock, "William Cecil Dampier," 61.

12. Whetham and Whetham, *Introduction,* 1. Francis Galton (1822–1911) was a polymath who specialized in statistics, anthropology, and sociology, among a number of other disciplines. He was also Charles Darwin's half cousin and was one of the earliest adopters of evolutionary theory. Galton was inspired by Darwin's *Origin of the Species,* particularly the chapter "Variation under Domestication" which

discussed animal breeding in great detail. The notion of developing new traits in a domesticated species through controlled breeding led him to start thinking about how that might be applied to human beings. It was Galton who coined the term "eugenics" in 1883 to describe the cultivation of good genes in humans. He served as Honorary President of the British Eugenics Society from 1907 to 1911. For biographical information see Bulmer, *Francis Galton*.

13. Whetham and Whetham, *Introduction*, 1.

14. Whetham and Whetham, *Introduction*, 1. Italics added.

15. Whetham and Whetham, *Introduction*, 61.

16. Hallanger, "Eugenics and the Question of Religion," 307.

17. Stoddard, *La amenaza del sub-hombre*; Stoddard, *Revolt against Civilization*.

18. Yudell, *Race Unmasked*.

19. Losurdo, "Towards a Critique," 48.

20. The translation was published by Editorial Nascimento, one of the most influential publishing houses in Chile during the twentieth century. It began as a bookshop in the 1870s. Carlos George-Nascimento inherited the business in 1917 and added a publishing house that then remained in business until the mid-1980s. Among its most important contributions to Chilean literature were the first editions of Gabriela Mistral's *Desolación* and Pablo Neruda's *Crepusculario* in 1923 (the same year as *La amenaza del sub-hombre*). It is unclear if Editorial Nascimento asked Sierra to translate Stoddard's work or if Sierra was already doing so of his own volition. Either way, Sierra agreed, which suggests he believed it would be marketable to a Chilean audience. For the history of Editorial Nascimento, see Memoria Chilena, "Editorial y librería Nascimento."

21. Museo Nacional de Medicina, "Lucas Sierra."

22. Museo Nacional de Medicina, "Lucas Sierra."

23. Stoddard, *La amenaza del sub-hombre*, 15–16.

24. Walsh, "Executioner's Shadow."

25. Stoddard, *La amenaza del sub-hombre*, 27. In the original English version: "Indeed, down to our own days, when the *new biological revelation* (for it is nothing short of that) has taught us the supreme importance of heredity, mankind tended to believe that environment rather than heredity was the main factor in human existence." See Stoddard, *Revolt against Civilization*, 34.

26. Sierra, *Bases de la higiene moderna*, 14.

27. There is quite a difference between *La amenaza del sub-hombre* and *The Revolt against Civilization*, primarily in length. It appears that Sierra decided to significantly shorten the book and to distill its main points. His active involvement as a translator for a Chilean audience certainly seems to have softened some of Stoddard's more objectionable ideas, but he did not misrepresent Stoddard's commitment to both racism and biological determinism.

28. Sierra, "Dos palabras," 11.

29. Stoddard, *La amenaza del sub-hombre*, 30. The English version reads: "the

same influences which profoundly affect lower forms have relatively little effect upon the higher animals and still less upon man himself. Man is, therefore, least affected by, and most independent of, environmental influences." See Stoddard, *Revolt against Civilization*, 46–47.

30. Stoddard, *La amenaza del sub-hombre*, 129. This passage in the Spanish version is different from the original English, which reads: "Hitherto all political and social philosophies, however much they might differ among themselves, have been agreed on certain principles: they have all believed that environment was of basic importance, and they have all proposed to improve mankind *from without*, by changing *existing individuals* through the action of various political and social agencies. Eugenics, on the other hand, believes that *heredity* is the basic factor, and plans to improve the race *from within*, by determining *which* existing individuals shall, and shall not, produce succeeding generations." The difference may in fact be the result of Sierra's trying to soften some of Stoddard's preference for biological determinism. In fact, the English version goes on: "This means the establishment of an *improved* social selection based upon *biological* considerations, instead of, as hitherto, upon environmental considerations." The Spanish version simply ends at the previous sentence. Regardless of version, Stoddard still had to rely on social selection (an environmental element) but hoped that it would be done according to biological considerations. See Stoddard, *Revolt against Civilization*, 239.

31. Darwin, *¿Qué es la eugenesia?*

32. Edwards, "Darwin, Leonard."

33. Pittard, "Introduction," 13.

34. One of the conundrums of the eugenics movement in Latin America was its obvious popularity—as indicated in the striking amount of press coverage and medical debates—existing alongside a relative lack of government support, particularly in contrast to the financial and administrative support received by eugenic programs in places such as the United States. This is the result of a number of different factors, one of the most concrete being significantly fewer financial resources available to most Latin American governments in this period. Of course, the entirety of this book is dedicated to better showing how other measures (such as prenuptial certificates and social worker home visits) could be considered part of the practical application of eugenics in Chile, which demonstrates a more robust administrative support than eugenic legislation alone might suggest. For discussions of how eugenic public health programs affected the lived experiences of Chileans, see Araya et al., *República de la salud*; Illanes, *Cuerpo y sangre*; Leyton, Palacios, and Sánchez, *Bulevar de los pobres*; Molina Bustos, *Institucionalidad sanitaria*; Zárate C., *Por la salud del cuerpo*. The expansion of the welfare state in the early twentieth century was also an important factor in furthering the reach of eugenics into Chileans' lives. See Fernández Darraz, *Estado y sociedad*; Illanes Oliva, *"En el nombre del pueblo"*; Naudon Figueroa, *La cuestión social*; Rosemblatt, *Gendered Compromises*; Yáñez Andrade, *Estado, consenso y crisis social*. Regional conferences dedicated to

eugenics, public health, and medical conferences beginning in the 1890s also speak to the popularity of the discipline and its links to racial thought in Chile and Latin America. See Reggiani, *Historia mínima*.

35. This was not an entirely fair belief on the part of Darwin. There were attempts to create coerced sterilization programs, to pass eugenic legislation, and to enact surveillance of Latin Americans' private lives. However, these attempts typically failed. Even when efforts were successful, such as when the state of Veracruz in Mexico passed sterilization legislation in 1932, laws of this sort often went unenforced. See Stern, "Hour of Eugenics."

36. The lack of proof led to what Julian Huxley referred to as the "eclipse of Darwinism" when biologists began to consider other possibilities to explain the evolution of different traits in the years before the modern synthesis in which Mendel's and Darwin's theories were finally reconciled. See Bowler, *Eclipse of Darwinism*; Huxley, *Evolution*.

37. Darwin, *¿Qué es la eugenesia?*, 37.

38. Darwin, *¿Qué es la eugenesia?*, 42.

39. Darwin, *¿Qué es la eugenesia?*, 80.

40. Darwin, *¿Qué es la eugenesia?*, 117–18.

41. Darwin, *¿Qué es la eugenesia?*, 161.

42. Hernández Alfonso, *Eugenesia y derecho a vivir*.

43. Sinclair, *Sex and Society*, 221.

44. Hernández Alfonso, *Eugenesia y derecho a vivir*, 16.

45. Hernández Alfonso, *Eugenesia y derecho a vivir*, 53–54.

46. Hernández Alfonso, *Eugenesia y derecho a vivir*, 67.

47. "Puericultura e hijiene antenatal," 283.

48. "Puericultura e hijiene antenatal," 283. The phrase "the right man in the right place" was originally written in English.

49. "Puericultura e hijiene antenatal," 287.

50. "Puericultura e hijiene antenatal," 288.

51. There were many religious leaders in the United States that supported eugenics, and eugenicists often attempted to work with them, assuming that this would only further their cause, but Catholic religious leaders were rarely included in these efforts. For more on this, see Rosen, *Preaching Eugenics*.

52. Millas Parada, *Eugenesia y derecho*, 11–12. Sparta as an example of long-standing eugenic practices was also mentioned in Middleton C., "Objetivacion del ideal de la salud," 813.

53. Millas Parada, *Eugenesia y derecho*, 13. This approach was quite unusual among Chilean eugenicists. Millas explicitly combined the theories of Darwinian and Lamarckian evolution whereas most Chilean eugenicists favored one or the other.

54. Millas Parada, *Eugenesia y derecho*, 16.

55. Millas Parada, *Eugenesia y derecho*, 42–43.

56. Millas Parada, *Eugenesia y derecho*, 17.

57. Some examples of the general feeling that positive eugenics were ethically sound from the period are Fisher, "Positive Eugenics" and J.L.C., "La eugenesia moderna."

58. Millas Parada, *Eugenesia y derecho*, 19.

59. For an overview of the history of utilitarianism, see Scarre, *Utilitarianism*.

60. Millas Parada, *Eugenesia y derecho*, 55.

61. Millas Parada, *Eugenesia y derecho*, 69. In November 1939, Allende also proposed legislation requiring a prenuptial certificate of health. This was designed to decrease the spread of venereal disease. See Stepan, *Hour of Eugenics*. León also discussed the potential use and value of this type of certificate in *La eugenesia*, 109.

62. Millas Parada, *Eugenesia y derecho*, 64.

63. León Palma, *La eugenesia*, 13.

64. For biographical information about Weismann, see Churchill, *August Weismann*.

65. León Palma, *La eugenesia*, 25.

66. León Palma, *La eugenesia*, 25.

67. León Palma, *La eugenesia*, 71.

68. León Palma, *La eugenesia*, 45.

69. For discussion of Betzhold's growing disillusionment with the concept of the Chilean superman, see Sánchez-Delgado and Cárcamo-Gebhardt, "Hans Betzhold." For further discussion of Betzhold's biography, see Cid, "Médicos, abogados y eugenesia negativa"; Farías, *Salvador Allende*.

70. Betzhold H., *Eugenesia*, 17–18.

71. Restat C., "El evolucionismo," 25.

72. Sánchez Gaete, *Historia de la Iglesia*, 215. Acción Católica was a loosely connected international collection of groups aimed at social reform that emerged in the late nineteenth and early twentieth centuries. For discussions of the development of Catholic Action movements in Latin America, see Bidegaín, *From Catholic Action to Liberation Theology*; Stewart-Gambino, *Church and Politics*, 4.

73. Restat C., "El evolucionismo," 26.

74. Restat C., "El evolucionismo," 29.

75. Restat C., "El evolucionismo," 29. Restat was building on a long tradition of using the eye (human and animal) as proof that evolution was not possible. One of the earliest appearances of this counterargument to evolution was in William Paley's *Natural Theology or Evidences of the Existence and Attributes of the Deity* (1802). Using the eye and other complex biological structures as proof of intelligent design had become so common in the first half of the nineteenth century that Darwin himself discussed the evolution of the eye through natural selection in the sixth chapter of *The Origin of Species* (1859). See Darwin, *Origin*, 186; Paley, *Natural Theology*, 18–42.

76. Restat C., "El evolucionismo," 31.

77. Restat C., "El evolucionismo," 32.

78. Restat C., "El evolucionismo," 35.

79. Restat C., "Estudios filosóficos" (August 2, 1924), 163.

80. Restat C., "Estudios filosóficos" (August 16, 1924), 257.

81. Duarte G., "El Doctor Roberto Barahona S.," 7.

82. Barahona Silva, "Los católicos," 36–37.

83. Vargas C., "170 años."

84. Barahona Silva, "Los católicos," 37.

85. Turda and Gillette, *Latin Eugenics*; Walsh, "Executioner's Shadow."

86. As soon as the Nazi Party took power in 1933, its leaders began implementing legislation that discriminated against German Jews and other ethnic minorities. Though the earliest laws did not protect Aryan racial purity in the strictly biological sense, they were about protecting the supposedly superior race from contamination. An example of this type of protection against Jewish influence was the Law for the Restoration of the Professional Civil Service passed on April 7, 1933, which prohibited German Jews from holding government jobs. The Nuremberg Laws, passed between 1935 and 1938, were more explicitly about protecting the presumed biological purity of the Aryan race. The Law for the Protection of German Blood and Honor criminalized sexual relationships and marriage between Aryans and Jews. See Ehrenrich, *Nazi Ancestral Proof.* Chileans were aware of the passage of this legislation in Germany. For example, in 1936, Ernesto Hechenleitner Trautmann submitted a thesis titled "Herencia morbosa y su correctivo eugenésico: 'la esterilización'" (Morbid inheritance and its eugenic corrective: 'Sterilization') to obtain his degree in law and political science from the Universidad de Chile. The general thrust of his thesis was to support the 1933 Law for the Prevention of Genetically Diseased Offspring, also known as the "Sterilization Law," which mandated the compulsory sterilization of any citizen deemed genetically unfit. See Hechenleitner Trautmann, *Herencia morbosa.*

87. Leon writes about American Catholics' rejection of eugenics and argues that their opinions began to carry more weight as awareness of Nazi atrocities grew. See Leon, *Image of God*; Turda and Gillette, *Latin Eugenics*.

88. Barahona, "Los católicos," 40.

89. Barahona, "Los católicos," 45.

90. Walsh, "Executioner's Shadow."

91. Grossi Aninat, *Eugenesia y su legislación*, 12.

92. Grossi Aninat, *Eugenesia y su legislación*, 23.

Chapter 4. "One of the Most Uniform Races of the Entire World"

I would like to thank Karin Rosemblatt, Warwick Anderson, and Hans Pols for feedback on an earlier version of this chapter, which appears in the *Journal of the History of Biology*.

1. Palacios, *Raza chilena* (1918), 34.

2. I refer here to Vasconcelos's *La raza cósmica* (*The Cosmic Race*), published in 1925, and Freyre's *Casa-grande & senzala* (*The Masters and the Slaves*) published in 1933. There are many more nationalist works regarding race mixing and the creation of specific national racial types, but these two are by far the most commonly discussed. Scholarly work on Vasconcelos's and Freyre's racial ideologies and nationalisms is vast; some representative examples include Andrade, *Outros perfis de Gilberto Freyre*; Burke and Pallares-Burke, *Gilberto Freyre*; Ocampo López, "José Vasconcelos y la educación mexicana"; Poole, "Image of 'Our Indian'"; Salvador Lara, *La lengua de la raza cósmica*; Stavans, *José Vasconcelos*; Tuna, *Gilberto Freyre*.

3. For Palacios, see Alvarado and Fernandez, "Una narración fundacional"; Alvarado Borgoño, "La modernidad maldita de Nicolás Palacios"; Calderón, "Un apostolado social"; Coletta, "Role of Degeneration Theory"; Gazmuri R., "Decadencia del espíritu"; Godoy P. and Galarce M., *Día de sangre*; Peralta Pizarro, *Idea de Chile*; Subercaseaux, "Raza y nación." Only three of these articles, and my own in the *Journal of the History of Biology*, attempt a full-scale analysis of Palacios's work and its impact.

4. Miranda and Vallejo, *Darwinismo*; Novoa and Levine, *From Man to Ape*; Stepan, *Hour of Eugenics*; Turda and Gillette, *Latin Eugenics*.

5. Céspedes and Garreaud, "Palacios Navarro, Nicolás"; Corti Cortés and Maltés Cortés, "Palacios Navarro, Nicolás"; Figueroa, "Palacios."

6. S. Palacios, "Nicolás Palacios: Recuerdos intimos," 12. Lastarria's *Don Guillermo* is often recognized as the first Chilean novel with socialist themes that also incorporated indigenous mythology.

7. S. Palacios, "Nicolás Palacios: Recuerdos intimos," 12.

8. Levine and Novoa, *Darwinistas*, 28.

9. Stepan discusses a similar trajectory of intellectual development for the Brazilian literary historian Sílvio Romero. See Stepan, *Picturing Tropical Nature*, 140.

10. S. Palacios, "Nicolás Palacios: Recuerdos intimos," 13.

11. Esposito, Rava, and Windrow, *Armies of the War*; Mellafe Maturana and Pelayo González, *La guerra del Pacífico*.

12. Alvarado and Fernández, "Una narración," 49; Godoy P. and Galarce M., *Día de sangre*.

13. Calderón, "Un apostolado social"; Céspedes and Garreaud, "Palacios Navarro, Nicolás"; Corti Cortés and Maltés Cortés, "Palacios Navarro, Nicolás"; Figueroa, "Palacios."

14. Palacios, *Raza chilena* (1918), 34.

15. Palacios, *Raza chilena* (1918), 31. Palacios was not alone in his suspicion of foreign immigration schemes. For more on anti-immigration sentiment in early twentieth-century Chile, see Walsh, "The Chilean Exception."

16. Collier and Sater, *History of Chile*, 95; Salazar and Pinto, *Historia contemporánea*, 78–81. These programs overlooked the fact that a significant portion of

the supposedly vacant zones were inhabited by indigenous peoples. See Frazier, *Salt in the Sand*. In some cases, these programs were designed to push indigenous groups even further away from their communal lands. In this respect, both Palacios and the Chilean government were in agreement: indigenous Chileans were to play no role in the modern Chilean nation.

17. The belief that southern Europeans were the most racially dubious racial type within Europe was widespread among eugenicists in the United States, United Kingdom, and northern Europe. Historical literature about eugenics in those places is vast. One of the most concise discussions of this antipathy for Latin races is in Ngai, *Impossible Subjects*. In the Latin American context, despite the supposed racial similarities, southern Europeans were also unwelcome migrants. See FitzGerald and Cook-Martín, *Culling the Masses*; Zarini, "La utopía eugenista."

18. Calderón, "Un apostolado social," 25.

19. "La superioridad de los anglo-sajones," 1.

20. Rodriguez paints a similar picture for Argentina between 1880 and 1930 in *Civilizing Argentina: Science, Medicine, and the Modern State*. Latin American intellectuals often wrote about the differences they perceived between Latin and Anglo-Saxon responses to modern life. Although European heritage was preferable to indigenous or African, southern European ancestry (associated with Latin origins) was not considered ideal for national modernization projects. See also Turda and Gillette, *Latin Eugenics*.

21. "La superioridad de los anglo-sajones," 1.

22. Palacios, *Raza chilena* (1918), 56.

23. Palacios, *Raza chilena* (1918), 34. Palacios is here referring to Charles Darwin's travels in Chile while on the *HMS Beagle* and to the American scholar Anson Uriel Hancock's *A History of Chile*, originally published in 1893 and translated into Spanish in 1896. See Hancock, *History of Chile*; Hancock, *Historia de Chile*.

24. Novoa and Levine, *From Man to Ape*, 5.

25. A number of Chilean historians and anthropologists wrote about the disappearance of indigenous groups in the wake of colonization. One of the most colorful examples of this was Edwards, *Peoples of Old*. Similar examples of obscuring the racial diversity of the past in the name of national homogeneity also happened in Argentina. Karush argues a similar case for Afro-Argentines in "Blackness in Argentina." Novoa and Levine also discuss this whitewashing of Argentine racial identity in *From Man to Ape*, 83, 122–24.

26. The idea of the "vanishing race" became especially prominent among scholars working in the United States, the origin of which is often attributed to Edward S. Curtis's *The North American Indian* series published between 1907 and 1930.

27. Palacios, *Raza chilena* (1918), 34.

28. Palacios, *Raza chilena* (1918), 43–44.

29. In fact, the Mapuche peoples would not be "pacified" until the 1880s. For more on this, see Crow, *Mapuche in Modern Chile*; Dillehay, *Monuments, Em-*

pires, and Resistance; Herr, *Contested Nation*; Hutchison et al., *Chile Reader*; Zavala
Cepeda et al., *Los parlamentos hispano-mapuches*.

30. Alvarado and Fernández, "Una narración," 49.

31. Stepan, *Picturing Tropical Nature*, 110.

32. "Razas que mueren," n.p.

33. "Razas que mueren," n.p.

34. Palacios, *Raza chilena* (1918), 4.

35. Claiming that an infusion of Germanic blood improved civilizations that
were primarily Latin was not only popular in Latin America. The German anthropologist Ludwig Woltmann made similar arguments about German influence in
Italy and France in a series of works published between 1906 and 1907 and so did
Anglo-German naturalist Houston Steward Chamberlain in his book *The Foundations of the Nineteenth Century* published in 1911. See Turda and Gillette, *Latin
Eugenics*, 17. Chamberlain's work and that of Arthur de Gobineau have been noted
as specifically influencing Palacios. See Calderón, "Un apostolado social, 28.

36. Palacios, *Raza chilena* (1918), 41.

37. Palacios, *Raza chilena* (1918), 37.

38. Palacios, *Raza chilena* (1918), 210.

39. Palacios, *Raza chilena* (1918), 198–212.

40. Palacios, *Raza chilena* (1918), 104.

41. Palacios, *Raza chilena* (1918), 201.

42. Palacios, *Raza chilena* (1918), 199–200. Body and facial hair became widespread metrics by which individuals were racially identified, and not only in Chile.
Although it always proved to be a somewhat divisive topic, many eugenicists discussed hair color and texture as secondary racial traits. Some examples of this type
of writing include Boas, "Eugenics"; Cane, "Hair and Its Heredity"; Davenport,
Eugenics. Green discusses body hair as a means of examining homosexual men in
Brazil in his book chapter "Doctoring the National Body." Facial hair in particular
was understood to be a defining characteristic of European heritage and something
that was universally lacking among indigenous men in Latin American countries.
See Castellanos, *El pelo en los Cubanos*; Coutts, Ahumada, and Bulnes, "Contribucion al estudio" (November 1929); Coutts, Ahumada, and Bulness, "Contribucion
al estudio" (December 1929).

43. Palacios, *Raza chilena* (1918), 212.

44. Novoa and Levine, *From Man to Ape*; Stepan, *Hour of Eugenics*.

45. Orel, *Gregor Mendel*.

46. Palacios, *Raza chilena* (1918), 213–14.

47. Palacios, *Raza chilena* (1918), 219.

48. Palacios, *Raza chilena* (1918), 57.

49. Palacios, *Raza chilena* (1918), 57.

50. The belief that the enslavement of African-descended peoples was not a
widespread practice in Chile remains firmly in place today, in both popular and

academic circles. The literature regarding this issue is relatively small. See Black-burn, *Overthrow of Colonial Slavery*; Blanchard, *Under the Flags of Freedom*; Collier and Sater, *History of Chile*, 9. Guillermo Feliú Cruz's *La abolición de la esclavitud* is considered one of the definitive works on the subject, despite its age. Some of the more recent scholarship on slavery in Chile comes from legal historians. See González Undurraga, *Esclavos y esclavas*; Palma G., *Abolición de la esclavitud*. There is virtually no coverage in English or Spanish in scholarly literature regarding Black identity in Chile that is not the result of relatively recent migration from other parts of the Americas or Africa. Popular discussion of this topic, however, is growing and is reflected in essays such as Doig-Acuña, "Recognizing Blackness in Chile." Similarly, groups aimed at speaking to the erasure of African heritage in Chile have been created in the past decade with the NGO Oro Negro being one of the most prominent.

51. Palacios, *Raza chilena* (1918), 221.

52. Darwin, *What Is Eugenics?*; Stoddard, *Revolt against Civilization*; Whetham and Whetham, *Introduction to Eugenics*.

53. Palacios, *Raza chilena* (1918), 221.

54. Palacios, *Raza chilena* (1918), 57–58.

55. Novoa and Levine, *From Man to Ape*, 129. The Argentine writer Vicente Quesada also believed that Afro-Argentines and criollos were slowly being absorbed into the population while Indians were disappearing entirely; he portrayed this in his stories such as *"Mi Tio Blas."* Novoa and Levine, *From Man to Ape*, 127.

56. Palacios, *Raza chilena* (1918), 58.

57. Palacios, *Raza chilena* (1918), 221–22.

58. Palacios, *Raza chilena* (1918), 89.

59. S. Palacios, "Nicolás Palacios: Recuerdos intimos," 18.

60. Galton, *Hereditary Genius*, 359.

61. Calderón, "Un apostolado social," 25.

62. Stepan, *Picturing Tropical Nature*, 125–26; Bronfman, *Measures of Equality* 50.

63. This is best encapsulated in the concept of the Black Legend, which a variety of different competing European powers popularized about Spain in order to portray their own colonial endeavors as benevolent. Work on this includes De-Guzmán, *Spain's Long Shadow*; Greer, Mignolo, and Quilligan, *Rereading the Black Legend*.

64. Barandiarán, "Researching Race in Chile." One of the most striking developments in Chile has been an increasingly strident anti-immigration discourse in the media and popular opinion aimed primarily at Haitian migrants who have arrived in increasing numbers since the 2010 earthquake. The overall feeling is that these individuals are not welcome because they do not speak Spanish, are unaware of traditional social customs, and rely on public welfare systems. Unsaid, but often palpable in this rhetoric, is the fear that the presence of a growing African-

descended immigrant community will encourage more African-descended migrants to arrive. See Tijoux, *Racismo en Chile.*

65. Calderón, "Un apostolado social," 25.

66. "Bibliografia: Raza chilena," 49.

67. Aguirre Sayago, "El Dr. Nicolás Palacios," 191.

68. "Se inauguró ayer el monumento al autor de *Raza chilena*," 1; Figueroa, "Palacios," 458.

69. Figueroa, "Palacios," 457–58.

70. Cubillos and Brucher, "Algunas caracteristicas," 314.

71. Alvarado and Fernández, "Una narración," 54; Calderón, "Un apostolado social," 25.

72. Memoria Chilena, "Nicolás Palacios"; Klubock, "Nationalism, Race, and the Politics of Imperialism," 236–37.

73. There were in total fifteen editions published in this period, all with the title *Resumen de la historia de Chile.* They appear to have been condensed and edited by Leopoldo Castedo.

Chapter 5. "Intimately Linked to the Issue of Sex"

1. Sánchez Delgado, "Sexo, eugenesia y política," 110–11.

2. Coutts, *A los jóvenes,* 4.

3. Stern, "Hour of Eugenics."

4. One such law, Decreto Ley No. 355, was actually entitled "En defensa de la raza." It outlined the creation of a series of different government offices aimed at limiting "social diseases" considered to be racially degenerative such as syphilis, tuberculosis, alcoholism, and prostitution. It was drafted and passed under the auspices of dictator General Carlos Ibañez del Campo in March 1925. See Decreto Ley No. 355—En defensa de la raza (March 17, 1925). That same year also saw the passing of the 1925 Código Sanitario, which created massive amounts of new laws related to public health and hygiene that many believed would have a beneficial and transcendent effect on the entire Chilean population. See Decreto Ley No. 602—Código Sanitario (October 13, 1925). In fact, this code was what created the División de Higiene Pública that Coutts directed. In 1939, Pedro Aguirre Cerda would pass Decreto Orgánico No. 4157 to found an institution dedicated to the defense of the Chilean race. The Institución Defensa de la Raza would ultimately include a model home and cultural center as well as parklands and offer a variety of different classes. See Decreto Orgánico No. 4157.

5. Besse, *Restructuring Patriarchy*; Caulfield, *In Defense of Honor*; Rosemblatt, *Gendered Compromises*; Vaughan, "Modernizing Patriarchy."

6. Much as indigenous women were overlooked in eugenic writing, indigenous men were not the focus of these texts. Here, the Chilean men being referred to were understood to be mestizo and somewhere on the pathway toward Whiteness.

7. De Santa Teresa, "El católico de hoy día también," 103.

8. De Santa Teresa, "El católico de hoy día también," 106.

9. Historians of the Catholic Church in Latin America have pointed to its feminization, women becoming the primary interlocutors for their families when it came to religious practice and church attendance, over the course of the nineteenth and early twentieth centuries. This is typically connected to the cultural movement toward secularization and anticlericalism. Chowning's "Catholic Church and the Ladies of the Vela Perpetua" is a concise distillation of these ideas.

10. Subercaseaux, *Historia de ideas*, 417.

11. Lenti, *Don Bosco, History and Spirit.*

12. Subercaseaux, *Historia de ideas*, 317.

13. Gentilini, *El libro del hombre varonil*, 35.

14. Gentilini, *El libro del hombre varonil*, 56.

15. Gentilini, *El libro del hombre varonil*, 53.

16. Gentilini, *El libro del hombre varonil*, 88.

17. Gentilini, *El libro del hombre varonil*, 84.

18. Fournier, *Para nuestros hijos*, 4.

19. Fournier, *Para nuestros hijos*, 4–5. For biographical information, see Beeson, "Alfred Fournier."

20. Fournier, *Para nuestros hijos*, 6.

21. Katz M., *Distrofias conjénitas*; Prado Tagle, "Sifilis conjenita tardia."

22. Fournier, *Para nuestros hijos*, 38.

23. Barbet, *Preparación*, 49.

24. Barbet, *Preparación*, 55.

25. Barbet, *Preparación*, 34.

26. Fournier also lamented this sexual double standard in "La sifilis de las mujeres honradas." See also Liga Chilena de Higiene Social, *Memorial de la Liga*; Edwards, *La continencia y la juventud.*

27. Barbet, *Preparación*, 43.

28. Gajardo, *La educacion sexual*, 7.

29. Gajardo, *La educacion sexual*, 10.

30. Gajardo, *La educacion sexual*, 15.

31. Gajardo, *La educacion sexual*, 114.

32. Gajardo, *La educacion sexual*, 51.

33. Gajardo, *La educacion sexual*, 47. Italics added.

34. Gajardo, *La educacion sexual*, 93.

35. Gajardo, *La educacion sexual*, 103.

36. Gajardo, *La educacion sexual*, 97.

37. Gajardo, *La educacion sexual*, 98. According to Gajardo, "when this phenomenon [first period] surprises her, the young girl observes it with alarm, believing herself victim of an unspeakable illness that she hides with fear" (98).

38. Sánchez Delgado, "Sexo, eugenesia y política," 112.

39. Coutts, *El instinto sexual*, 5.

40. Coutts, *El instinto sexual*, 7.

41. Coutts, *El instinto sexual*, 8. Coutts here posited that a higher marriage rate reduces crime, much as Gajardo did.

42. Coutts, *El instinto sexual*, 41.

43. Gentilini, *¡Sed puros!*, 63.

44. Gentilini, *¡Sed puros!*, 76.

45. Gentilini, *¡Sed puros!*, 88.

46. Gentilini, *¡Sed puros!*, 114.

47. Gentilini, *¡Sed puros!*, 110.

48. Gentilini, *¡Sed puros!*, 7–8.

49. Del Campo (Ramirez), "María," 185.

50. Salazar et al., *Historia contemporánea de Chile IV*, 79; Salazar Vergara, *Patriarcado mercantil*.

51. Out of 387 documents concerning idealized gender norms and behaviors that I surveyed during my research, almost 65 percent (251) were about women. Just under 13 percent (50) focused on male misbehavior.

52. Del Campo, "María," 188.

53. Lamy, "La mujer de mañana," 970.

54. Lamy, "La mujer de mañana," 971.

55. Lamy, "La mujer de mañana," 972.

56. Options were still relatively limited, but the early decades of the twentieth century saw a significant expansion of public education for women at all levels. For further discussions of women's education in Chile, see Egaña, *La educación primaria*; Sánchez Manríquez, "El ingreso de la mujer"; Serrano, *Historia de la educación*.

57. "La mujer católica," 5.

58. Maza Valenzuela, "Catolicismo,"; Power, *Right-Wing Women*; Verba, *Catholic Feminism*; Voekel, *Alone before God*.

59. Gentilini, *El libro de la mujer*, 14–15.

60. Gentilini, *El libro de la mujer*, 9.

61. Gentilini, *El libro de la mujer*, 37.

62. Gentilini, *El libro de la mujer*, 93.

63. Showing that this amount of education did not protect her from the dangers of womanhood, she died at the hands of her lover in 1931 as part of a murder-suicide. "Patrimonio: Cora Mayers," 23.

64. Mayers, *La mujer*, 12.

65. One of the more illustrious Chilean physicians to address the issue of illegitimacy was Salvador Allende in his book *La realidad medico-social chilena* (1939). He wrote: "The first aspect of this problem is that illegitimacy implies the deficient physiological conditions of children—in large part—of single mothers deprived

of the economic support of a father. . . . From there arises the Ministry's preoccupation with a policy of protection for single mothers and the normalization of working-class families, by which we mean the future of the mother and child" (105).

66. Maza Valenzuela, "Catolicismo," 166–67. Figures for the size of the Cruz Blanca are from Lavrin, *Women, Feminism, and Social Change*, 305.

67. Edwards de Salas, "Nuestros pobres y sus hijos," 173.

68. It is unclear if Edwards de Salas got her own mothers' school, but the notion of a *centro de madres* became quite popular over the course of the twentieth century. For more information regarding these developments and the concrete efforts made by these centers, see Memoria Chilena, "Los centros de madres."

69. Edwards de Salas, "Nuestros pobres y sus hijos," 354.

70. Edwards de Salas, "Nuestros pobres y sus hijos," 355.

71. The separation of indigenous children from their families likely occurred throughout Latin America, but the historical scholarship related to this practice appears to be in a nascent stage. There has been more historical research on this phenomenon in other settler colonial societies. See Jacobsen, *White Mother to a Dark Race*; Jacobsen, *Generation Removed*; Read, *Stolen Generations*.

72. Verónica, "La enseñanza doméstica," 1.

Chapter 6. Picturing *la raza chilena*

1. Banta and Hinsley, *From Site to Sight*; Edwards, *Anthropology and Photography*; Edwards and Morton, *Photography, Anthropology and History*; Hight and Sampson, *Colonialist Photography*; Oksiloff, *Picturing the Primitive*; Rogers, *Delia's Tears*.

2. Bancel, David, and Thomas, *Invention of Race*; Ciarlo, *Advertising Empire*.

3. Poole, *Vision, Race, and Modernity*.

4. Sontag, *On Photography*.

5. Lloréns, *Imaging the Great Puerto Rican Family*, xx.

6. Lloréns, *Imaging the Great Puerto Rican Family*, xxi.

7. Cánepa Koch and Kummels, *Photography in Latin America*.

8. I surveyed a total of 1,434 separate texts (books, articles, essays) during this research. The vast majority did not include any type of image or illustration beyond the front matter or cover page.

9. "Nuestra primera palabra," 1.

10. "Nuestra primera palabra," 2.

11. Forsythe, *Humanitarians*.

12. "Antecedentes sobre la Cruz Roja Chilena."

13. "Antecedentes sobre la Cruz Roja Chilena," 2.

14. McEvoy, *Guerreros civilizadores*; Parodi Revoredo, *Lo que dicen de nosotros*; Sater, *Andean Tragedy*; Skuban, *Lines in the Sand*.

15. "La X Conferencia Internacional de la Cruz Roja," 50.

16. "Sofía Francisca del Carmen Eastman Cox."

17. Phillip, "El hombre deberia avergonzarse de estar enfermo."

18. Phillip, "El hombre deberia avergonzarse de estar enfermo," 309–10.

19. Phillip, "El hombre deberia avergonzarse de estar enfermo," 315.

20. Reggiani, "Eugenics and Physical Culture"; Vimieiro Gomes, "Rise of Biotypology."

21. Front cover, *Revista de Salud Pública de la Cruz Roja Chilena*, December 1928.

22. "La Escuela de Servicio Social," 9. The first school of social work in Spain was founded at the Universitat de Barcelona in 1932, so this claim seems likely to be true. See Fullana, Serra, and Pallisera, "Social Professions in Spain," 36–37.

23. "La Escuela de Servicio Social," 10.

24. Castañeda M. and Salamé C., "A 90 años," 403; Memoria Chilena, "Alejandro del Río."

25. Castañeda M. and Salamé C., "A 90 años," 403.

26. Eilers, "René Sand."

27. "La Escuela de Servicio Social," 17–21.

28. San Cristóbal and San Cristóbal, "Servicio medico," 27.

29. San Cristóbal and San Cristóbal, "Servicio medico," 26.

30. San Cristóbal and San Cristóbal, "Servicio medico," 29.

31. San Cristóbal and San Cristóbal, "Servicio medico," 33.

32. Mayers, "Plan de organizacion," 574.

33. Mayers, "Plan de organizacion," 575.

34. Mayers, "Plan de organizacion," 574.

35. Mayers, "Plan de organizacion," 576.

36. CEPAL and MINSAL, *Atlas sociodemográfico*.

37. Prieto, "El patronato nacional de la infancia," 22.

38. Prieto, "El patronato nacional de la infancia," 23.

39. MacMillan, "Forms So Attenuated," 344.

40. Cádiz Oyarzun, "Algunas observaciones clinicas," 524.

41. Castillo Vejar, "Historia Hospital 'Enrique Deformes.'"

42. MacMillan, "Forms So Attenuated," 344.

43. MacMillan, "Forms So Attenuated," 332–33.

44. Cádiz Oyarzun, "Algunas observaciones clinicas," 527.

45. Cádiz Oyarzun, "Algunas observaciones clinicas," 525.

46. Cádiz Oyarzun, "Algunas observaciones clinicas," 528.

47. Cádiz Oyarzun, "Algunas observaciones clinicas," 529.

48. Cádiz Oyarzun, "Algunas observaciones clinicas," 529.

49. Cádiz Oyarzun, "Algunas observaciones clinicas," 529.

50. Cádiz Oyarzun, "Algunas observaciones clinicas," 530.

51. MacMillan, "Forms So Attenuated," 346.

52. Cádiz Oyarzun, "Algunas observaciones clinicas," 531.

53. Zárate Campo, *Dar a luz.*

54. Cádiz Oyarzun, "Algunas observaciones clinicas," 530.

55. Cádiz Oyarzun, "Algunas observaciones clinicas," 525.

56. Cádiz Oyarzun, "Algunas observaciones clinicas," 531.

57. MacMillan, "Forms So Attenuated."

58. Cádiz Oyarzun, "Algunas observaciones clinicas," 534.

59. Although this is not mentioned in "Algunas observaciones," O.B.B. ultimately prevailed upon Cádiz to remove her testes and create an artificial vagina for her prior to her marriage. Efforts at having children, however, proved fruitless. See MacMillan, "Forms So Attenuated," 348.

60. Cádiz Oyarzun, "Algunas observaciones clinicas," 534.

61. Cádiz Oyarzun, "Algunas observaciones clinicas," 535. Acromegaly is a hormonal condition affecting adults in which too much growth hormone is produced generally affecting the size of the hands, feet, and face.

62. Cádiz Oyarzun, "Algunas observaciones clinicas," 535.

63. Cádiz Oyarzun, "Algunas observaciones clinicas," 536.

64. Cádiz Oyarzun, "Algunas observaciones clinicas," 534.

65. Cádiz Oyarzun, "Algunas observaciones clinicas," 536.

66. Cádiz Oyarzun, "Algunas observaciones clinicas," 541.

67. Cádiz Oyarzun, "Algunas observaciones clinicas," 541.

68. Cádiz Oyarzun, "Algunas observaciones clinicas," 544.

69. The article included case studies of six individuals who presented as women but whom Cádiz identified as intersexual.

Conclusion

1. Aggio, "La cultura política"; Barr-Melej, *Reforming Chile*; Berenguela, *El ultimo gran grito radical*; Milos Hurtado, *Frente popular*; Reyes Alvarez, *Los presidentes radicales*; Rosemblatt, *Gendered Compromises*; Snow, *Radicalismo chileno.*

2. Geary, *Beyond Civil Rights*; Greenbaum, *Blaming the Poor*; Lewis, *Five Families*; Wallerstein, *Modern World-System.*

3. Elkins, *Slavery*; Tannenbaum, *Ten Keys.*

4. There is a vast literature on the rise of Allende, the coup of September 11, 1973, the Pinochet regime, and the return to democracy. Some examples include Dorfman, *Chile, the Other September 11*; Huneeus, *El regimen de Pinochet*; Spooner, *General's Slow Retreat*; Winn, *Weavers of Revolution.*

5. Salgado and Castillo, "Differential Status Evaluations."

6. Amorós, *Pinochet.*

7. Allende Gossens, *Higiene mental y delicuencia.*

8. Farías, *Salvador Allende.* Farías's book caused quite an uproar in Chile upon its publication, and most of his claims have been refuted. One of the more recent efforts to contextualize Allende's support of sterilization in the late 1930s is Sánchez Delgado, "Salvador Allende."

9. Amorós, *Allende*.

10. Allende, *La realidad médico-social chilena*.

11. Vial Correa, *Pinochet*.

12. Pius XII, *Humani generis*.

13. Fleet, *Rise and Fall*; Luna, Monestier, and Rosenblatt, "Religious Parties."

14. Contreras Vejar and Casanova, *Catholicism and Democracy*.

15. Contreras-Vejar, "Unorthodox Fate."

Bibliography

A.F.L. "Crónica científica—los trabajos de P. Wasmann SJ." *La Revista Católica* 599 (September 18, 1926): 446–49.

Aedo-Richmond, Ruth. *La educación privada en Chile: un estudio histórico-analítico desde el período colonial hasta 1990*. Santiago: Red Internacional del Libro, 2000.

Aggio, Alberto. "La cultura política del radicalismo chileno en clave de revolución pasiva." *Ayer* 70 (2008): 141–68.

Aguirre Sayago, A. "El Dr. Nicolás Palacios." *Revista Médica Chilena* 6 (June 1911): 191–93.

Alberto, Paulina L., and Eduardo Elena. *Rethinking Race in Modern Argentina*. New York: Cambridge University Press, 2016.

Allende, Salvador. *La realidad médico-social chilena*. Edited by Hernán Soto, María Angélica Illanes, and Mariano Requena. Santiago, Chile: Editorial Cuarto Propio, 1999 [1939].

Allende Gossens, Salvador. *Higiene mental y delicuencia: tesis para optar al título de medico cirujano de la Universidad de Chile*. Santiago: Ediciones Chile América CESOC, 2005.

Alonso, Luis. "Ciencia y religion." *Mente y cerebro* (December 2005): 93–95.

Alvarado, Miguel, and Héctor Fernandez. "Una narración fundacional para una antropología filosófica chilena: *Raza chilena* de Nicolás Palacios." *Cinta moebio* 40 (2011): 47–63.

Alvarado Borgoño, Miguel. "La modernidad maldita de Nicolás Palacios: apuntes sobre *Raza chilena*." *Gazeta de Antropología* 20 (2004): 1–9.

Álvarez Hernández, Fernanda. "La república parlamentaria de Chile: perspectivas historiográficas." *Universum* 27, no. 1 (2012): 209–22.

Amorós, Mario. *Allende: la biografía*. Madrid: Ediciones B, 2013.

Amorós, Mario. *Pinochet: biografía militar y política*. Barcelona: Ediciones B, 2019.

Andersen, Lisa. *The Politics of Prohibition: American Governance and the Prohibition Party, 1869–1933*. Cambridge: Cambridge University Press, 2013.

Andes, Stephen J. C. *The Vatican and Catholic Activism in Mexico and Chile: The Politics of Transnational Catholicism, 1920–1940.* Oxford: Oxford University Press, 2014.

Andrade, Ana Luiza. *Outros perfis de Gilberto Freyre: voltas duras, dóceis ao cotidiano dos brasileiros.* Sao Paulo: Nankin Editorial, 2007.

Ankelen H., Federico. "La esterilidad femenina." *Medicina Moderna* 7, no. 6 (January 1934): 209–15.

"Antecedentes sobre la Cruz Roja Chilena." *Revista de la Salud Pública de la Cruz Roja Chilena* 1 (July/August 1922): 2–5.

Appelbaum, Nancy P., Anne S. Macpherson, and Karin Alejandra Rosemblatt, eds. *Race and Nation in Modern Latin America.* Chapel Hill: University of North Carolina Press, 2003.

Araya, Claudia, César Leyton, Marcelo López, Cristián Palacios, and Marcelo Sánchez, eds. *República de la salud: fundación y ruinas de un país sanitario, Chile siglos XIX y XX.* Santiago: Ocho Libros, 2016.

Aspe Armella, María Luisa. *La formación social y política de los católicos mexicanos: la Acción Católica Mexicana y la Unión Nacional de Estudiantes Católicos, 1929–1958.* Mexico City: Universidad Iberoamericana, A.C., 2008.

Astorquizo Sazzo, Juan. "Eugenesia." *Medicina Moderna* 9 (April 1938): 415–35.

Attridge, Harold W., and Ronald L. Numbers. *The Religion and Science Debate: Why Does It Continue?* New Haven, CT: Yale University Press, 2009.

Bancel, Nicolas, Thomas David, and Dominic Thomas. *The Invention of Race: Scientific and Popular Representations.* New York: Routledge, 2014.

Banta, Melissa and Curtis M. Hinsley. *From Site to Sight: Anthropology, Photography, and the Power of Imagery.* Cambridge, MA: Harvard University Press, 2017.

Barabino, Santiago E., and Nicolás Besio Moreno, eds. *Congreso Científico Internacional Americano,* 1:194. Buenos Aires: Imprenta de Coni Hermanos, 1910.

Barahona Silva, Roberto. "Los católicos ante el problema científico de la eugenesia." *Estudios* 47 (October 15, 1936): 35–45.

Barandiarán, Javiera. "Researching Race in Chile." *Latin American Research Review* 47, no. 1 (2012): 161–76.

Barbet, Pierre. *La passion de N.-S. Jésus-Christ selon le chirurgien.* Issoudun: Dillen, 1950.

Barbet, Pierre. *Preparación del joven al matrimonio.* Santiago: Liga Chilena de Higiene Social, 1924.

Barr-Melej, Patrick. *Reforming Chile: Cultural Politics, Nationalism, and the Rise of the Middle Class.* Chapel Hill: University of North Carolina Press, 2001.

Beeson, B. Barker. "Alfred Fournier, His Life and Works." *Archive of Dermatology and Syphilology* 10, no. 3 (1924): 297–303.

Bennett Leay, Hernan. *El alcoholismo y las enfermedades mentales: estudio médico-social.* Santiago: Imp. El Imparcial, 1940.

Berenguela, Luis. *El último gran grito radical.* Santiago: Lubec, 1996.

Besa de Díaz, M. "Ideas que vivifican, ideas que matan." *El Mercurio* 17747 (June 22, 1933): 7.

Besse, Susan K. *Restructuring Patriarchy: The Modernization of Gender Inequality in Brazil, 1914–1940.* Chapel Hill: University of North Carolina, 1996.

Betzhold H., Hans. *Eugenesia.* Santiago: Sociedad Imprenta y Litografía Universo, 1939.

"Bibliografía: Raza chilena." *La Revista Católica* 97 (August 5, 1905): 49–50.

Biblioteca del Congreso Nacional de Chile. "Paulino Alfonso del Barrio." https://www.bcn.cl/historiapolitica/resenas_parlamentarias/wiki/Paulino_Alfonso_del_Barrio.

Biblioteca del Congreso Nacional de Chile. "Ricardo Cox Méndez." https://www.bcn.cl/historiapolitica/resenas_parlamentarias/wiki/Ricardo_Cox_Méndez.

Bidegaín, Ana María. *From Catholic Action to Liberation Theology: The Historical Process of the Laity in Latin America in the Twentieth Century.* Notre Dame: Kellogg Institute for International Studies, 1985.

Blackburn, Robin. *The Overthrow of Colonial Slavery, 1776–1848.* New York: Verso, 1988.

Blacker, C. P. *Eugenics: Galton and After.* Westport: Hyperion Press, 1987.

Blanchard, Peter. *Under the Flags of Freedom: Slave Soldiers and the Wars of Independence in Spanish South America.* Pittsburgh: University of Pittsburgh Press, 2008.

Bliss, Katherine. *Compromised Positions: Prostitution, Public Health, and Gender Politics in Revolutionary Mexico City.* University Park: Pennsylvania State University Press, 2001.

Block, Sharon. *Colonial Complexions: Race and Bodies in Eighteenth-Century America.* Philadelphia: University of Pennsylvania Press, 2018.

Boas, Franz. "Eugenics." *Scientific Monthly* 3, no. 5 (November 1916): 471–78.

Bonner, Michelle D. *Policing Protest in Argentina and Chile.* Boulder: First Forum Press, 2013.

Bowler, Peter J. *The Eclipse of Darwinism: Anti-Darwinian Evolution Theories in the Decades around 1900.* Baltimore, MD: Johns Hopkins University Press, 1992.

Bowler, Peter J. *The Mendelian Revolution: The Emergence of Hereditarian Concepts in Modern Science and Society.* London: Athlone Press, 1989.

Bowler, Peter J. *Reconciling Science and Religion: The Debate in Early Twentieth-Century Britain.* Chicago: University of Chicago Press, 2001.

Bowler, Peter J., and Iwan Rhys Morus. *Making Modern Science: A Historical Survey.* Chicago: University of Chicago Press, 2005.

Brace, C. Loring. *Race Is a Four-Letter Word: The Genesis of a Concept.* New York: Oxford University Press, 2005.

Bronfman, Alejandra. *Measures of Equality: Social Science, Citizenship, and Race in Cuba, 1902–1940.* Chapel Hill: University of North Carolina Press, 2004.

Brooke, John H., Margaret Osler, and Jitse M. van der Meer. *Science in Theistic Contexts: Cognitive Dimensions*. Osiris series no. 16. Chicago: University of Chicago Press, 2001.

Brown, B. Ricardo. *Until Darwin: Science, Human Variety, and the Origins of Race*. London: Pickering and Chatto, 2010.

Buchenau, Jürgen. *Plutarco Elías Calles and the Mexican Revolution*. Lanham, MD: Rowman and Littlefield, 2007.

Buckley, Eve. "Overpopulation Debates in Latin America during the Cold War." *Oxford Research Encyclopedia of Latin American History*, February 26, 2018. https://doi.org/10.1093/acrefore/9780199366439.013.338.

Bulmer, Michael G. *Francis Galton: Pioneer of Heredity and Biometry*. Baltimore: Johns Hopkins University Press, 2003.

Burke, Peter, and Maria Lúcia G. Pallares-Burke. *Gilberto Freyre: Social Theory in the Tropics*. Oxford: Peter Lang, 2008.

Butler, Matthew. *Popular Piety and Political Identity in Mexico's Cristero Rebellion: Michoacán, 1927–29*. New York: Oxford University Press, 2004.

Cádiz Oyarzun, Romeo. "Algunas observaciones clinicas de estados intersexuales en la especie humana." *Medicina Moderna* 11 (June 1930): 524–54.

Cádiz Oyarzun, Romeo. *Sexo anormal: hermafroditisimo-pseudohermafroditisimo, ginecomastia, homosexualidad y otros estados intersexuales y anomolías de sexo: estudio general, clínico y terapeútico*. Santiago: N.p., 1958.

Calderón, Alfonso. "Un apostolado social." *Vida médica* (1982): 24–30.

Campos Menendez, Enrique. *Biblioteca nacional*. Santiago: Ediciones DIBAM, 1982.

Cane, Maurice H. "Hair and Its Heredity." *Eugenics Review* 4, no. 3 (October 1912): 257–83.

Cánepa Koch, Gisela, and Ingrid Kummels, eds. *Photography in Latin America: Images and Identities across Time and Space*. Bielefeld, Germany: Verlag, 2016.

Cañizares-Esguerra, Jorge. *Nature, Empire, and Nation: Explorations of the History of Science in the Iberian World*. Stanford, CA: Stanford University Press, 2006.

Caro R., José María. "Conferencia sobre el origen del hombre dada por el Sr. Obispo D. José María Caro R." *La Revista Católica* 17, no. 370 (January 6, 1917): 5–19.

Castañeda M., Patricia, and Ana María Salamé C. "A 90 años de la creación de la primera escuela de trabajo social en Chile y Latinoamérica, por el Dr. Alejandro del Río." *Revista Médica de Chile* 143, no. 3 (March 2015): 403–4.

Castaño, Carlos Alberto. "El alcoholismo aristocrático y la cura de hambre para adelgazar." *Estudios* 30 (May 1935): 46–49.

Castedo, Leopoldo, and Ricardo Lagos Escobar. *Chile: vida y muerte de la República Parlamentaria*. Santiago: Sudamericana, 2001.

Castellanos, Israel. *El pelo en los cubanos*. Havana: Carasa y Companía, 1933.

Castillo Infante, Fernando. *La flecha roja: relato histórico sobre la Falange Nacional*. Santiago: Editorial Francisco de Aguirre, 1997.

Castillo Vejar, Myriam. "Historia Hospital 'Enrique Deformes.'" http://www .bibliotecaminsal.cl/wp/wp-content/uploads/2011/09/Historia-Hospital -Enrique-Deformes.pdf.

Castillo Velasco, Jaime. *Las fuentes de la democracia cristiana*. Santiago: Ediciones Rumbos, 1999.

Caulfield, Sueann. *In Defense of Honor: Sexual Morality, Modernity, and Nation in Early Twentieth-Century Brazil*. Durham, NC: Duke University Press, 2000.

Celis Brunet, Ana María, René Cortínez Castro S.J., and Maria Elena Pimstein Scroggie. "Religion and Law in the Non-Confessional Chilean State." In *Religion and the Secular State: Interim Reports*, edited by W. Cole Durham Jr. and Javier Martínez-Torrón, 213–35. Provo: International Center for Law and Religion Studies, Brigham Young University, 2010.

Céspedes, Mario, and Lelia Garreaud. "Palacios Navarro, Nicolás." In *Gran diccionario de Chile (biográfico-cultural)*, 532–33. Santiago: Importadora Alfa Limitada, 1988.

Chamberlain, Houston Steward. *The Foundations of the Nineteenth Century*. New York: John Lane, 1899.

Charlín, Carlos. "Las dos verdades." *Estudios* 15 (February 1934): 3–14.

Chowning, Margaret. "The Catholic Church and the Ladies of the Vela Perpetua: Gender and Devotional Change in Nineteenth-Century Mexico." *Past & Present* 221, no. 1 (November 2013): 197–237.

Chowning, Margaret. *Rebellious Nuns: The Troubled History of a Mexican Convent, 1752–1863*. New York: Oxford University Press, 2006.

Chresfield, Michell. "To Improve the Race: Eugenics as a Strategy for Racial Uplift, 1900–1940." Master's thesis, Vanderbilt University, Nashville, TN, 2013.

Churchill, Frederick B. *August Weismann: Development, Heredity, and Evolution*. Cambridge, MA: Harvard University Press, 2015.

Ciarlo, David. *Advertising Empire: Race and Visual Culture in Imperial Germany*. Cambridge, MA: Harvard University Press, 2011.

Cid, Gabriel. "Médicos, abogados y eugenesia negativa en Chile, 1933–1941." *Anales de Historia de la Medicina* 19, no. 1 (2009): 35–46.

Cifuentes Grez, Antonio. "El Proyecto de Represión del Alcoholismo." *Estudios* 56 (July 1937): 4–8.

Coletta, Michela. "The Role of Degeneration Theory in Spanish American Public Discourse at the *Fin de Siècle*: *Raza Latina* and Immigration in Chile and Argentina." *Bulletin of Latin American Research* 30, no. 1 (2011): 87–103.

Collier, Simon. "Religious Freedom, Clericalism, and Anti-clericalism in Chile, 1820–1920." In *Freedom and Religion in the Nineteenth Century*, edited by Richard J. Helmstadter, 302–38. Stanford, CA: Stanford University Press, 1997.

Collier, Simon, and William F. Sater. *A History of Chile, 1808–2002*. New York: Cambridge University Press, 2004.

Comisión Económica para América Latina y el Caribe (CEPAL) and Ministerio de Salud Chile (MINSAL). *Atlas sociodemográfico de la población y pueblos indígenas: Región Metropolitana e Isla de Pascua, Chile*. Santiago: Contempo Gráfica, 2010.

Congar, Yves. *The Catholic Church and the Race Question*. Paris: UNESCO, 1953.

Connelly, Matthew. *Fatal Misconception: The Struggle to Control World Population*. Cambridge, MA: Belknap Press of Harvard University Press, 2008.

Contreras-Vejar, Yuri. "Unorthodox Fate: The Rise of Chile's Christian Democratic Party." *Journal of Religious and Political Practice* 1, no. 1 (2015): 58–72.

Contreras Vejar, Yuri, and Jose Casanova. *Catholicism and Democracy: The Ideological Origins of the Chilean Christian Democratic Party, 1920–1945*. Ann Arbor, MI: University Microfilms, 2009.

Cordemans, Leo. "De la caridad al servicio social." *Servicio Social* 1–2 (March–June 1927): 3–7.

Corti Cortés, Lucía, and Julio Maltés Cortés. "Palacios Navarro, Nicolás." In *Enciclopedia histórica de Chile*, 476. Barcelona: Bibliografica Internacional, 2003.

Coutts, W. E. *A los jóvenes*. Santiago: Talleres de San Vicente, 1929.

Coutts, W. E. *El instinto sexual y la vida contemporánea: su influencia en los actos delictuosos*. Buenos Aires, Argentina: Talleres Gráficos de la Penitenciaría Nacional, 1926.

Coutts, W. E., G. Ahumada, and R. Bulnes. "Contribucion al estudio del significado biológico de los caracteres pilosos en la especie humana." *Revista Médica Chilena* 11 (November 1929): 852–60.

Coutts, W. E., G. Ahumada, and R. Bulnes. "Contribucion al estudio del significado biológico de los caracteres pilosos en la especie humana." *Revista Médica Chilena* 12 (December 1929): 975–86.

Cox Méndez, Ricardo. "Orientaciones contemporáneas del catolicismo." *El Mercurio* 4323 (September 17, 1909): 5.

"La crisis matrimonial." *El Mercurio* 6402 (January 13, 1918): 5.

Crow, Joanna. *The Mapuche in Modern Chile: A Cultural History*. Gainesville: University Press of Florida, 2012.

Cubillos, Luis, and Eduardo Brucher. "Algunas caracteristicas bio-psicologicas y raciales de nuestros delincuentes araucanos." *Medicina Moderna* (January 1939): 314–17.

Cunin, Elizabeth, and Odile Hoffman. *Blackness and Mestizaje in Mexico and Central America*. Trenton, NJ: Africa World Press, 2014.

Curley, Robert. "Transnational Subaltern Voices: Sexual Violence, Anticlericalism, and the Mexican Revolution." In *Local Church, Global Church: Catholic Activism in Latin America from Rerum Novarum to Vatican II*, edited by Stephen J. C. Andes, 91–116. Washington, DC: Catholic University of America Press, 2016.

Currell, Susan, and Christina Codgell. *Popular Eugenics: National Efficiency and American Mass Culture in the 1930s*. Athens: Ohio University Press, 2006.

"Current Comment—Ineffectiveness of Contraceptive Methods." *Journal of the American Medical Association* 107, no. 19 (November 7, 1936): 1564.

Curtis, Edward S. *The North American Indian: The Complete Portfolios.* Köln, Germany: Taschen, 2019.

Dampier, William Cecil, and Catherine Durning Whetham. *The Family and the Nation: A Study in Natural Inheritance and Social Responsibility.* New York: Longmans, Green, 1909.

Darwin, Charles. *On the Origin of Species by Means of Natural Selection, or the Preservation of Favoured Races in the Struggle for Life.* London: John Murray, 1859.

Darwin, Leonard. *¿Qué es la eugenesia? Modo de mejorar la raza humana.* Translated by Juan Comas Camps and Margarita Dellenbach. Madrid: Ediciones Morata, 1930.

Darwin, Leonard. *What Is Eugenics?* London: Watts, 1928.

Davenport, Charles Benedict. *Eugenics: The Science of Human Improvement by Better Breeding.* New York: Henry Holt, 1910.

Dávila, Jerry. *Diploma of Whiteness: Race and Social Policy in Brazil, 1917–1945.* Durham, NC: Duke University Press, 2003.

Dawes, Gregory W. *Galileo and the Conflict between Religion and Science.* New York: Routledge, 2019.

de la Cadena, Marisol. *Indigenous Mestizos: The Politics of Race and Culture in Cuzco, Peru, 1919–1991.* Durham, NC: Duke University Press, 2003.

de la Luz, Clara. *La mujer y la especie (trabajo leido en el Centro Demócrata de Santiago el 3 de Mayo de 1913).* Santiago: Imprenta Lee y CA., 1913.

"De nuevo la generación espontánea." *La Revista Católica* 305 (April 18, 1914): 634–35.

de Santa Teresa, P. Samuel. "El católico de hoy día también es el hombre de hoy día." *La Revista Católica* 218 (August 20, 1910): 101–8.

de Santa Teresa, Samuel. "El católico de hoy." *La Revista Católica* 214 (June 18, 1910): 836.

de Tezanos-Pinto S., Sergio. "Valparaíso y sus medicos: una historia digna de publicar." In *Quintas jornadas de historia de la medicina,* edited by Alejandro Goic G. and Ricardo Cruz-Coke M., 125–30. Santiago: LOM Ediciones, 2002.

Debré, Patrice. *Louis Pasteur.* Baltimore, MD: Johns Hopkins University Press, 2000.

Decreto Ley No. 355—En defensa de la raza (17 March 1925).

Decreto Ley No. 602—Código Sanitario (October 13, 1925).

Decreto Orgánico No. 4157 (August 18, 1939), Secretaría General de la Defensa de la Raza, *Defensa de la raza, 1939–1941, Santiago de Chile.* Santiago: Empresa Editora Zig-Zag, 1941.

DeGuzmán, María. *Spain's Long Shadow: The Black Legend, Off-Whiteness, and Anglo-American Empire.* Minneapolis: University of Minnesota Press, 2005.

del Campo, Sofia (pseud. Juan Ramon Ramirez). "María y la mujer chilena." *La Revista Católica* 87 (March 4, 1905): 185–205.

Depassier, Victor. *La muerte del materialismo: conferencia dedicada a las clases dirigentes y a los estudiantes de ambas universidades.* Santiago: Imprenta de San José, 1919.

DeYoung, Ursula. *A Vision of Modern Science: John Tyndall and the Role of the Scientist in Victorian Culture.* New York: Palgrave Macmillan, 2011.

Díaz Avilez, Mónica. *To Be Indio in Colonial Spanish America.* Albuquerque: University of New Mexico Press, 2017.

Díaz Nieva, José. *Chile: de la Falange Nacional a la democracia cristiana.* Madrid: Universidad Nacional de Educación a Distancia, 2001.

Dillehay, Tom D. *Monuments, Empires, and Resistance: The Araucanian Polity and Ritual Narratives.* New York: Cambridge University Press, 2007.

Doig-Acuña, Maya. "Recognizing Blackness in Chile." Guernica, March 2, 2020. https://www.guernicamag.com/recognizing-blackness-in-chile.

Dorfman, Ariel, ed. *Chile, the Other September 11: An Anthology of Reflections on the 1973 Coup.* New York: Ocean Press, 2016.

Dorr, Gregory Michael. *Segregation's Science: Eugenics and Society in Virginia.* Charlottesville: University of Virginia Press, 2008.

Dorr, Gregory Michael, and Angela Logan. "'Quality, Not Mere Quantity, Counts': Black Eugenics and the NAACP Baby Contests." In *A Century of Eugenics in America: From the Indiana Experiment to the Human Genome Era*, ed. Paul Lombardo, 68–92. Bloomington: Indiana University Press, 2011.

Dorsaz, Armand, Andre Rendu, and Raoul de Guchteneere. *Le contrôle rationnel des naissances.* Uvrier-St-Léonard, Valais: Prof. M. Issele, 1935.

Douglass, Frederick. "The Color Line." *North American Review* (June 1, 1881): 567–77.

Doyle, Don Harrison, and Marco Antonio Villela Pamplona. *Nationalism in the New World.* Athens: University of Georgia Press, 2006.

Draper, John William. *Historia de los conflictos entre la religion y la ciencia.* Translated by Augusto T. Arcimís. Madrid: Aribau y Companía, 1876.

Draper, John William. *History of the Conflict between Religion and Science.* New York: D. Appleton, 1874.

Drinot, Paulo. *The Sexual Question: A History of Prostitution in Peru, 1850s–1950s.* New York: Cambridge University Press, 2020.

Duarte G., Ignacio. "El Doctor Roberto Barahona S." *Boletín Escuela de Medicina P. Universidad Católica de Chile* 31 (1983): 7–8.

DuBois, W. E. B. *The Souls of Black Folk.* Chicago: A. C. McClurg, 1903.

Dueñas, Alcira. *Indians and Mestizos in the "Lettered City": Reshaping Justice, Social Hierarchy, and Political Culture in Colonial Peru.* Boulder: University Press of Colorado, 2010.

Durst, Dennis L. *Eugenics and Protestant Social Reform: Hereditary Science and Religion in America, 1860–1940*. Eugene, OR: Wipf and Stock, 2017.

E. M. S. "La Iglesia católica acepta el birth control." *Boletin Médico Social* 25 (June 1936): 246–49.

Eagleton, Terry. *Materialism*. New Haven, CT: Yale University Press, 2017.

Eakin, Marshall C. *Becoming Brazilians: Race and National Identity in Twentieth-Century Brazil*. New York: Cambridge University Press, 2017.

Earle, Rebecca. *The Body of the Conquistador: Food, Race and the Colonial Experience in Spanish America, 1492–1700*. Cambridge: Cambridge University Press, 2012.

Edelson, Edward. *Gregor Mendel and the Roots of Genetics*. Oxford: Oxford University Press, 2001.

Edwards, A. W. F. "Darwin, Leonard (1850–1943)." In *Oxford Dictionary of National Biography*. New York: Oxford University Press, 2004. https://doi.org/10.1093/ref:odnb/54078.

Edwards, Agustín. *Peoples of Old*. London: Ernest Benn, 1929.

Edwards, Elizabeth. *Anthropology and Photography, 1860–1920*. New Haven, CT: Yale University Press, 1997.

Edwards, Elizabeth, and Christopher A. Morton. *Photography, Anthropology and History: Expanding the Frame*. New York: Routledge, 2016.

Edwards, Rafael. *La continencia y la juventud*. Santiago: Librería y Casa Editorial de la Federación de Obras Católicas, 1918.

Edwards de Salas, Adela. "Nuestros pobres y sus hijos." *La Revista Católica* 208 (March 19, 1910): 353–56.

Edwards de Salas, Adela. "Nuestros pobres y sus hijos—escuelas maternales." *La Revista Católica* 206 (February 18, 1910): 170–74.

Egaña, Loreto. *La educación primaria en Chile, 1860–1930: una aventura de niñas y maestras*. Santiago: LOM Ediciones, 2003.

Ehrenrich, Eric. *The Nazi Ancestral Proof: Genealogy, Racial Science, and the Final Solution*. Bloomington: Indiana University Press, 2007.

Eilers, Kerstin. "René Sand (1877–1953) and His Contribution to International Social Work, IASSW President (1946–1953)." *Social Work and Society* 5, no. 1 (2007): 102–9.

Eiss, Paul K., and Joanne Rappaport. *Politics and Performance of Mestizaje in Latin America: Mestizo Acts*. London: Routledge, 2018.

Elkins, Stanley M. *Slavery: A Problem in American Institutional and Intellectual Life*. Chicago: University of Chicago Press, 1959.

Elsey, Brenda. *Citizens and Sportsmen: Fútbol and Politics in Twentieth-Century Chile*. Austin: University of Texas Press, 2011.

English, Daylanne K. *Unnatural Selections: Eugenics in American Modernism and the Harlem Renaissance*. Chapel Hill: University of North Carolina Press, 2004.

Errázuriz, Crescente, Luis Antonio Castro Alvarez, Gilberto Fuenzalida Guzmán, Carlos Silva Cotapos, and Rafael Edwards Salas. "Circular colectiva del Episcopado Chileno sobre la obligación grave de inscribir los matrimonios en el registro civil." *La Revista Católica* 442 (January 3, 1920): 5–9.

"La escuela de servicio social de Santiago de Chile." *Servicio Social* 1–2 (March–June 1927): 8–41.

Esposito, Gabriele, Giuseppe Rava, and Martin Windrow. *Armies of the War of the Pacific 1879–83: Chile, Peru & Bolivia.* Oxford: Osprey, 2016.

"Estatua de Pasteur." *El Diario Popular* 17 (September 22, 1902): 2.

"Eugenesia nacional." *Boletín del Ministerio de Higiene, Asistencia y Previsión Social* 6 (October 1927): 5–6.

Farías, Víctor. *Salvador Allende: antisemitismo y eutanasia.* Santiago: Maye, 2005.

Farley, John. *The Spontaneous Generation Controversy from Descartes to Oparin.* Baltimore, MD: Johns Hopkins University Press, 1977.

Feliú Cruz, Guillermo. *La abolición de la esclavitud en Chile: estudio histórico y social.* Santiago: Universidad de Chile, 1942.

Fernandez Abara, Joaquin. *El ibañismo (1937–1952): un caso de populismo en la política chilena.* Santiago: Instituto de Historia, Pontificia Universidad Católica de Chile, 2008.

Fernández Darraz, Enrique. *Estado y sociedad en Chile, 1891–1931: el estado excluyente, la lógica estatal oligárquica y la formación de la sociedad.* Santiago: LOM Ediciones, 2003.

Fernández Labbé, Marcos. *Bebidas alcohólicas en Chile: una historia económica de su fomento y expansion 1870–1930.* Santiago: Universidad Alberto Hurtado, 2010.

Ferrer, Ada. *Insurgent Cuba: Race, Nation, and Revolution, 1868–1898.* Chapel Hill: University of North Carolina Press, 1999.

Figueroa, Virgilio. "Palacios." In *Diccionario histórico, biográfico y bibliográfico de Chile,* 457–58. Santiago: Balcells, 1931.

Fisher, Andrew B., Matthew D. O'Hara, and Irene Silverblatt, eds. *Imperial Subjects: Race and Identity in Colonial Latin America.* Durham, NC: Duke University Press, 2009.

Fisher, R. A. "Positive Eugenics." *Eugenics Review* 9, no. 3 (1917): 206–12.

FitzGerald, David, and David Cook-Martin. *Culling the Masses: The Democratic Origins of Racist Immigration Policy in the Americas.* Cambridge, MA: Harvard University Press, 2014.

Fitzgerald, Keith A. *The Face of the Nation: Immigration, the State, and the National Identity.* Stanford, CA: Stanford University Press, 1996.

Fleet, Michael. *The Rise and Fall of Chilean Christian Democracy.* Princeton, NJ: Princeton University Press, 2014.

Foote, Nicola. *Military Struggle and Identity Formation in Latin America: Race, Nation, and Community during the Liberal Period.* Gainesville: University Press of Florida, 2013.

Foote, Nicola, and Michael Goebel. *Immigration and National Identities in Latin America*. Gainesville: University Press of Florida, 2016.

Forsythe, David P. *The Humanitarians: The International Committee of the Red Cross*. Cambridge: Cambridge University Press, 2005.

Fournier, Alfred. *Para nuestros hijos cuando tengan 18 años: algunos consejos del Profesor Fournier*. Translated by Emilio R. Coni. Buenos Aires: Liga Argentina de Profilaxis Social, 1921.

Fournier, Alfred. "La sífilis de las mujeres honradas." *Revista Médica de Chile* 11 (November 1906): 341–43.

Frazier, Lessie Jo. *Salt in the Sand: Memory, Violence, and the Nation-State in Chile, 1890 to the Present*. Durham, NC: Duke University Press, 2007.

French, John D., and Daniel James. *The Gendered Worlds of Latin American Women Workers: From Household and Factory to the Union Hall and Ballot Box*. Durham, NC: Duke University Press, 1997.

Freyre, Gilberto. *Casa-grande & senzala: formação da família brasileira sob o regime de economia patriarchal*. Rio de Janeiro: Maia and Schmidt, 1933.

Frye Jacobson, Matthew. *Whiteness of a Different Color: European Immigrants and the Alchemy of Race*. Cambridge, MA: Harvard University Press, 1998.

Fuenzalida Guzmán, Gilberto. *El deber electoral de los católicos: circular del Obispo de Concepción en que se ordenan preces por el buen resultado de las próximas elecciones*. Concepción: Soulodre, 1920.

Fuenzalida Guzmán, Gilberto. "Deberes de los católicos en los momentos actuales." *La Revista Católica* 462 (November 6, 1920): 688–709.

Fuenzalida Guzmán, Gilberto. *Qué es la Acción Católica? Su naturaleza, sus finalidades, su campo de trabajo, sus obras, organización, su necesidad y sus relaciones con las asociaciones puramente religiosas y con la política: instrucciones dadas a los socios por el obispo de Concepción*. Santiago: Imprenta Chile, 1932.

Fullana, Judit, Carles Serra, and Maria Pallisera. "The Social Professions in Spain: Past and Present." *European Journal of Social Education* 20/21 (2011): 35–45.

Gajardo, Samuel. *La educacion sexual del niño y del adolescente*. Santiago: Dirección General de Prisiones, 1940.

Galton, Francis. *Hereditary Genius: An Inquiry into Its Laws and Consequences*. London: Macmillan, 1869.

García González, Armando. *Las trampas del poder: sanidad, eugenesia y migración, Cuba y Estados Unidos (1900–1940)*. Madrid: Consejo Superior de Investigaciones Científicas, 2007.

García González, Armando, and Raquel Álvarez Peláez. *En busca de la raza perfecta: eugenesia e higiene en Cuba (1898–1958)*. Madrid: CSIC, 1999.

García González, Armando, and Raquel Álvarez Peláez. "Eugenesia e imperialismo: las relaciones Cuba–Estados Unidos, 1921–1940." In *Darwinismo social y eugenesia en el mundo latino*, ed. Marisa Miranda and Gustavo Vallejo, 193–230. Buenos Aires: Siglo XXI de Argentina Editores, 2005.

Gayon, Jean. *Darwinism's Struggle for Survival: Heredity and the Hypothesis of Natural Selection.* Translated by Matthew Cobb. New York: Cambridge University Press, 1998.

Gazmuri, Cristián. *El '48' chileno: igualitarios, reformistas, radicales, masons y bomberos.* Santiago: Editorial Universitaria, 1992.

Gazmuri R., Cristián. "Decadencia del espíritu de nacionalidad." In *El Chile del centenario, los ensayistas de la crisis,* edited by R. Cristián Gazmuri and E. Rodríguez Mendoza. Santiago: Instituto de Historia, Pontificia Universidad Católica de Chile, 2001.

Geary, Daniel. *Beyond Civil Rights: The Moynihan Report and Its Legacy.* Philadelphia: University of Pennsylvania Press, 2015.

Geison, Gerald L. *The Private Science of Louis Pasteur.* Princeton, NJ: Princeton University Press, 1995.

Gentilini, Bernardino. *El libro de la mujer: como cristiana, esposa, madre, educadora y apóstol.* Santiago: Apostolado de la Prensa, 1917.

Gentilini, Bernardo. *El libro del hombre varonil: como cristiano y caballero, esposo, padre y educador, hombre de profesión y de negocios, ciudadano y apóstol social.* Santiago: Apostolado de la Prensa, 1918.

Gentilini, Bernardo. *¡Sed puros! Educación de la castidad: gobierno de las pasiones.* Santiago de Chile: Apostolado de la Prensa, 1936.

Gibbon, Sahra, Mónica Sans, and Ricardo Ventura Santos, eds. *Racial Identities, Genetic Ancestry and Health in South America: Argentina, Brazil, Colombia, and Uruguay.* New York: Palgrave Macmillan, 2011.

Gilbert, James. *Redeeming Culture: American Religion in an Age of Science.* Chicago: University of Chicago Press, 1997.

Gilson, Gregory D., and Irving W. Levinson, eds. *Latin American Positivism: New Historical and Philosophical Essays.* Lanham, MD: Lexington Books, 2013.

Glick, Thomas F. "Cultural Issues in the Reception of Relativity." In *The Comparative Reception of Relativity,* edited by Thomas F. Glick, 381–400. Boston: D. Reidel, 1987.

Glick, Thomas F. "Relativity in Spain in the Comparative Reception of Relativity." In *The Comparative Reception of Relativity,* edited by Thomas F. Glick, 231–64. Boston: D. Reidel, 1987.

Glick, Thomas F. "Science in Twentieth-Century Latin America." In *Ideas and Ideologies in Twentieth Century Latin America,* edited by Leslie Bethell, 287–360. New York: Cambridge University Press, 1996.

Glick, Thomas F., Miguel Angel Puig-Samper, and Rosaura Ruiz, eds. *The Reception of Darwinism in the Iberian World: Spain, Spanish America, and Brazil.* Boston: Kluwer Press, 2001.

Gobat, Michel. "The Invention of Latin America: A Transnational History of Anti-imperialism, Democracy, and Race." *American Historical Review* 118, no. 5 (December 2013): 1345–75.

Godoy P., Pedro, and Gustavo Galarce M. *Día de sangre: Nicolás Palacios y el genocidio de Iquique 21.12.1907.* Iquique: Universidad Arturo Prat, 2007.

González Quijano, Humberto, and Rosa Margarita Suárez Díaz. "Semblanza del General de Brigada Eusebio Hernández Pérez." *Revista cubana de medicina militar* 46, no. 2 (April–June 2017): 196–205.

González Undurraga, Carolina. *Esclavos y esclavas demandando justicia Chile, 1740–1823, documentación judicial por carta de libertad y papel de venta.* Santiago: Editorial Universitaria, 2014.

Gorostarzu, M. "El problema social del matrimonio." *La Revista Católica* 678 (May 3, 1930): 618–23.

Gould, Stephen Jay. *The Mismeasure of Man.* New York: Norton, 1996.

Green, James N. "Doctoring the National Body: Gender, Race, Eugenics, and the 'Invert' in Urban Brazil, ca. 1920–1945." In *Gender, Sexuality, and Power in Latin America since Independence,* ed. William E. French and Katherine sElaine Bliss, 187–211. Lanham, MD: Rowman and Littlefield, 2007.

Greenbaum, Susan D. *Blaming the Poor: The Long Shadow of the Moynihan Report on Cruel Images about Poverty.* New Brunswick, NJ: Rutgers University Press, 2015.

Greer, Margaret R., Walter D. Mignolo, and Maureen Quilligan *Rereading the Black Legend: The Discourses of Religious and Racial Difference in the Renaissance Empires.* Chicago: University of Chicago Press, 2008.

Grossi Aninat, Amanda. *Eugenesia y su legislación.* Santiago: Editorial Nascimento, 1941.

"Guerra al alcoholismo." *La Revista Católica* 10 (December 15, 1901): 458–59.

Guitarte, Arturo. "Esterilidad fisiologica," *Medicina Moderna* 7, no. 6 (January 1934): 361–66.

Guy, Donna. *Sex and Danger in Buenos Aires: Prostitution, Family, and Nation in Argentina.* Lincoln: University of Nebraska Press, 1991.

Hallanger, Nathan. "Eugenics and the Question of Religion." In *The Evolution of Evil,* edited by Gaymon Bennett, Martinez J. Hewlett, Ted Peters, and Robert John Russell, 301–17. Gottingen: Vandenhoeck and Ruprecht, 2008.

Hanchard, Michael George. *Orpheus and Power: The Movimento Negro of Rio de Janeiro and Sao Paulo, Brazil, 1945–1988.* Princeton, NJ: Princeton University Press, 1994.

Hancock, Anson Uriel. *Historia de Chile . . . traducida del inglés por J. Casado.* Translated by José Casado. Madrid: N.p., 1896.

Hancock, Anson Uriel. *A History of Chile.* Chicago: C. H. Sergel, 1893.

Hanlon, Joseph. "Christ under the Microscope." *New Scientist* 80, no. 1124 (October 12, 1978): 96–98.

Harris, Henry. *Things Come to Life: Spontaneous Generation Revisited.* New York: Oxford University Press, 2002.

Haught, John F. "Darwinism and Catholicism." In *Cambridge Encyclopedia of Dar-*

win and Evolutionary Thought, edited by M. Ruse, 485–92. New York: Cambridge University Press, 2013.

Hechenleitner Trautmann, Ernesto. *Herencia morbosa y su correctivo eugenesico: 'la esterilizacion.'* Santiago: Impresa Periodistica "El Imparcial," 1936.

Heise Gonzalez, Julio. *Historia de Chile: el periodo parlamentario, 1861–1925.* Santiago: Editorial Andrés Bello, 1974.

"Henry Charlton Bastian, M.A., M.d.lond., F.R.C.P., F.R.S., Emeritus Professor of Medicine and Clinical Medicine, University College, London." *British Medical Journal* 2, no. 2865 (November 27, 1915): 795–96.

Hering Torres, Max Sebastián, María Elena Martínez, and David Nirenberg, eds. *Race and Blood in the Iberian World.* Berlin: LIT Verlag, 2012.

Hernández, Eusebio, and Domingo F. Ramos. *Homicultura.* Havana: Secretaria de Sanidad y Beneficencia, 1911.

Hernández Alfonso, Luis. *Eugenesia y derecho a vivir.* Madrid: Ediciones Morata, 1933.

Herr, Pilar M. *Contested Nation: The Mapuche, Bandits, and State Formation in Nineteenth-Century Chile.* Albuquerque: University of New Mexico Press, 2019.

Hess, Peter M. J. "Evolution, Suffering, and the God of Hope in Roman Catholic Thought after Darwin." In *The Evolution of Evil,* edited by Gaymon Bennett et al., 234–56. Gottingen: Vandenhoeck and Ruprecht, 2008.

Hess, Peter M. J., and Paul L. Allen. *Catholicism and Science.* Westport, CT: Greenwood Press, 2008.

Hierarchy of the Catholic Church. "José María Caro Rodríguez." http://www.cath olic-hierarchy.org/bishop/bcaro.html.

Hight, Eleanor M., and Gary D. Sampson, eds. *Colonialist Photography: Imag(in) ing Race and Place.* London: Routledge, 2002.

Hogarth, Rana A. *Medicalizing Blackness: Making Racial Difference in the Atlantic World, 1780–1840.* Chapel Hill: University of North Carolina, 2017.

Holder, Rodney Dennis, and Simon Mitton. *Georges Lemaître: Life, Science, and Legacy.* New York: Springer 2015.

Holt, Thomas C. "Foreword." In *Race and Nation in Modern Latin America,* edited by Nancy P. Appelbaum, Anne S. Macpherson, and Karin Alejandra Rosemblatt, vii–xiv. Chapel Hill: University of North Carolina Press, 2003.

Hooker, Juliet. *Theorizing Race in the Americas: Douglass, Sarmiento, DuBois, and Vasconcelos.* New York: Oxford University Press, 2017.

Htun, Mala. *Sexo y estado: aborto, divorcio y familia bajo dictaduras y democracias en América Latina.* Santiago: Universidad Diego Portales, 2010.

Huneeus, Carlos. *El regimen de Pinochet.* Santiago: Editorial Sudamericana, 2000.

Huneeus Cox, Alejandro. "Birth-control o la limitación de la Natalidad." *Estudios* 11 (August 1933): 28–33.

Hutchison, Elizabeth Q., Thomas Miller Klubock, Nara B. Milanich, and Peter

Winn. *The Chile Reader: History, Culture, Politics*. Durham, NC: Duke University Press, 2014.

Hutchison, Elizabeth Quay. *Labors Appropriate to Their Sex: Gender, Labor, and Politics in Urban Chile, 1900–1930*. Durham, NC: Duke University Press, 2001.

Huxley, Julian. *Evolution: The Modern Synthesis*. London: Allen and Unwin, 1942.

Illanes, María Angélica. *Cuerpo y sangre de la política: la construcción histórica de las visitadoras sociales (1887–1940)*. Santiago: LOM Ediciones, 2006.

Illanes Oliva, María Angélica. *"En el nombre del pueblo, del estado y de la ciencia": historia social de la salud pública, Chile 1880–1973*. Santiago: Colectivo de Atención Primaria, 1993.

Ivey, Paul Eli. *Radiance from Halcyon: A Utopian Experiment in Religion and Science*. Minneapolis: University of Minnesota Press, 2013.

J.L.C. "La eugenesia moderna." *La Revista Católica* 761 (February 17, 1934): 76–80.

Jacobsen, Margaret D. *A Generation Removed: The Fostering and Adoption of Indigenous Children in the Postwar World*. Lincoln: University of Nebraska Press, 2014.

Jacobsen, Margaret D. *White Mother to a Dark Race: Settler Colonialism, Maternalism, and the Removal of Indigenous Children in the American West and Australia, 1880–1940*. Lincoln: University of Nebraska Press, 2009.

Jodock, Darrell. *Catholicism Contending with Modernity: Roman Catholic Modernism and Anti-modernism in Historical Context*. New York: Cambridge University Press, 2011.

Johnson, Lyman L. *Workshop of Revolution: Plebeian Buenos Aires and the Atlantic World, 1776–1810*. Durham, NC: Duke University Press, 2011.

Jones, Richard H. *For the Glory of God: The Role of Christianity in the Rise and Development of Modern Science*. Lanham, MD: University Press of America, 2011.

Jordan, Winthrop D. "Historical Origins of the One-Drop Racial Rule in the United States." *Journal of Critical Mixed Race Studies* 1, no. 1 (2014): 98–132.

Jörinssen, Luisa. "El concepto de caridad en la asistencia social." *La Revista Católica* 699 (April 11, 1931): 321–27.

Jouve Martín, José Ramón. *The Black Doctors of Colonial Lima: Science, Race, and Writing in Colonial and Early Republican Peru*. Montreal: McGill-Queen's University Press, 2014.

Karush, Matthew B. "Blackness in Argentina: Jazz, Tango and Race before Perón." *Past and Present* 216 (2012): 215–45.

Katz M., Carmela. *Distrofias conjénitas*. Santiago: Imprenta y En. "Victoria" 1910.

Kellogg, Susan. *Weaving the Past: A History of Latin America's Indigenous Women from the Prehispanic Period to the Present*. New York: Oxford University Press, 2005.

Kelly, Michael. "'Catholicisme ondoyant': Catholic Intellectual Engagement and the Crisis of Civilization in the 1930s." In *God's Mirror: Renewal and En-*

gagement in French Catholic Intellectual Culture in the Mid-Twentieth Century, edited by Katherine Davies and Toby Garfitt, 28–49. New York: Fordham University Press, 2015.

Kevles, Daniel J. In the Name of Eugenics: Genetics and the Uses of Human Heredity. New York: Knopf, 1985.

Keymer F., Eduardo. "Uso de anticoncepcionales—problema económico-social." In Estudios Médicos, 239–52. Santiago de Chile: Imprenta W. Gnadt, 1938.

Kline, Wendy. Building a Better Race: Gender, Sexuality, and Eugenics from the Turn of the Century to the Baby Boom. Berkeley: University of California Press, 2001.

Klubock, Thomas Miller. Contested Communities: Class, Gender and Politics in Chile's El Teniente Copper Mine, 1904–1951. Durham, NC: Duke University Press, 1998.

Klubock, Thomas Miller. "Nationalism, Race, and the Politics of Imperialism: Workers and North American Capital in the Chilean Copper Industry." In Reclaiming the Political in Latin American History: Essays from the North, edited by Gilbert M. Joseph, 231–67. Durham, NC: Duke University Press, 2001.

Kragh, Helge. Cosmology and Controversy: The Historical Development of Two Theories of the Universe. Princeton, NJ: Princeton University Press, 1999.

Kragh, Helge, and Malcolm S. Longair, eds. The Oxford Handbook of Modern Cosmology. New York: Oxford University Press, 2019.

Lake, Marilyn, and Henry Reynolds. Drawing the Global Colour Line: White Men's Countries and the International Challenge of Racial Equality. Cambridge: Cambridge University Press, 2008.

Lamarck, Jean-Baptiste. Philosophie Zoologique. Paris: Musée d'Histoire Naturelle, 1809.

Lamy, Esteban. "La mujer de mañana." La Revista Católica 261 (June 15, 1912): 970–78.

Langley, Lester D. The Americas in the Age of Revolution, 1750–1850. New Haven, CT: Yale University Press, 1996.

Larson, Edward J. Summer for the Gods: The Scopes Trial and America's Continuing Debate over Science and Religion. New York: Basic Books, 1997.

Lasso, Marixa. Myths of Harmony: Race and Republicanism during the Age of Revolution, Colombia, 1795–1831. Pittsburgh: University of Pittsburgh Press, 2007.

Lastarria, José Victorino. Don Guillermo: historia contemporanea. Santiago: Impresor del Correo, 1860.

Lavrin, Asunción. Sexuality and Marriage in Colonial Latin America. Lincoln: University of Nebraska Press, 1992.

Lavrin, Asunción. Women, Feminism, and Social Change in Argentina, Chile and Uruguay: 1890–1940. Lincoln: University of Nebraska Press, 1995.

Lenti, Arthur J. Don Bosco, History and Spirit: Beginnings of the Salesian Society and Its Constitutions. Rome: Libreria Ateneo Salesiano, 2008.

León, Marco Antonio. "Crisis del Partido Conservador en Chile (1945–1953): un estudio a través de 'Política y Espíritu.'" In *Anuario de Historia de la Iglesia en Chile* 12 (1994): 127–52.

León, Marco Antonio. "La crisis del Partido Conservador en Chile: un estudio a través de 'Política y Espíritu.' Segunda parte: El conservadurismo bajo Ibáñez." In *Anuario de Historia de la Iglesia en Chile* 13 (1995): 155–80.

Leon, Sharon. *An Image of God: The Catholic Struggle with Eugenics*. Chicago: University of Chicago Press, 2013.

León Palma, Julio. *La eugenesia*. Concepción: Impresor "El Aguila," 1937.

Levine, Alex, and Adriana Novoa. *¡Darwinistas! The Construction of Evolutionary Thought in Nineteenth-Century Argentina*. Boston: Brill, 2012.

Lewis, Oscar. *Five Families: Mexican Case Studies in the Culture of Poverty*. New York: Basic Books, 1959.

Leyton, César, Cristián Palacios, and Marcelo Sánchez, eds. *Bulevar de los pobres: racismo científico, higiene, y eugenesia en Chile e Iberoamérica siglos XIX y XX*. Santiago: Ocho Libros, 2015.

Liga Chilena de Higiene Social. *Memoria de la Liga Chilena de Higiene Social sobre el problema de la esclavitud blanca en relación con el Título IV del Nuevo Código Sanitario de Chile*. Santiago: Imprenta Nascimento, 1926.

Lloréns, Hilda. *Imaging the Great Puerto Rican Family: Framing Nation, Race, and Gender during the American Century*. Lanham, MD: Lexington Books, 2014.

Logan, Enid Lynette. "Each Sheep with Its Mate: Marking Race and Legitimacy in Cuban Catholic Parish Archives, 1890–1940." *New West Indian Guide/Nieuwe West-Indische Gids* 84, no. 1–2 (2010): 5–39.

Lopes, Maria Margaret, and Irina Podgorny. "The Shaping of Latin American Museums of Natural History, 1850–1990." In *Nature and Empire: Science and the Colonial Enterprise*, edited by Roy MacLeod, 108–18. Ithaca, NY: Cornell University Press, 2001.

Losurdo, Domenico. "Towards a Critique of the Category of Totalitarianism." *Historical Materialism* 12, no. 2 (2004): 25–55.

Luna, Juan Pablo, Felipe Monestier, and Fernando Rosenblatt. "Religious Parties in Chile: The Christian Democratic Party and the Independent Democratic Union." *Democratization* 20, no. 5 (August 2013): 917–38.

Lund, Joshua. *The Mestizo State: Reading Race in Mexico*. Minneapolis: University of Minnesota Press, 2012.

Lyell, Charles. *Principles of Geology; or, The Modern Changes of the Earth and Its Inhabitants Considered as Illustrative of Geology*. Project Gutenberg, 2010.

MacMillan, Kurt. "'Forms So Attenuated That They Merge into Normality Itself': Alexander Lipschütz, Gregorio Marañón, and Theories of Intersexuality in Chile, Circa 1930." In *A Global History of Sexual Science, 1880–1960*, edited by Veronika Fuechtner, Douglas E. Haynes, and Ryan M. Jones, 330–52. Berkeley: University of California Press, 2018.

Marantz Henig, Robin. *The Monk in the Garden: The Lost and Found Genius of Gregor Mendel, the Father of Genetics*. New York: Houghton Mifflin Harcourt, 2017.

Maritain, Jacques. *The Rights of Man and Natural Law*. New York: Scribner, 1943.

Maxwell, Anne. *Picture Imperfect: Photography and Eugenics, 1870–1940*. Brighton: Sussex Academic Press, 2008.

Mayers, Cora. "La educacion higiénica de la nacion." *Revista de Beneficencia Pública* 3 (September 1924): 199–202.

Mayers, Cora. *La mujer: defensora de la raza*. Santiago: Imprenta Santiago, 1925.

Mayers, Cora. "Plan de organizacion de la 'Liga de Madrecitas.'" *Boletín Sanitario* 9 (September 1927): 574–85.

Maza Valenzuela, Erika. "Catolicismo, anticlericalismo y la tensión del sufragio a la mujer en Chile." *Estudios Públicos* 58 (Fall 1995): 137–95.

Mazumdar, Pauline M. H. *The Eugenics Movement: An International Perspective*. New York: Routledge, 2007.

McEvoy, Carmen. *Guerreros civilizadores: política, sociedad y cultura en Chile durante la guerra del Pacífico*. Lima: PUCP, 2016.

McGirr, Lisa. *The War on Alcohol: Prohibition and the Rise of the American State*. New York: W. W. Norton, 2016.

McNamara, Patrick J. *Sons of the Sierra: Juárez, Díaz, and the People of Ixtlán, Oaxaca, 1855–1920*. Chapel Hill: University of North Carolina Press, 2007.

Mellafe Maturana, Rafael, and Mauricio Pelayo González. *La guerra del Pacífico: en imágenes, relatos y testimonios*. Lima: Legatum Editores, 2019.

Memoria Chilena. "Alejandro del Río (1867–1939)." http://www.memoriachilena .gob.cl/602/w3-article-94680.html.

Memoria Chilena. "Los centros de madres en Chile (1930–1989)." http://www .memoriachilena.gob.cl/602/w3-article-100688.html#presentacion.

Memoria Chilena. "Editorial y librería Nascimento (1875–1986)." http://www.me moriachilena.gob.cl/602/w3-article-3363.html#presentacion.

Memoria Chilena. "Jaime Eyzaguirre." http://www.memoriachilena.cl/602/w3-ar ticle-656.html.

Memoria Chilena. "Nicolás Palacios." In "Reforma y nacionalismo en Chile (1910–1931)." http://www.memoriachilena.cl/602/w3-article-97363.html.

Merlin, "Un problema social," *El Mercurio* 6401 (January 12, 1918): 3.

Middleton C., Luis G. "Objetivacion del ideal de la salud: su desenvolvimiento en la Comuna, sus proyecciones nacionales e internacionales." *Revista Médica de Chile* 11 (November 1932): 813–28.

Millas Parada, Guillermo. *Eugenesia y derecho*. Santiago: Empresa Periodistica "La Nacion," 1936.

Miller, Marilyn Grace. *Rise and Fall of the Cosmic Race: The Cult of Mestizaje in Latin America*. Austin: University of Texas Press, 2004.

Milos Hurtado, Pedro. *Frente Popular en Chile: su configuración, 1935–1938*. Santiago: LOM Ediciones, 2008.

Miranda, Marisa, and Gustavo Vallejo. *Darwinismo social y eugenesia en el mundo latino*. Buenos Aires: Siglo XXI de Argentina Editores, 2005.

Miranda T., Rene. "Clinica ginecológica." *Revista Médica de Chile* 1 (January 1937): 43–44.

Molina Bustos, Carlos Antonio. *Institucionalidad sanitaria chilena, 1889–1989*. Santiago: LOM Ediciones, 2010.

Moore, Stephen T. *Bootleggers and Borders: The Paradox of Prohibition on a Canada-US Borderland*. Lincoln: University of Nebraska Press, 2014.

"La mujer católica." *La Cruzada* 106 (March 15, 1917): 5.

Muñoz Sougarret, Jorge, and Francisco Ther Ríos. "El pescador en el imaginario científico durante la etapa de formación de la academia ictiológica chilena, 1829–1909." *História, Ciências, Saúde—Manguinhos 73* 20, no. 4 (2013): 1621–33.

Museo Nacional de Medicina. "Lucas Sierra." http://www.museomedicina.cl/home /index.php/component/content/article/46-s-a-v/125-dr-lucas-sierra-1866 -1937.html.

Naudon Figueroa, Andrés. *La cuestión social y el derecho: orígenes de la primera codificación laboral chilena*. Santiago: RIL Editores, 2013.

Ngai, Mae M. *Impossible Subjects: Illegal Aliens and the Making of Modern America*. Princeton, NJ: Princeton University Press, 2004.

Noé, Giovanni. *La ciencia i los sentimientos humanitarios: conferencia leida en el Club de Señoras el sábado 25 de noviembre de 1916*. Santiago: Imprenta Universitaria, 1916.

Nogueira Joyce, Samantha. *Brazilian Telenovelas and the Myth of Racial Democracy*. Lanham, MD: Lexington Books, 2012.

Novoa, Adriana, and Alex Levine. *From Man to Ape: Darwinism in Argentina, 1870–1920*. Chicago: University of Chicago Press, 2010.

"Nuestra primera palabra." *Revista de la Salud Pública de la Cruz Roja Chilena* 1 (July/August 1922): 1–2.

Numbers, Ronald. *The Creationists: From Scientific Creationism to Intelligent Design*. Cambridge, MA: Harvard University Press, 2006.

Numbers, Ronald L., ed. *Galileo Goes to Jail and Other Myths about Science and Religion*. Cambridge, MA: Harvard University Press, 2009.

Ocampo López, Javier. "José Vasconcelos y la educación mexicana." *Revista Historia de la Educación Latinoamericana* 7 (2005): 137–57.

Oksiloff, Assenka. *Picturing the Primitive: Visual Culture, Ethnography, and Early German Cinema*. New York: Palgrave, 2001.

Olavarrieta, J. B. *Higiene del matrimonio*. Santiago: Librerias "Cultura," 1933.

O'Leary, Don. *Roman Catholicism and Modern Science: A History*. London: Continuum, 2007.

Olson, Richard. "Series Foreword." In *Religion and the Physical Sciences*, edited by Kate Grayson Boisvert, xiii–xx. Westport, CT: Greenwood Press, 2008.

Orbegoso, Arturo. "Eugenesia, tests mentales y degeneración racial en el Perú." *Revista de Psicología* 14 (2012): 230–43.

Orel, Vitezslav. *Gregor Mendel: The First Geneticist.* Translated by Stephen Finn. New York: Oxford University Press, 1996.

O'Toole, Rachel Sarah. *Bound Lives: Africans, Indians, and the Making of Race in Colonial Peru.* Pittsburgh: University of Pittsburgh Press, 2012.

Painter, Nell Irvin. *The History of White People.* New York: W. W. Norton, 2010.

Palacios, Nicolas. *Raza chilena: libro escrito por un chileno i para los chilenos.* Valparaiso: Imprenta i Litografia Alemana, 1904.

Palacios, Nicolás. *Raza chilena: libro escrito por un chileno y para los chilenos.* Vol. 1. Santiago: Imprenta Universitaria, 1918.

Palacios, Senén. "Nicolás Palacios: Recuerdos intimos." In *Raza chilena: libro escrito por un chileno y para los chilenos,* 1:7–30. 2 vols. Santiago: Imprenta Universitaria, 1918.

Paley, William. *Natural Theology: or, Evidences of the Existence and Attributes of the Deity.* 12th ed. London: J. Faulder.

Palma, Héctor A. "Consideraciones historiográficas, epistemológicas y prácticas acerca de la eugenesia." In *Darwinismo social y eugenesia en el mundo latino,* edited by Marisa Miranda and Gustavo Vallejo, 115–44. Buenos Aires: Siglo XXI de Argentina Editores, 2005.

Palma, Héctor A., ed. *Darwin y el darwinismo: 150 años después.* Buenos Aires: UNSA Medita, 2012.

Palma G., Eric Eduardo. *Abolición de la esclavitud en el constitucionalismo del siglo XIX: Colombia, Chile, Perú y Portugal.* Santiago: Editorial Jurídica de Chile, 2016.

Parodi Revoredo, Daniel. *Lo que dicen de nosotros: la guerra del Pacífico en la historiografía y textos escolares chilenos.* Frankfurt: Editorial UPC, 2017.

"Patrimonio: Cora Mayers." *Sociedad Chilena de Pediatría,* 23. https://sochipe.cl/v3/esteto_articulo_solo.php?id=866.

Patton, Pamela A. *Envisioning Others: Race, Color, and the Visual in Iberia and Latin America.* Leiden: Koninklijke Brill, 2016.

Peralta Pizarro, Ariel. *Idea de Chile.* Concepción: Ediciones Universidad de Concepción, 1993.

Phillip, R. "El hombre deberia avergonzarse de estar enfermo." *Revista de la Salud Pública de la Cruz Roja Chilena* 4–6 (1923): 309–25.

Pickering, Mary. *Auguste Comte.* 3 vols. Cambridge: Cambridge University Press, 2010.

Pinto Duran, Carlos, ed. "Bernardino Quijada Burr." In *Diccionario personal de Chile,* 210–11. Santiago: Imprenta Claret, 1921.

Pittard, Eugene. "Introduction." In *¿Qué es la eugenesia? Modo de mejorar la raza humana,* edited by Juan Comas Camps, translated by Margarita Dellenbach, 10–15. Madrid: Ediciones Morata, 1930.

Pius XI. *Casti connubii: On Christian Marriage.* December 31, 1930. https://w2 .vatican.va/content/pius-xi/en/encyclicals/documents/hf_p-xi_enc_1930 1231_casti-connubii.html.

Pontificia Universidad Católica de Chile. Office of the President. "Monsignor Rodolfo Vergara Antúnez." https://rectoria.uc.cl/acerca-de-rectoria/rectores -anteriores/monsenor-rodolfo-vergara-antunez.

Poole, Deborah. "An Image of 'Our Indian': Type Photographs and Racial Sentiments in Oaxaca, 1920–1940." *Hispanic American Historical Review* 84, no. 1 (2004): 37–82.

Poole, Deborah. *Vision, Race, and Modernity: A Visual Economy of the Andean Image World.* Princeton, NJ: Princeton University Press, 1997.

Pope Leo XIII. *Rerum novarum: On Capital and Labor.* Rome: Libreria Editrice Vaticana, 1891.

Pope Pius XII. *Humani generis: Encyclical Letter of Pope Pius XII: Concerning Some False Opinions which Threaten to Undermine the Foundations of Catholic Doctrine.* Washington, DC: National Catholic Welfare Conference, 1950.

Poska, Alison M. *Regulating the People: The Catholic Reformation in Seventeenth-Century Spain.* Boston: Brill, 1998.

Power, Margaret. *Right-Wing Women in Chile: Feminine Power and the Struggle against Allende, 1964–1973.* University Park: Pennsylvania State University, 2002.

Prado Tagle, Dr. E. "Sifilis conjenita tardia." *Revista Médica de Chile* 12 (December 1915): 440–45.

Priego Martínez, Natalia. *Positivism, Science, and "The Scientists" in Porfirian Mexico: A Reappraisal.* Liverpool: Liverpool University Press, 2016.

Prieto, I. "El patronato nacional de la infancia." *Medicina Moderna* 8 (March 1, 1928): 22–28.

"Puericultura e hijiene antenatal." *Revista Médica de Chile* 9 (September 1915): 283–88.

Quijada B., Bernardino. *La teoría de la evolucion.* Santiago: Imprenta Universitaria, 1917.

Rappaport, Joanne. *The Disappearing Mestizo: Configuring Difference in the Colonial New Kingdom of Granada.* Durham, NC: Duke University Press, 2014.

"Razas que mueren." *Zig-Zag* 101 (January 27, 1907): n.p.

Read, Peter. *The Stolen Generations: The Removal of Aboriginal Children in New South Wales, 1883 to 1969.* Surrey Hills: NSW Department of Aboriginal Affairs, 2010.

Reggiani, Andrés. "Eugenics and Physical Culture: Biotypology, Sports and the Body in Latin America, 1930s–1940s." *Contemporanea* (Bologna) 21, no. 3 (2018): 325–50.

Reggiani, Andrés Horacio. *Historia mínima de la eugenesia en América Latina.* Mexico City: El Colegio de México, 2019.

Restall, Matthew. *Beyond Black and Red: African–Native Relations in Colonial Latin America*. Albuquerque: University of New Mexico Press, 2005.

Restat C., Julio. "Estudios filosóficos—el evolucionismo frente a la existencia de Dios demostrada por el origen de la vida." *La Revista Católica* 552 (August 2, 1924): 163–72.

Restat C., Julio. "Estudios filosóficos—el evolucionismo frente a la existencia de Dios demostrada por el origen de la vida." *La Revista Católica* 553 (August 16, 1924): 250–57.

Restat C., Julio. "El evolucionismo frente a la existencia de Dios demostrada por el origen de la vida." *La Revista Católica* 550 (July 5, 1924): 24–37.

Reyes Alvarez, Jaime. *Los presidentes radicales y su partido: Chile 1938–1952*. Santiago: Centro de Estudios Públicos, 1989.

Robins, Nicholas A. *Of Love and Loathing: Marital Life, Strife, and Intimacy in the Colonial Andes, 1750–1825*. Lincoln: University of Nebraska Press, 2015.

Rodriguez, Daniel A. "'The Dangers that Surround the Child': Gender, Science, and Infant Mortality in Postindependence Havana." *Cuban Studies* 45 (2017): 297–318.

Rodriguez, Julia. *Civilizing Argentina: Science, Medicine, and the Modern State*. Chapel Hill: University of North Carolina Press, 2006.

Rogers, Molly. *Delia's Tears: Race, Science, and Photography in Nineteenth-Century America*. New Haven, CT: Yale University Press, 2010.

Rorabaugh, W. J. *Prohibition: A Very Short Introduction*. New York: Oxford University Press, 2020.

Rosemblatt, Karin Alejandra. *Gendered Compromises: Political Cultures and the State in Chile, 1920–1950*. Chapel Hill: University of North Carolina Press, 2000.

Rosemblatt, Karin Alejandra. *The Science and Politics of Race in Mexico and the United States, 1910–1950*. Chapel Hill: University of North Carolina Press, 2018.

Rosemblatt, Karin Alejandra. "Sexuality and Biopower in Chile and Latin America." *Political Power and Social Theory* 15 (2002): 229–62.

Rosen, Christine. *Preaching Eugenics: Religious Leaders and the American Eugenics Movement*. New York: Oxford University Press, 2004.

Rosental, Paul-André. "Eugenics and Social Security in France before and after the Vichy Regime." *Journal of Modern European History* 10 (2012): 540–61.

Rucker S., M. "Orientaciones de acción social con motivo del XXV aniversario de la encíclica Rerum Novarum." *La Revista Católica* 371 (January 20, 1917): 93–108.

Ruiz Gutiérrez, Rosaura, Ricardo Noguera Solano, Juan Manuel Rodríguez Caso, and M. J. S. Hodge, eds. *Darwin en (y desde) México*. Mexico City: Siglo Ventiuno Editores, 2015.

Saint Augustine. *On the Literal Interpretation of Genesis: An Unfinished Book*. Translated by Roland J. Teske. Washington, DC: Catholic University of America Press, 2001.

Salazar, Gabriel, and Julio Pinto. *Historia contemporánea de Chile II: actores, identidad y movimiento.* Santiago: LOM Ediciones, 1999.

Salazar, Gabriel, Julio Pinto Vallejos, María Stella Toro, and Victor Muñoz. *Historia contemporánea de Chile IV: hombría y feminidad.* Santiago: LOM Ediciones, 2002.

Salazar Vergara, Gabriel. *Patriarcado mercantil y liberación femenina: Chile 1810–1930.* Santiago: Debate, 2019.

Salgado, Mauricio, and Javier Castillo. "Differential Status Evaluations and Racial Bias in the Chilean Segregated School System." *Sociological Forum* 33, no. 2 (June 2018): 354–77.

Salvador Lara, Jorge. *La lengua de la raza cósmica: ensayos sobre el español, las academias y los escritores.* Quito: Publicaciones de la Academia Ecuatoriana de la Lengua, 2007.

Sánchez Delgado, Marcelo. "Salvador Allende, esterilización de alienados y debate eugénico chileno." *Izquierdas (Santiago)* 35 (September 2017): 260–86.

Sánchez Delgado, Marcelo. "Sexo, eugenesia y política: Waldemar Coutts (Chile, 1895–1959)." *Revista de Historia* 25, no. 1 (2018): 109–30.

Sánchez-Delgado, Marcelo, and Nicolás Cárcamo-Gebhardt. "Hans Betzhold and the Chilean 'Superman': A Tale of Disillusion, 1938–1943." *História, Ciências, Saúde-Manguinhos* 25, no. 1 (August 68–51 :(2018.

Sánchez Gaete, Marcial. *Historia de la Iglesia de Chile: una sociedad en cambio.* Santiago: Editorial Universidad de Chile, 2014.

Sánchez Manríquez, Karin. "El ingreso de la mujer chilena a la universidad y los cambios en la costumbre por medio de la ley, 1872–1877." *Historia (Santiago)* 39, no. 2 (December 2006): 497–529.

San Cristóbal, Laura, and Blanca San Cristóbal. "Servicio medico y asistencia social en la escuela." *Servicio Social* 1 (March 1928): 25–33.

San Francisco, Alejandro. *La guerra civil de 1891.* Santiago: Centro de Estudios Bicentenario, 2010.

Sarmiento, Domingo Faustino. *Facundo: Civilization and Barbarism.* Buenos Aires: Editorial Claridad, 1845.

Sater, William F. *Andean Tragedy: Fighting the War of the Pacific, 1879–1884.* Lincoln: University of Nebraska Press, 2007.

Scarre, Geoffrey. *Utilitarianism.* London: Routledge, 2020.

Schelkens, Karim, John A. Dick, and Jürgen Mettepenningen. *Aggiornamento? Catholicism from Gregory XVI to Benedict XVI.* Boston: Brill, 2013.

Schell, Patience A. "Eugenics Policy and Practice in Cuba, Puerto Rico, and Mexico." In *The Oxford Handbook of the History of Eugenics,* edited by Alison Bashford and Philippa Levine. Oxford: Oxford University Press, 2010. https://doi.org/10.1093/oxfordhb/9780195373141.013.0029.

Schell, Patience A. "An Honorable Vocation for Ladies: The Work of the Mexico City Unión de Damas Católicas Mexicanas, 1912–1926." *Journal of Women's History* 10, no. 4 (1999): 78–103.

Schell, Patience A. *The Sociable Sciences: Darwin and His Contemporaries in Chile.* New York: Palgrave Macmillan, 2013.

Schofield, Robert E. *Mechanism and Materialism: British Natural Philosophy in an Age of Reason.* Princeton, NJ: Princeton University Press, 2015.

Schwaller, Robert C. *Géneros de gente in Early Colonial Mexico: Defining Racial Difference.* Norman: University of Oklahoma Press, 2016.

Seed, Patricia. *To Love, Honor, and Obey in Colonial Mexico: Conflicts over Marriage Choice, 1574–1821.* Stanford, CA: Stanford University Press, 1988.

"Se inauguró ayer el monumento al autor de *Raza chilena.*" *El Mercurio* (January 2, 1926): 1.

Serrano, Sol. *Historia de la educación en Chile (1810–2010).* Vol. 2, *La educación nacional (1880–1930).* Santiago: Taurus, 2012.

Serrano, Sol. *¿Que hacer con Dios en la República? Política y secularización en Chile (1845–1885).* Santiago: Fondo de Cultura Económica, 2008.

Serrano, Sol. *Universidad y nación: Chile en el siglo XIX.* Santiago: Editorial Universitaria, 1993.

Seth, Suman. *Difference and Disease: Medicine, Race and the Eighteenth-Century British Empire.* New York: Cambridge University Press, 2018.

Sherman, Shantella Y. *In Search of Purity: Popular Eugenics and Racial Uplift among New Negroes.* Bloomington: Xlibris Corp, 2016.

Sierra, Lúcas. *Bases de la higiene moderna: papel que en la difusión de sus principios debe desempeñar la mujer (Conferencia dictada en el Club de Señoras el 11 de noviembre de 1916).* Santiago: Imprenta Universitaria, 1916.

Sierra, Lúcas. *Cien años de la enseñanza de la medicina en Chile.* Santiago: Prensas de la Universidad de Chile, 1934.

Sierra, Lúcas. "Dos palabras." In *La amenaza del sub-hombre* by Lothrop Stoddard. Translated by Lucas Sierra, 7-13. Santiago: Impresor Nascimento, 1923.

Silva, Bárbara, and Rodrigo Henríquez. "El Frente Popular: representaciones sobre la ciudadanía en Chile, 1950–1930." *European Review of Latin American and Caribbean Studies* 103 (2017): 91–108.

Silva, Patricio. *In the Name of Reason: Technocrats and Politics in Chile.* University Park: Pennsylvania State University Press, 2008.

Silva Bascuñán, Alejandro. *Una experiencia social cristiana: formación de la falange.* Santiago: Ediciones CESOC, 2008.

Silverblatt, Irene. *Modern Inquisitions: Peru and the Colonial Origins of the Civilized World.* Durham, NC: Duke University Press, 2004.

Sinclair, Alison. *Sex and Society in Early Twentieth-Century Spain: Hildegart Rodríguez and the World League for Sexual Reform.* Cardiff: University of Wales Press, 2007.

Skidmore, Thomas E. *Black into White: Race and Nationality in Brazilian Thought.* New York: Oxford University Press, 1974.

Skuban, William E. *Lines in the Sand: Nationalism and Identity on the Peruvian-Chilean Frontier.* Albuquerque: University of New Mexico Press, 2007.

Smith, Brian H. *The Church and Politics in Chile.* Princeton, NJ: Princeton University Press, 2014.

Snow, Peter G. *Radicalismo chileno: historia y doctrina del Partido Radical.* Translated by Ana Noboa de Dufaux. Santiago: Francisco de Aguirre, 1972.

Sociedad Chilena de Oftamologia. "Historia." https://www.sochiof.cl/historia.

"Sofía Francisca del Carmen Eastman Cox." https://www.geni.com/people/Sof%C3%ADa-Francisca-del-Carmen-Eastman-Cox/6000000001699591646.

Sontag, Susan. *On Photography.* New York: Picador, 1973.

Spickard, Paul R. *Almost All Aliens: Immigration, Race, and Colonialism in American History and Identity.* New York: Routledge, 2007.

Spongberg, Mary. *Feminizing Venereal Disease: The Body of the Prostitute of Nineteenth-Century Medical Discourse.* Basingstoke: Macmillan Press, 1997.

Spooner, Mary Helen. *The General's Slow Retreat: Chile after Pinochet.* Berkeley: University of California Press, 2011.

Stavans, Ilan. *José Vasconcelos: The Prophet of Race.* New Brunswick, NJ: Rutgers University Press, 2011.

Stepan, Nancy Leys. *"The Hour of Eugenics": Race, Gender, and Nation in Latin America.* Ithaca, NY: Cornell University Press, 1991.

Stepan, Nancy Leys. *Picturing Tropical Nature.* Ithaca, NY: Cornell University Press, 2001.

Stern, Alexandra Minna. *Eugenic Nation: Faults and Frontiers of Better Breeding in Modern America.* Berkeley: University of California Press, 2005.

Stern, Alexandra Minna. "'The Hour of Eugenics' in Veracruz, Mexico: Radical Politics, Public Health, and Latin America's Only Sterilization Law." *Hispanic American Historical Review* 91, no. 3 (2011): 431–43.

Stewart-Gambino, Hannah. "Redefining the Changes and Politics in Chile." In *Conflict and Competition: The Latin American Church in a Changing Environment,* edited by Edward L. Cleary and Hannah Stewart-Gambino, 21–44. Boulder: Lynne Rienner, 1992.

Stewart-Gambino, Hannah W. *The Church and Politics in the Chilean Countryside.* Boulder, CO: Westview Press, 1992.

Stoddard, Lothrop. *La amenaza del sub-hombre.* Translated by Lucas Sierra. Santiago: Impresor Nascimento, 1923.

Stoddard, Lothrop. *The Revolt against Civilization: The Menace of the Under Man.* London: Chapman and Hall, 1922.

Stoddard, Lothrop. *The Rising Tide of Color: The Threat against White World Supremacy.* New York: Charles Scribner's Sons, 1922.

Strick, James. "Darwinism and the Origin of Life: The Role of H. C. Bastian in the

British Spontaneous Generation Debates, 1868–1873." *Journal of the History of Biology* 32, no. 1 (Spring 1999): 51–92.

Strick, James Edgar, and Joshua Lederberg. *Sparks of Life: Darwinism and the Victorian Debates over Spontaneous Generation.* Cambridge, MA: Harvard University Press, 2002.

Suárez y Lopez-Guazo, Laura. "The Mexican Eugenics Society: Racial Selection and Improvement." In *The Reception of Darwinism in the Iberian World*, edited by Thomas F. Glick, Miguel Angel Puig-Samper, and Rosaura Ruiz, 143–51. Boston: Kluwer Academic Publishers, 2001.

Subercaseaux, Bernardo. *Historia de las ideas y de la cultura en Chile: fin de siglo, la época de Balmaceda.* Vol. 2. Santiago: Editorial Universitaria, 1997.

Subercaseaux, Bernardo. "Raza y nación: el caso de Chile." *A Contra Corriente* 5, no. 1 (2007): 29–63.

"La superioridad de los anglo-sajones." *El Diario Popular* (December 2, 1902): 1.

Sussman, Robert W. *The Myth of Race: The Troubling Persistence of an Unscientific Idea.* Cambridge, MA: Harvard University Press, 2014.

Tamayo Hurtado, Manuel, and Francisco González García. "La enseñanza de la evolución en Chile: historia de un conflict documentado en los textos de estudio de enseñanza media." *Investigações em Ensino de Ciências* 15, no. 2 (2010): 310–36.

Tannenbaum, Frank. *Slave and Citizen: The Negro in the Americas.* New York: Knopf, 1946.

Tannenbaum, Frank. *Ten Keys to Latin America.* New York: Vintage Books, 1962.

Taylor, Geoffrey I., and E. H. E. Havelock. "William Cecil Dampier (1867–1952)." *Obituary Notices of Fellows of the Royal Society* 9, no. 1 (November 1954): 55–63.

Telles, Edward, ed. *Pigmentocracies: Ethnicity, Race, and Color in Latin America.* Chapel Hill: University of Carolina Press, 2014.

Thompson, Phillip M. *Between Science and Religion: The Engagement of Catholic Intellectuals with Science and Technology in the Twentieth Century.* New York: Lexington Books, 2009.

Thonet Ingles, Carlos. "Sobre patologia del fraude sexual." *Medicina Moderna/Revista de Medicina* 4 (November 1943): 201–5.

Tijoux, Maria Emilia, ed. *Racismo en Chile: la piel como marca de la inmigración.* Santiago: Editorial Universitaria, 2016.

Tinsman, Heidi. *Partners in Conflict: The Politics of Gender, Sexuality, and Labor in the Chilean Agrarian Reform, 1950–1973.* Durham, NC: Duke University Press, 2002.

Tuna, Gustavo Henrique. *Gilberto Freyre: entre tradição e ruptura.* Sao Paulo: Grupo Editorial Cone Sul, 2000.

Turda, Marius, and Aaron Gillette. *Latin Eugenics in Comparative Perspective.* Sydney: Bloomsbury Academic, 2014.

Turner, Frank M. "Science and Religious Freedom." In *Freedom and Religion in the Nineteenth Century*, edited by Richard J. Helmstadter, 54–86. Stanford, CA: Stanford University Press, 1997.

Twinam, Ann. *Public Lives, Private Secrets: Gender, Honor, Sexuality, and Illegitimacy in Colonial Spanish America*. Stanford, CA: Stanford University Press, 2007.

Twinam, Ann. *Purchasing Whiteness: Pardos, Mulattos, and the Quest for Social Mobility in the Spanish Indies*. Stanford, CA: Stanford University Press, 2015.

Universidad de Chile. "Carlos Charlín Correa." http://www.uchile.cl/portal/presen tacion/historia/rectores-de-la-u-de-chile/4711/carlos-charlin-correa-1927.

Universidad de Valparaíso. Escuela de Obstetricia y Puericultura. "Historia." https://obstetricia.uv.cl/inicio/index.php/nosotros/historia.

Vaamonde, Gustavo Adolfo. *Oscuridad y confusión: el pueblo y la política venezolana del siglo XIX en las ideas de Antonio Guzmán Blanco*. Caracas: Universidad Católica Andrés Bello Fundación Polar, 2004.

Vaggione, Juan Marco, and José Manuel Morán Faúndes, eds. *Laicidad and Religious Diversity in Latin America*. Cham: Springer, 2016.

Van Lennep, Dr. "Esterilidad del matrimonio." *Revista Médica de Chile* 9 (September 1917): 340–47.

Vargas C., Nelson A. "170 años de la Escuela de Medicina de la Universidad de Chile: su aporte a la salud infantil y del adolescente en Chile." *Revista Chilena de Pediatría* 74, no. 2 (2003): 141–48.

Vasconcelos, José. *La raza cósmica: misión de la raza iberoamericana: notas de viajes a la América del Sur*. Barcelona: Agencia Mundial de Libreria, 1925.

Vaughan, Mary Kay. "Modernizing Patriarchy: State Policies, Rural Households, and Women in Mexico, 1930–1940." In *Hidden Histories of Gender and the State in Latin America*, edited by Elizabeth Dore and Maxine Molyneux, 194–214. Durham, NC: Duke University Press, 2000.

Verba, Ericka. *Catholic Feminism and the Social Question in Chile, 1910–1917: The Liga de Damas Chilenas*. Lewiston, NY: Edwin Mellen Press, 2003.

Verdaguer Tarradella, Juan. "Reseña histórica del Departamento de Oftamologia," http://www.uchile.cl/postgrados/82585/resena-historica.

Vergara, Angela. *Copper Workers, International Business, and Domestic Politics in Cold War Chile*. University Park: Pennsylvania State University Press, 2008.

Vergara Antúnez, Rodolfo. "El materialismo y la origen de las cosas." *La Revista Católica* 212 (May 21, 1910): 632–41.

Verónica. "La enseñanza doméstica." *El Eco de la Liga de Damas Chilenas* 26 (September 15, 1913): N.p.

Vial Correa, Gonzalo. *Pinochet: la biografía*. Santiago: Aguilar, 2002.

Vieira Powers, Karen. *Women in the Crucible of Conquest: The Gendered Genesis of Spanish American Society, 1500–1600*. Albuquerque: University of New Mexico Press, 2005.

Vimieiro Gomes, Ana Carolina. "The Rise of Biotypology in Brazil: Measuring and Classifying the Morphology, Physiology and Character of Brazilians in the 1930s." *Ciências Humanas* 7, no. 3 (2012): 705–19.

Vinson, Ben. *Before Mestizaje: The Frontiers of Race and Caste in Colonial Mexico.* New York: Cambridge University Press, 2018.

Vitzthum, Richard C. *Materialism: An Affirmative History and Definition.* Amherst: Prometheus Books, 1995.

Voekel, Pamela. *Alone before God: The Religious Origins of Modern Mexico.* Durham, NC: Duke University Press, 2002.

von Germeten, Nicole. *Violent Delights, Violent Ends: Sex, Race, and Honor in Colonial Cartagena de Indias.* Albuquerque: University of New Mexico Press, 2013.

Wade, Peter. *Degrees of Mixture, Degrees of Freedom: Genomics, Multiculturalism, and Race in Latin America.* Durham, NC: Duke University Press, 2017.

Wade, Peter. *Race and Sex in Latin America.* New York: Pluto Press, 2009.

Wade, Peter, Carlos López Beltrán, Eduardo Restrepo, and Ricardo Ventura Santos, eds. *Mestizo Genomics: Race Mixture, Nation, and Science in Latin America.* Durham, NC: Duke University Press, 2014.

Wade Chambers, David. "Locality and Science: Myths of Centre and Periphery." In *Mundialización de la ciencia y cultural nacional: Actas del Congreso Internacional "Ciencia, descubrimiento y mundo colonial,"* edited by Antonio Lafuente, Alberto Elena, and María Luisa Ortega, 605–18. Madrid: Ediciones Doce Calles, 1993.

Walker, Tamara J. *Exquisite Slaves: Race, Clothing, and Status in Colonial Lima.* New York: Cambridge University Press, 2017.

Wallerstein, Immanuel Maurice. *The Modern World-System.* New York: Academic Press, 1974.

Walsh, James J. *Catholic Churchmen in Science: Sketches of the Lives of Catholic Ecclesiastics Who Were among the Great Founders in Science.* Philadelphia: American Ecclesiastical Review, Dolphin Press, 1910.

Walsh, Sarah. "The Chilean Exception: Racial Homogeneity, Mestizaje and Eugenic Nationalism." *Journal of Iberian and Latin American Studies* 25, no. 1 (2019): 105–25.

Walsh, Sarah. "The Executioner's Shadow: Coerced Sterilization and the Creation of 'Latin' Eugenics in Chile," *History of Science* (2018). https://doi.org/10.1177/0073275318755533.

Walsh, Sarah "'One of the Most Uniform Races of the Entire World': Creole Eugenics and the Myth of Chilean Racial Homogeneity." *Journal of the History of Biology* 48, no. 4 (2015): 613–39.

Walsh, Sarah. "Restoring the Chilean Race: Catholicism and Latin Eugenics in Chile." *Catholic Historical Review* 105, no. 1 (Winter 2019): 116–38.

Weikart, Richard. *From Darwin to Hitler: Evolutionary Ethics, Eugenics, and Racism in Germany.* New York: Palgrave Macmillan, 2004.

Weinstein, Barbara. *The Color of Modernity: Sao Paulo and the Making of Race and Nation in Brazil.* Durham, NC: Duke University Press, 2014.

Whetham, Catherine Durning. *The Upbringing of Daughters.* New York: Longmans, Green, 1917.

Whetham, W. C. D., and C. D. Whetham, *An Introduction to Eugenics.* London: Macmillan, 1912.

White, Andrew Dickson. *Historia de la lucha entre la ciencia y la teología.* Translated by José de Caso. Madrid: La España Moderna, 1910.

White, Andrew Dickson. *A History of the Warfare of Science with Theology in Christendom.* New York: Dover Publications, 1896.

Widdance Twine, Frances. *Racism and Racial Democracy: The Maintenance of White Supremacy in Brazil.* New Brunswick, NJ: Rutgers University Press, 1998.

Wilson, Juan. "De los hijos, fin primario del matrimonio." In *Estudios Médicos,* 223–38. Santiago de Chile: Imprenta W. Gnadt, 1938.

Winn, Peter. *Weavers of Revolution: The Yarur Workers and Chile's Road to Socialism.* New York: Oxford University Press, 1989.

Woltmann, Ludwig. *Die Germanen in Frankreich eine Untersuchung über den Eina fluss der germanischen Rasse auf die Geschichte und Kulture Franreichs.* Jena, Germany: E. Diedrichs, 1907.

Woltmann, Ludwig. *Die Germanen und die Renaissance in Italien.* Leipzig: Thüringische Verlagsanstalt, 1905.

Worth, Richard. *Teetotalers and Saloon Smashers: The Temperance Movement and Prohibition.* Berkeley Heights, NJ: Enslow, 2009.

"La X Conferencia Internacional de la Cruz Roja." *Revista de la Salud Pública de la Cruz Roja Chilena* 1 (July/August 1922): 48–51.

Yañez Andrade, Juan Carlos. *Estado, consenso y crisis social: el espacio público en Chile, 1900–1920.* Santiago: LOM Ediciones, 2003.

Yudell, Michael. *Race Unmasked: Biology and Race in the Twentieth Century.* New York: Columbia University Press, 2014.

Zárate C., María Soledad. *Por la salud del cuerpo: historia y políticas sanitarias en Chile.* Santiago: Ediciones Universidad Alberto Hurtado, 2008.

Zárate Campo, María Soledad. *Dar a luz en Chile, siglo XIX: de la "ciencia de hembra" a la ciencia obstétrica.* Santiago: Editorial Universidad Alberto Hurtado, 2008.

Zarini, Pedro. "La utopía eugenista en la Argentina (1900–1950)." In *El mosaico argentino: modelos y representaciones del espacio y de la población, siglos XIX–XX,* edited by Hernán Otero, 425–66. Buenos Aires: Siglo Veintiuno, 2004.

Zavala Cepeda, José Manual, Cristián Lineros Pérez, Gertrudis Payàs Puigarnau, Laura Hillock Damm, Angélica Cardemil Lastra, Armando Luza Melo, and Italo Salgado Ismodes, eds. *Los parlamentos hispano-mapuches, 1593–1803: textos fundamentales.* Temuco: Ediciones Universidad Católica de Temuco, 2015.

Zeitlin, Maurice. *The Civil Wars in Chile (or the Bourgeois Revolutions that Never Were)*. Princeton, NJ: Princeton University Press, 2016.

Zugibe, Frederick T. *The Crucifixion of Jesus: A Forensic Inquiry*. New York: M. Evans, 2005.

Index

Note: Page numbers in *italics* indicate illustrative material.